PSYCHOSOMATICS TODAY

PSYCHOANALYTIC IDEAS AND APPLICATIONS SERIES

Other titles in the Series

The Art of Interpretation: Deconstruction and New Beginning in the Psychoanalytic Process
  Wolfgang Loch
  edited and commentary by Peter Wegner

The Unconscious: Further Reflections
  edited by José Carlos Calich & Helmut Hinz

Escape from Selfhood: Breaking Boundaries and Craving for Oneness
  Ilany Kogan

The Unconscious in Psychoanalysis
  Antonio Alberti Semi

From Impression to Inquiry: A Tribute to the Work of Robert Wallerstein
  edited by Wilma Bucci & Norbert Freedman; associate editor Ethan A. Graham

Talking About Supervision: 10 Questions, 10 Analysts = 100 Answers
  edited by Laura Elliot Rubinstein

Envy and Gratitude Revisited
  edited by Priscilla Roth and Alessandra Lemma

The Work of Confluence: Listening and Interpreting in the Psychoanalytic Field
  Madeleine & Willy Baranger
  edited and commentary by Leticia Glocer Fiorini
  Foreword by Cláudio Laks Eizink

The Analyzing Situation
  by Jean-Luc Donnet, translated by Andrew Weller

Good Feelings: Psychoanalytic Reflections in Positive Emotions and Attitudes
  edited by Salman Akhtar

PSYCHOSOMATICS TODAY

A Psychoanalytic Perspective

edited by
Marilia Aisenstein and
Elsa Rappoport de Aisemberg

Psychoanalytic Ideas and Applications Series

KARNAC

First published in 2010 by
Karnac Books Ltd
118 Finchley Road, London NW3 5HT

British Library Cataloguing in Publication Data

A C.I.P. for this book is available from the British Library

ISBN 978 1 85575 861 2

Edited, designed and produced by The Studio Publishing Services Ltd
www.publishingservicesuk.co.uk
e-mail: studio@publishingservicesuk.co.uk

Printed in Great Britain

www.karnacbooks.com

CONTENTS

THE INTERNATIONAL PSYCHOANALYSIS LIBRARY   vii
  IPA Publications Committee

ACKNOWLEDGEMENTS   ix

ABOUT THE EDITORS AND CONTRIBUTORS   xi

PREFACE   xv
  Marilia Aisenstein and Elsa Rappoport de Aisemberg

INTRODUCTION   xxi
  Cláudio Laks Eizirik

CHAPTER ONE
Thoughts on the Paris School of Psychosomatics   1
  André Green

CHAPTER TWO
The mysterious leap of the somatic into the psyche   47
  Marilia Aisenstein

CHAPTER THREE
Psychosomatics: the role of unconscious phantasy   63
  Catalina Bronstein

CHAPTER FOUR
A rash of a different colour: somatopsychic eruptions   77
from the other side
  Lila J. Kalinich

CHAPTER FIVE
Adolescence: the body as a scenario for   93
non-symbolized dramas
  Ruggero Levy

CHAPTER SIX
Psychosomatic conditions in contemporary psychoanalysis   111
  Elsa Rappoport de Aisemberg

CHAPTER SEVEN
Particular vicissitudes of the drive confronted with   131
mourning: sublimation and somatization
  Evelyne Sechaud

CHAPTER EIGHT
The place of affect in the psychosomatic economy   145
  Claude Smadja

CHAPTER NINE
The capacity to say no and psychosomatic   163
disorders in childhood
  Gerard Szwec

CHAPTER TEN
Symbolism, symbolization, and trauma in   181
psychosomatic theory
  Graeme J. Taylor

AFTERWORD   201
Madeleine Baranger

INDEX   205

PSYCHOANALYTIC IDEAS AND APPLICATIONS SERIES

IPA Publications Committee

The Publications Committee of the International Psychoanalytical Association continues, with this volume, the series "Psychoanalytic Ideas and Applications".

The aim is to focus on the scientific production of significant authors whose works are outstanding contributions to the development of the psychoanalytic field and to set out relevant ideas and themes, generated during the history of psychoanalysis, that deserve to be discussed by present psychoanalysts.

The relationship between psychoanalytic ideas and their applications has to be put forward from the perspective of theory, clinical practice, technique, and research so as to maintain their validity for contemporary psychoanalysis.

The Publication Committee's objective is to share these ideas with the psychoanalytic community and with professionals in other related disciplines, in order to expand their knowledge and generate a productive interchange between the text and the reader.

Psychosomatic diseases represent many of the problems that the psychoanalyst must deal with at the present time. Debates on psychosomatic diseases explore, among other topics, what cannot be symbolized by the patient, and cover important controversies in contemporary psychoanalysis.

Special thanks are due to the editors, Marilia Aisenstein and Elsa Rappoport de Aisemberg, as well as to the contributors to this volume, who accepted the challenge to update these debates, including their remarkable clinical experience.

Leticia Glocer Fiorini
Series Editor
Chair of the Publications Committee of the
International Psychoanalytical Association

ACKNOWLEDGEMENTS

Marilia Aisenstein and Elsa Rappoport de Aisemberg, in our character of co-editors of this book, wish to express our gratitude to Leticia Glocer Fiorini, Chair of the Publications Committee of the International Psychoanalytical Association, for her support in producing a book on our theoretical and clinical field: *Psychosomatics Today: A Psychoanalytic Perspective*.

At the same time we wish to extend our appreciation to the members of the former Publications Committee that accepted unanimously our project once submitted: Salman Akhtar, Thierry Bokanowski, Sergio Lewkowicz, and Mary K. O'Neil.

The same applies to the present Committee, also chaired by Leticia Glocer Fiorini, and especially to her, for her professional expertise and assistance and her unconditional availability in guiding us in this exciting task in organizing this international book within the framework of the IPA.

Last, but not least, our gratitude to all those persons that contributed to make this publication possible.

Elsa Rappoport de Aisemberg is a member and training analyst of the Argentine Psychoanalytic Association. She is the former Vice-president of the Argentine Psychoanalytic Association, member of the IPA Allied Centre Committee, past Chair of Scientific Collo-quiums and Adviser for the Scientific Department of the Argentine Psychoanalytic Association, and Chair of the Research Group on Psychosomatics at the Argentine Psychoanalytic Association. She is the author of many papers and publications on psychosomatics.

Marilia Aisenstein is a member and training analyst of the Paris Psychoanalytical Society and of the Hellenik Psychoanalytical Society. A past President of the Paris Psychoanalytical Society, past President of IPSO, Paris Psychosomatic Institute, former European representative to the Board, and former Chair of IPA International New Groups, she is the author of many papers and publications about psychosomatics and received the Bouvet Award in 1992.

Madeleine Baranger is a member and training analyst of the Argentine Psychoanalytic Association. She was co-founder of the Uruguayan Psychoanalytic Association, where she created and directed the Institute of Psychoanalysis. She is co-author of the Training Plan for the Institute of Psychoanalysis of the Argentine Psychoanalytic Association, and an ex member of the Executive Committee and the Training Committee of the Argentine Psycho-analytic Association. She has received the Mary Sigourney Award, and is the author of several publications and books.

Catalina Bronstein is a member and training analyst of the British Psychoanalytic Society, is a Senior Lecturer at UCL, and works at the Brent Adolescent Centre. She edited *Kleinian Theory. A Contemporary Perspective*. She is also London Editor of the *International Journal of Psychoanalysis*.

Cláudio Laks Eizirik is a member and training analyst of the Brazilian Psychoanalytical Society of Porto Alegre. He is a past President of the International Psychoanalytic Association, past President of the Federation of Psychoanalytic Societies of Latin America, past President and Institute Director of the Brazilian Psychoanalytical Society of Porto Alegre, and ex Vice-president and Chair of the House of Delegates of IPA. He is Professor of Psychiatry at the University of Rio Grande do Sul, and is the author of four books and several papers.

Leticia Glocer Fiorini is a training psychoanalyst of the Argentine Psychoanalytic Association. She is the current Chair of the Publications Committee of the International Psychoanalytical Association (since 2005), former Chair of the Publications Committee of the Argentine Psychoanalytic Association, former editor of the *Revista de Psicoanálisis*, Buenos Aires, and current General Editor of IPA Publications Committee's Series. She was awarded the Celes Cárcamo Prize (APA, 1994) for her paper: "The feminine position: a heterogeneous construction", and is the author of *Deconstructing the Feminine. Psychoanalysis, Gender, and Theories of complexity* (Karnac, 2007), published in Spanish as *Lo femenino y el pensamiento complejo* (Lugar Ed., 2001). She is also co-editor of *On Freud's Mourning and Melancholia* (Karnac, 2007) and of *The Experience of Time* (Karnac, 2009), and Editor in Spanish of *The Other in the Intersubjective Field* (2004); *Time, History and Structure* (2006); *Labyrinths of Violence* (2008); and *The Body: Languages and Silences* (2008). She has also published numerous papers about femininity in books and in psychoanalytic journals in Spanish, English, Portuguese, and Italian.

André Green is a member and training analyst of the Paris Psychoanalytical Society, past President and past Director of the Institute of the Paris Psychoanalytical Society, and past Vice-president of the International Psychoanalytical Association. He has received several awards among which the Mary Sigourney Award, and IPA Outstanding Scientific Award. He is the author of a huge number of books and publications.

Lila Kalinich is a member and training analyst of Columbia University Centre for Psychoanalytic Training and Research, Professor of Psychiatry at Columbia University, and past President of The Association for Psychoanalytic Medicine in New York. She is the author of clinical and theoretical works, and editor of *The Dead Father. A Psychoanalytical Inquiry*. She received the Daniel Award for distinguished contribution to psychoanalysis.

Ruggero Levy is a member and training analyst of the Brazilian Psychoanalytical Society of Porto Alegre, Director of the Institute and Former President of the Brazilian Psychoanalytical Society of Porto Alegre, and Professor of Children, Adolescents' and Adults' Psychotherapy. He is the author of many papers and publications.

Evelyne Sechaud is a member and training analyst of the French Psychoanalytic Association, past President of the French Psychoanalytic Association, and former President of the European Psychoanalytic Federation. She started a research group on the specificity of psychoanalytic treatment today, and is Maître de Conférences at the Paris V University and Consultant at the La Salpétrière Hospital. She has written many papers, in particular on transference and sublimation.

Claude Smadja is a member and training analyst of the Paris Psychoanalytical Society, a psychiatrist, Director of IPSO, Paris Psychosomatic Institute, and President of the IPSO Pierre Marty International Association. He is the author of many books and articles.

Gerard Szwec is a member and training analyst of the Paris Psychoanalytical Society, a psychiatrist and child analyst, and Director of the Child and Adolescent Department of IPSO, Paris Psychosomatic Institute. He is the Editor of the *Revue Francaise de Psychosomatique*, the author of several papers and books, and received the Bouvet Award.

Graeme J. Taylor is a member of the Toronto Institute of Contemporary Psychoanalysis, Professor of Psychiatry at the University of Toronto, a psychiatrist at the Mount Sinai Hospital, Toronto, and a Fellow of the American Academy of Psychoanalysis and Dynamic Psychiatry, among others. He has received the Mary Sigourney Award, and has conducted empirical research on alexithymia and published several papers and books about psychosomatic medicine and contemporary psychoanalysis.

PREFACE

This book, composed of a collection of articles on present-day psychosomatics, proposes to be both contemporary and thoroughly Freudian. Our objective is to present in it representatives of the major currents initiated by the pioneers in the field of psychosomatics. The contributions that they offer are all theoretical and clinical, original and personal, and each one of the contributors figures in his or her own particular framework.

It has often been said that Freud was not interested in psychosomatics; he rather showed some ambivalence in tackling this subject. Nevertheless, he extensively studied the different states of the body. All his papers concerning corporeal expressions are in the line of his theoretical concern relating to drives. Studying Freud's oeuvre, one can describe four kinds of somatic symptoms: conversion hysteria symptoms, the somatic symptoms of the actual neurosis, hypochondriac symptoms, and organized organic ailments.

Conversion hysteria symptoms are memory symbols converted into the body and underlying unconscious fantasies in which sexuality plays a crucial role. Conversion implies a certain number of conditions: a relatively complete Oedipal organization, a dynamic unconscious responsible for symbolization, and the existence of repression.

In contrast, the *somatic symptoms of the actual neurosis* cover the category of the functional disorders of classic medicine and do not generally have any symbolic signification. They are typically accompanied by anxiety and are viewed as the result of an erotic hypercathexis of the somatic function . Freud's hypothesis concerning libido theory is the double association of the drive of each organ or somatic function. An organ is cathected by the drives of self-preservation, as much as through the sexual drives. Thus, there exists an organ eroticism which is illustrated in the feeling of a good functioning of the body. However, if there exists within an organ an imbalance between the two forms of drive cathexis, the organ will be disturbed in its physiological functioning.

Hypochondriac symptoms are somatic complaints for which there exists no organic lesion. They originate in a stasis of narcissistic libido which has not found a psychical use. Hypochondriac anxieties projected on to bodily organs witness an insufficiency of psychic representations of these organs.

Organic ailments are the specific domain of psychosomatics. Freud approached the study of organic ailments on two different levels. The first is that of narcissistic regression, occurring when the illness becomes somatically established. Freud was interested in the modifications in libidinal economy tied to the presence of a somatic occurrence. The return of narcissistic libido towards the sick organ constitutes, for Freud, a regular feature of somatically ill subjects. The second is always related to his two drive theories.

In 1920, he had noticed some enigmatic relationships between pathological states of the body and psychopathological psychic states; he mentions the effacement of a neurotic or even psychotic state during the establishment of a somatic disease and concludes that it must related to some movements of the libido.

Post-Freudian currents in psychosomatics

Sandor Ferenczi worked on the psychoanalysis of organic ailments. His notion of pathoneurosis sought to account for neurotic, psychotic, or narcissistic alternations arising following an somatic illness.

Georg Groddeck proposed a psychoanalytic theory of organic illness, according to which the id could produce a neurotic symptom or character trait as well as a somatic illness. All somatic illness is, thus, seen as having a symbolic value and may be treated by psychoanalysis.

In the USA, around the thirties, psychiatrists and psychoanalysts carried out research that laid down the bases for psychosomatic medicine. Their observations were diffused widely in Europe and South America, and contributed to the development of diverse currents of psychosomatics. Flanders Dunbar, whose contribution is crucial, founded a methodology of clinical investigation, at once psychological and physiological, which enabled her to elaborate personality profiles. Franz Alexander is the author whose work is most widely known in France, in particular *Fundamentals of Psychoanalysis* (1948) and *Psychosomatic Medicine* (1950). A student of Ferenczi, Alexander created the Chicago School of Psychosomatic Medicine. His approach to somatic disease associates a psychoanalytical point of view and a physiopathological perspective. Psychosomatic medicine is built on two theoretical entities. First, the theory of organ neurosis, originating in the Freudian conception of the actual neurosis, considers that long-standing repressed emotions on the psychic level are first conveyed by nerve pathways towards the organs, which they alter in their functioning. This can lead to functional disorders and then to organic ailments. Second, the hypothesis of specificity postulates that a specific physiopathological syndrome corresponds to each emotion. The work of Alexander and his colleagues of the Chicago school, in addition to that of other North American thinkers, underlined the role of emotional conflict in relation to the somatic symptom. The observations and works concerning a number of diseases, such as bronchial asthma, arterial hypertension, gastro-duodenal ulcers, remain of great interest; moreover, they paved the way for the later work of psychosomaticists.

The spread in France of the work of the North American psychosomaticists and the discussions on their theoretical positions led to new conceptions. Refocusing psychoanalytic practice with somatic patients on the relationship and the transference allowed the proposal of a psychoanalytically orientated approach to psychosomatic occurrences. The theoretical debate that took place between the different schools was mostly focused on the question of the symbolic meaning of the somatic symptom.

J.-P. Valabrega worked out the concept of generalized conversion, which reposes on the idea of the existence of a conversion nucleus in each individual. The body is thought of as overloaded with a signifying memory, and all somatic symptoms contain meaning that the psychoanalytic cure aims at discovering.

Joyce McDougall contributed to the psychosomatic field excellent clinical material of her patients with somatic symptoms whom she was treating within the psychoanalytical framework. She created several hypotheses to explain this praxis: somatic vulnerability, as an early functioning towards which we can return if quantity invades us; psychosomatosis, as madness in the body, based in Winnicott's concept of psyche–soma splitting; foreclosure of the intolerable and painful representation and desaffectation, among others.

The Paris Psychosomatic School was founded in the late 1940s and the early 1950s by certain analysts of the Paris Psychoanalytical Society, essentially Pierre Marty, Michel Fain, Michel de M'Uzan, and Christian David. The first papers focused on cephalic, rachialgic, or allergic illnesses. They emphasized the insufficiency of neurotic defence mechanisms and attributed to somatic symptoms a substitutive value. At the beginning of the 1960s, *Psychosomatic Investigation* is published, co-written by Marty, de M'Uzan, and David (1963). This volume may be viewed as the founding act of psychosomatics as a strictly psychoanalytic discipline. Some new clinical notions are described: essential depression, mechanical thinking, the mechanism of projective reduplication, and a new perspective—the economic perspective—based on the psychosomatic investigation of patients suffering from somatic diseases. In this perspective, all human creations are studied in their transformation in relation to each other. Such is the case with mental creations: neurotic and psychotic symptoms, character traits, perversions, but also behaviour and somatizations.

Pierre Marty's contribution is an evolutionist doctrine of psychosomatic economy. This reposes on the coexistence and alternation of two opposite forms of drive-motion. The first, "life motions", are motions of organization. The second, "death motions", are motions of disorganization. Individual evolution leads in all humans to the edification of systems of fixation–regression that are more or less resistant. In a long-lasting general way, severe somatizations can be seen as the result of failures of these defence systems.

In Latin America, specifically in Buenos Aires, psychosomatics was in the interest of the pioneers. Consequently, Arnaldo Rascovsky, Ángel Garma, and Enrique Pichon Rivière left a profound inscription by adding the body to the psyche as the object of research of psychoanalysts, each with their particular way.

First, there was an interdisciplinary search towards psychosomatic medicine, especially in Rascovsky, and, later on, with Garma, an inclusion in the psychoanalytical field. In 1943, Rascovsky presented a paper about this subject and, in 1948, compiled the first book, *Psychosomatic Pathology*, with the writings of several local authors.

Ángel Garma, as well as Arnaldo Rascovsky, holds a subtle clinical vision, and theoretically uses the ideas of his time. He understands somatic symptoms as conversions, as psychoneurosis. His numerous works and books about the asthmatic patient, or those with headaches or gastro-duodenal ulcer symptoms, account for his interest in this subject making him a referent in the field.

At the same time, Pichon Rivière formulates the idea that the unconscious expresses itself in three areas: mind, body, and the external world.

In the 1970s, David Liberman researched by using clinical material of "atypical" patients, which resulted in his work *Overadapted*, on those persons overadapted to the formal aspects of external reality, concluding that these patients hold a non-neurotic structure that can lead to a severe somatosis or even sudden death. He presented his findings in Helsinski in 1981.

As the reader will find, this book wishes to pay homage to the work of the early psychosomaticians, but is not a collection of fundamental papers. It brings together varied papers from the subsequent generations. It can be thought of as an *Après-coup* that is rooted in the revolutionary views of the pioneers and attempts to reconsider them within our psychoanalytical everyday practice.

Marilia Aisenstein and Elsa Rappoport de Aisemberg
June 2010

Introduction

Cláudio Laks Eizirik

Marilia Aisenstein and Elsa Rappoport de Aisemberg assembled a distinguished group of analytic thinkers and clinicians with the aim of reflecting on and discussing one of the most challenging areas of our field, something that was referred to by Freud as that enigmatic leap from psyche to soma, from a contemporary perspective.

As in any other psychoanalytic realm, what the reader will find here is a well-balanced dialogue between past and present, Freudian ideas and those of his main followers, and specifically on psychosomatics, the main insights put forward by such relevant thinkers as Franz Alexander, Pierre Marty, Joyce McDougall, Arnaldo Rascovsky, Ángel Garma, Enrique Pichon Rivière, David Liberman, and André Green. In each of the chapters, these authors are in a very lively conversation with other current contributors to this field, in such a way that we can see one of the main trends of contemporary psychoanalysis: its pluralism and the challenge to listen to the other.

The book, despite several different approaches that cover the main theories of the field, however, has as a central reference: the contributions from the Paris Psychosomatic School developed by Pierre Marty and his followers. The paradigmatic chapter written by André Green shows the close connection of Marty's ideas with Freud's views, but also highlights that some of his main concepts, such as mechanical thinking, the mechanical life, essential depression, and progressive disorganizations are lasting contributions that make it at least easier to understand the psychic functioning of psychosomatic patients. Other points strongly stressed by Green are the pioneering use of the idea of mentalization by Marty, and the notion of prepsychic mozaik in his theorization.

Marilia Aisenstein, one of the main contributors to contemporary literature on the subject, revises Freud's developments, as well as other authors, to show how the contributions of the Paris School are in tune with, and an evolution of, what was previously understood and proposed. In her chapter on the drive destiny confronted with mourning, between somatization and sublimation, Evelyne Séchaud also follows a Freudian line to develop and illustrate her relevant ideas. Elsa Rappoport de Aisemberg, in her chapter on psychosomatic conditions in contemporary psychoanalysis, shows the presence of several remarkable Latin American analytic thinkers in the field, as well as her own ideas, developed through several previous papers. Claude Smadja, another frequent contributor to this field, puts forward his ideas on affect and somatization. Catalina Bronstein, using mainly Kleinian and post-Kleinian concepts, mainly unconscious fantasy, shows how these contributions can be extremely useful in understanding and approaching psychosomatic conditions. Lila Kalinish addresses one of the most disturbing of these symptoms in her paper on a rash of different colour. Adolescence is a time when, particularly, the body is used as a theatre for non-symbolized dramas, as Ruggero Levy shows very clearly. Following similar lines, Graeme Taylor discusses symbolism, symbolization, and trauma. Psychosomatic disorders in childhood, and the capacity to say no, are presented by Gerard Szwec.

Each chapter presents a double face, which, in my view, makes it both intellectually stimulating and clinically useful: each of the authors not only develops his/her own view on the subject, but also offers detailed clinical material which allows the reader to follow the argument and compare these situations with his/her own clinical practice. Since we are seeing more and more psychosomatic patients in our current practice, this is one of the strengths of this book. Another relevant contribution derives from a long time of maturation and testing of these ideas. Since the discussions on whether these conditions are asymbolic or have primary symbolic meaning, until recent developments that show how mentalization operates and how each analytic field will produce its specific story (and here we have the joy of reading the concluding remarks by Madeleine Baranger), psychoanalysis has come a long way, in both its theorization and clinical skills, so that currently we are more able to face so many challenging situations with less fear and a great deal of gratitude to our colleagues who opened this way and gave us their reflections, and the account of their attempts, failures, and possibilities.

I cannot conclude without a note on the two organizers of this remarkable book: both Marilia and Elsa are among the most gifted analysts of our time, in several dimensions. They are not only master clinicians, but also inspired and inspiring writers and thinkers, as well as extremely active participants in the institutional life of their societies, regions, and also relevant players in the international psychoanalytic scene, where they are contributing with energy and passion to the development of psychoanalysis in new frontiers and new territories. The fact that they belong to different analytic cultures, together with the fact that they are giving life in this book to a long mutual work, collaboration and inter-influence between French and Latin American psychoanalysis, is to be celebrated as another among their many achievements. It is also another achievement of the IPA's Publication Committee, in its policy of expanding our frontiers and helping analysts from different latitudes to listen and learn from different voices and experiences.

For all these reasons, it is for me a great pleasure to strongly recommend *Psychosomatics Today: A Psychoanalytical Perspective* as a book of reference and as an eloquent update that will certainly help us all to understand better and to face with our patients that enigmatic leap from psyche to soma.

CHAPTER ONE

Thoughts on the Paris School of Psychosomatics*[1]

André Green

The return of the theoretical repressed of psychosomatics

The explanations given *a posteriori* with regard to the Conference in Geneva[2] have not, in my opinion, entirely clarified
the situation. I would like to make some preliminary
remarks in an attempt to justify the diverse and successive formulations concerning the French title announcing it, for this evolution
is significant. During the sole meeting I had with Marty, in preparation for this conference, the theme I proposed was the following:
"How is the primitive material of the mind whose transformation
gives birth to representation to be conceived, and how can this
hypothetical material be used in psychoanalytic practice?" To my
mind, this somewhat enigmatic title had the interest of bringing us
back to the notion of the *psychical representative of the drive.*

I would simply point out that when I speak of primitive material, I do not understand this in terms of what would be found at
the origin of the developmental process of a baby. I have certain

*Translated by Andrew Weller

1

reservations about the mode of explanation that consists in constructing a genesis that exists first and foremost in the head of the theoretician who postulates it and that one then tries to pass off as reality because it is based on something observable. I am speaking of primitive material as it can be inferred from clinical experience with a patient whoever he/she is: adult or child.

"Psychosomatics: a border concept": this title I will return to its rightful owner, that is, Nicolaïdis, because it is his. Nicolaïdis concluded his paper by speaking of the fundamental unity of the human being. One never speaks so much about unity as when it is not obvious, or when it is constantly called into question. There is, indeed, a form of unity between two concepts that are separated by such a fundamental difference that no one would dream for a moment of saying that "psychic" and "somatic" are interchangeable terms. I will try to clarify the nature of this "in-between" zone that separates and unites them. Should "psychosomatic" be written as one word or with a hyphen, a synapse? Here it is written as one word. What, then, is "psychosomatic"? It is worth noting that we always say "psychosomatic" and not "somatopsychic", whereas Freudian theory begins with the soma and then moves towards the psyche. So we should say: "somato-psychic", but the term is not employed. When we speak of an area "between" somatic and psychic, I think that this was an inspirational idea of Marty's and, perhaps, a point of discord between him and me; the problem of the *prepsychic* was being posed, this expression being coined after that of the preconscious.

Just as an agency was invented that is called the preconscious, which is not the unconscious but is closely linked to it because it is the portion of the unconscious that is capable of becoming conscious, so one can postulate *the hypothesis of a prepsychic* as a somatic sphere that is, or is not, capable of becoming psychic. That is the question. The pertinence of certain definitions Freud gave of the drive in the last part of his work will be recognized here.

I think that Marty's work can be understood—and the more I read it, the more this is how I understand it—as an attempt to describe what is in the order of a "fore psychic" (*avant-psychique*). For some years now, I have been attentive to the problem of the language of psychoanalysts, not of the language in the *cure* (enough has been said about this in France), but of the problem of *theoretical language*. Not enough consideration has been given to this point. When one witnesses the confrontations between diverse theories which have a common object, one realizes that there is a level of discussion where conceptual issues are at stake, which is translated by the language used in the theorization. Call that the preconscious of the theoretician, if you will. The language used reflects the ideology that is behind the theory, whether acknowledged or not, precisely in the same way as the subject's preconscious representations reveal a sort of ideology that is constitutive of his mind. Now it is here that we are in the presence of a singular theoretical language in Marty's work, whose particular character has not been sufficiently noted.

As for the second title proposed, "The relevance of the theoretical model of neurosis in the face of non-neurotic and more particularly psychosomatic states", this was mine. I formulated it after Marty had died. Proposing such a title was already a way of introducing, it seems to me, one of the issues of debate, which was a source of the controversy. It is my contention—and I am going to repeat it throughout this paper—that Marty's thinking came up against the following difficulty in his theorization, if not in his clinical descriptions. *For Marty, the model of neurosis provides the sole term of comparison with psychosomatic praxis.* In my opinion, he chose, for historical reasons, to overlook the non-neurotic structures, because he built his system before the authors to whom I am going to refer appeared on the theoretical horizon in France. He ignored the work of the Anglo-Saxon analysts who have had a great impact on contemporary psychoanalytic thinking; I am thinking mainly of Winnicott and Bion. I do not think you will ever find these authors cited in Marty's work. Now this is more than a theoretical symptom: it is a sign of French insularity. There is a regrettable negligence here of the models which emerged from the study of borderline cases and of forms akin to psychosis that now frequently haunt our couches. I say forms *akin* to psychosis, because psychoanalysts need to come down to earth a little and realize that the psychotics they have on their couches are not the same as those in psychiatric hospitals! This evolution was predicted by Freud. Whereas the beginnings of his work are marked by the relations between perversion and neurosis, the end of his work reveals, in my view, a different concern, which is the comparison between psychosis and neurosis. So it is perfectly normal that so much interest was shown thereafter in borderline cases. Psychoanalytic praxis shifted its centre of gravity beyond the context of neurosis. Marty was not aware of this. He did not take it into account, in spite of the work of his friend Bouvet, who drew attention to pregenital structures.

My relations with Pierre Marty were always both ultra simple and rather complicated; I believe that we had mutual respect for each other. He never failed to send me his books with extremely touching dedications in the style: "I am told, dear André Green, that you are the one who is most likely to understand me . . ." Who told him that? And if it was the case, why did he not engage in discussion with me? Now, I fear that Marty was reluctant to have such a debate, but why? Those who were closer to him than I was may be able to tell you, but, personally, I have never understood what the reason was. What would have been my position in such an exchange? Let me reiterate the positions that I have already defended: it is my belief that borderline cases cannot be elucidated by the application of the model of neurosis arising from Freud's work and I have even proposed, in the paper that I presented in London in 1975, a model which is specific to them. I envisage the mind in terms of its frontiers: I try to define it between the bounds or limits of psychical activity. I place the psyche between the soma on one side and reality on the other. And within the psychical field, I see two fundamental mechanisms: depression and splitting. By "depression", I mean a *primary depression*, which is not unrelated to what Marty describes in the form of essential depression. I define it in terms that are close to his, as a lowering of psychical tonus, which I distinguish from neurotic or melancholic depression as we know them.

At the opposite pole, we have *splitting*. I consider it to be a fundamental activity of mental life, because it is with splitting that differentiation begins. The possibility of dividing the universe in two is the first psychical act by which it can be signified: good–bad, inside–outside, etc. In short, all the essential pairs that underlie mental life imply a fundamental (I do not say primitive) and matrix process of splitting. To these fundamental splits, underlying the mind, others must be added. The split psyche/soma—which is part of normal experience—can take a very pathological turn. This is what we observe in psychosomatics. Marty asserts something that is not very far removed from what I am saying. He contends that in the structures he treats, there is a sort of reduction of the whole psychic field, that is, of the inner world, with, on the other hand, a hypercathexis of the factual and of reality, which seem to play a very important role. In other words, the psychosomatic patient puts his soma and external reality in communication, while crushing everything that pertains to the mind. I have argued that the mind can be considered as an intermediate formation between these two poles. This collision between soma and reality raises problems for us that Marty had foreseen. However, should this crushing of the psychic field really be seen in relation to neurosis, or rather in relation to non-neurotic structures, that is, to forms akin to psychosis or borderline cases, where, precisely, another mode of functioning than neurosis obtains, and where the mind avoids this crushing by employing other defensive manoeuvres? Go crazy or die: this is the dilemma in which borderline cases are caught, in my view. But here we are concerned with something else that is more difficult to define.

Let us move on during now to the third title. This title came to my mind during the day of tribute paid to him, during a very interesting paper given by Michel de M'Uzan on Marty's career. At one point, as he was describing a psychosomatic mechanism, he added in passing, "which is not altogether different from what can be observed in certain psychoses or certain borderline cases". I came out of the session feeling quite pleased with what I had heard, and I said to Nicolaïdis, "There you are, now we have the title: the *Return of the theoretical repressed of psychosomatics*." In other words, psychosomatics chose to overlook psychosis and the borderline cases, but the tribute to Marty raised questions that cannot be found in the work of the late master. It was a case of ideas coming back through the window after being refused entry via the door.

On this occasion, I made the following remark to myself: psychosomatics was born in Sainte-Anne where Marty was, at the time, the leading practitioner, at the end of a programme of psychiatric studies. At the time, some doctors in general hospitals were looking for psychiatrists who were able to make a contribution because they had the feeling, faced with certain patients, that something was going on that was beyond them which belonged to psychic, if not psychiatric, pathology. This interested Marty, and so he got involved first by forming an initial core of collaborators, which gave rise later to a foundational book on psychosomatic investigation (Marty, M'Uzan, & David, 1963). Now, in this first group Marty was the only psychiatrist. Neither Fain, de M'Uzan, nor David were psychiatrists. De M'Uzan had frequented the hospital Henri-Rousselle to a certain extent, but I do not think I will offend him if I say that his psychiatric training at that time was certainly not comparable with that of psychiatrists who had worked for four years in psychiatric hospitals and open psychiatric services, and who had a panoramic view of psychiatry and psychopathology which was by no means lacking in depth.

I think that this is what is returning today, at a time when psychosomatic pathology is compared not with Freud's psychoanalytic theory, but with post-Freudian psychoanalytic theory.

Marty's pioneering work, which deserves our full tribute as such, also has the merit of having been capable of jettisoning received ideas and of opening up new paths. A corpus of psychosomatic theory existed before Marty, which he examined very closely, concluding that it did not account for the phenomena that it studied. His work is of considerable importance and was created by a remarkable man. Marty's intellectual honesty and generosity—fundamental qualities for a theoretician—should be emphasized, and we know that it is perfectly possible in psychoanalysis to produce fake works, that is, works that are not marked by any intellectual probity but impress and dazzle because they produce an aesthetic shock effect. I think that Marty stands in complete contrast to this form of intellectual seduction. I would even say that his work has something invigorating about it. It comprises unquestionable discoveries, such as the concepts of "operational thinking" (pensée opératoire), a term which was subsequently replaced by "operational life" (vie opératoire), essential depression, and progressive disorganizations. I am personally convinced that these acquisitions will remain. The criticisms that I would formulate today are not intended to contest these discoveries, but, rather, to ask whether there is not another way of seeing things or if there is not another field, different and yet comparable with the one Marty described, which should be set in parallel with the field he described. None the less, I would differentiate between Marty's *clinical discoveries*, which can be called into question, such as those I have just mentioned, and their *theoretical counterpart*, that is, the explanation that he proposes for these clinical phenomena as well as the overall conception within which they are included.

The germ and its development

Marty says somewhere, I think it is in his book *La Psychosomatique de l'adulte* (1990), that *L'investigation psychosomatique* (his first book, published in 1963, with the collaboration of de M'Uzan and David) contains the embryonic germ of the whole of psychosomatic theory. Indeed, when one re-reads this book, one can say that all the essential points are there. It is at this juncture, however, that I am going to introduce the application of some of the ideas that I have put forward to you. I do not think I am betraying a secret if I say that when one reads the conclusion of *L'investigation psychosomatique* and one sees the description of what was called at the time "operational thinking", de M'Uzan's signature is noticeable. The style is of importance concerning the formulation of ideas.

What does this conclusion tell us? It speaks to us about the person who, at that time, was called the psychosomatic patient. This meant a *psychically normal subject* (a subject who is neither neurotic nor psychotic). Today, we know that this "normal subject" is not at all "normal", and is sometimes a *normopath*. In fact, he is "abnormally normal" (to use the expression an expert had used for the poisoner Marie Besnard[3]), for the so-called normal, as we know, is not as normal as all that. He is not the slightest bit mad, unlike the psychoanalyst who is always a bit crazy. This is why the psychosomatician is disconcerted because he cannot find in the patient the germ of madness that he has within himself, and because he considers he is a bit more normal than others because he recognizes that he is not completely normal and that he is a bit crazy! Joking apart, the psychosomatic subject is cut off from his unconscious, we are told. His id is frozen in somatic forms. He seems more sensitive to the quantitative than qualitative aspects of mental life without possessing a sufficient distinction of "drive values". It is here that there is a remarkable description of which one finds few echoes in the rest of Marty's work, which is that of *projective reduplication*. This projective reduplication is a preoccupation that I would tend to associate more with de M'Uzan. It is remarkable because it indicates, in the psychosomatic patient, a compulsive relationship to the same, the need to find in the other what one is oneself. In short, something which, as far as the functioning of otherness is concerned, can only rediscover the same, and, when it does not succeed in doing so, finds itself in a destabilizing situation. In other words, *it involves a relationship with a "stereotyped" alterity*, in the strict sense of the term, that is, conforming to a stereotype. And here, already, we can see looming the reference to behaviour, which is not at all common in psychoanalytic thinking. We had a few glimpses of it with Reich. It is true that character neurosis, according to this author, implies references to behaviour. As you know, in order to get things moving in some of his analyses, he would say to the patient, "Do you want me to show you what you look like?", and he would lie down on the floor mimicking the patient's attitude on the couch. Here, we are really at the level of behaviour. Let me ask a question: what does behaviour mean in the context of a problem that refers to the relations between the mental and the somatic? Our curiosity remains unsatisfied: is it something that is signified through the ego? Some psychoanalysts are accustomed to referring to personality, or to character. There, the reference to behaviour would already be a way of signifying a certain automation of the mind. (It is worth recalling that in biology the designation of behaviour applies to the animal and clearly plays the role of avoiding recourse to the term "mind or mental life" [*psychisme*].) We are faced with the necessity of taking into consideration a subject in action. However, the action will be linked neither to desire nor to the drive, where, in any case, nothing of this order is noticeable. What is the meaning of what occurs? I have used the word "meaning", but the sense of the meaning is not very clear here. I think I can recall certain expressions such as "money, women, cars . . .", which Marty used to refer to what motivated the existence of certain patients; this was the picture he gave by way of illustration. He was alluding, of course, to a sort of psychic impoverishment and conformism in the individual who follows a prevailing social model, but whose own singular desire cannot be identified in his fantasy life.

So, we can see that a new finding has been introduced into psychoanalysis: sensory-motricity. When we consider things from the angle of sensory-motricity, it takes us back to a kind of reflexological model. In the best of cases, it is a Piagetian model. In psychoanalytic vocabulary, this supposes a theoretical context that is discussed, moreover, by Marty and Fain (1955) in their study devoted to the *role of motricity in the object-relation*. Here, we have the introduction of a foreign body into psychoanalytic thought; I am not saying that it needs to be evacuated, but its dissonant character must be noted. Another observation that deserves further exploration is the *poverty of language.*

All this dates back to 1963. You will see that the main pillars of the theory were already there. Already, at this time, Marty's ambition was to elaborate a similar system in psychosomatics to that of metapsychology in psychoanalysis. This means that the psychoanalytic metapsychology is not applicable, because its counterpart needs to be created for psychosomatics. Metapsychology is beyond psychology; should one speak here of "metasomatics"? One can sense, from the very beginning of this work, the investigator's preoccupation for synthesis, which is quite different from the analytic attitude. The analyst is not concerned with synthesis; he tries to give prominence to elements that he has analysed which belong to the mind alone. Synthesis is subject to the psychoanalyst's spontaneity. Marty constantly stresses this: one has to pay attention to the way the subject enters the consulting room, how he is dressed, how he moves, how he settles down into the chair, and so on; in short, aspects which the analyst will also notice, though he will tend to play down their meaning in relation to others. You will say to me, "But that's all we have to go on with these patients." Perhaps, but here there is a deviation towards the exteriority or the phenomenology of a mode of being.

I want to cite now an interesting paragraph concerning the case study which is presented. The authors say,

Initially, we feared we would not be able to become attached to this apparently dull character, often strictly realistic, somewhat cursory, who acted as if everything was evident and exuded a vague air of sadness. But very quickly, we became aware of a gap in this subject, who was physically ill, of a rupture between this smooth surface, this often uneventful daily life, and an obscure, far off region which was none the less permeated by brutal forces which were likely to erupt into the open episodically, almost without any nuances. Even so, most of the time, we could only grasp this *shadow zone* via the observation of a lack. It was impossible for a human being to be as

flat and resourceless as his way of being tended to make one to
believe. [Marty, de M'Uzan, & David, 1963, p. 262]

Yet, this depth remained opaque until the end, perhaps due to a
lack of appropriate theoretic tools.

This inaugural stylistic formulation was subsequently followed
up in Marty's work when he proceeded to undertake a reformula-
tion of psychoanalytic theory. We do not have, as one might suppose, a psychoanalytic theory that is intact and a psychosomatic
theory alongside it, in addition. In fact, what we have is a reformu-
lation of psychoanalytic theory, but is it acceptable to everybody?
In my view, Marty took a direction that I would call "presignifi-
cative signification": in other words, looking in the mind for what
comes "before" . . . before what? Before. Everyone is looking for the
before, the primal! Melanie Klein looks for this "before" in the
paranoid–schizoid and depressive positions, at the beginning of
life. Piera Aulagnier also looks for the "before", which is why she
speaks of pictograms. For my part, I do not look for this "before",
for a very simple reason, which is that I do not know how I could
find it. So, rather than looking under the street lamp, where there is
more light, for the key that I lost on the pavement on the opposite
side of the road, I try to go on looking for it on the pavement where
I lost it, even if there is no street lamp!

What are these street lamps? They are existing theories. No
researcher invents a theory all by himself. In other words, each
theory is created from a new field of experience and pre-existing
theories. Innovators modify pre-existing theories in the light of
what they think they have found in the new field of experience. But
the way they modify them is by no means innocent. If I wanted to
characterize the nature of the psychosomatic phenomenon according to Marty, I would say that he is concerned with the *prepsychic*
Among the different definitions of the drive, there is one that suits
me well, which consists in saying that the drive is anchored in the
somatic but that the latter, according to Freud, is already part of the
psychical realm "in forms unknown to us" (Freud, 1938, p. 145). I
think that it is this dimension of what is already psychic "*in forms
unknown to us*" that is the issue here, which means that it is not the
forms that we are generally familiar with that will reveal it to us.
Which psychical realm are we referring to? In the "synapsis", or at

the crossroads of the somatic and the psychic, it is a matter of describing the prepsychic psychic, the mind "in an unknown form", but how? The task is to imagine a realm prior to the psychic, or a native mind whose specific qualities have not yet blossomed and still bears the mark of the biologism from which it has barely separated itself. Are we going to describe it in the same way as the psychic already known to us is described or, in order to conceive this unknown prepsychic, are we going to use a description that is more orientated towards the biological? Marty's theorization involves a biologization of psychoanalytic thinking. One gets the impression that Marty was stimulated by his patients into making an extraordinary effort of imagination that led him to create what I will permit myself to call a *fictional biology*. This is not a reproach, for it is not possible to do otherwise; it is exactly the same as when one speaks of the primitive, of the before . . . it is a fictional genetics. I myself am obliged to do so when I have to speak about it.

Marty's biologizing formulation

Let us return to the fictional biology of Marty's theorization. Where can it be identified? It can be seen in the direction taken by the theory, which tips psychoanalysis towards the side of non-meaning, of force, and of everything that the subject evacuates, as if the subject was no longer an affair of the psychical, and, thus, of the psychoanalyst. You will, no doubt, be able to contest this assertion, but I will, none the less, give you some arguments to support my point of view.

For example: Marty re-establishes the notion of instinct; he says, "there is the drive, but there is also the instinct". It is quite clear that when he speaks of instinct, it refers to something that belongs to a reality that is more biological than psychical, yet without being identical with what biology calls instinct. Moreover, Marty characterizes instinct in terms of two activities: automation and programming.

Automatism: it may be objected here that Marty is making connections with psychoanalytic theory by recalling the repetition automatism. But is it the repetition automatism or the repetition compulsion? This is where problems of language, terminology, and style become fundamental. If we are speaking of repetition automatism, it is quite clear that we are closer to the automatism of a biological function, devoid of any form of intentionality. Compulsion, which remains a constraint, is more in the order of the psychical. Next: *programming*. We know the extent to which the notion of programme infiltrated modern biology, only to be contested subsequently. Marty's thinking seems to be a sort of over-biologizing reinterpretation of the conceptual indefiniteness of Freudian biologism. Freud has his biology, but it is a biology that is more metaphorical than real, perhaps a "metabiology" (I have defended the necessity of such a conception in Green, 2000), whereas Marty does away with this metaphor. In other words, he de-metaphorizes in an attempt to delineate a form of realism. In the short biographical note of his last book, *Mentalisation et psychosomatique* (1991), the following words are written about him: "Interested very early on in the relations between the body and the mind of individuals, P. Marty, a doctor, then a psychiatrist, then a psychoanalyst, and always an evolutionist, pursued research . . .". The importance of evolutionist theory on Marty's thinking was considerable. It goes hand in hand with another aspect of his thinking: hierarchization. In fact, there is the soma, there is behaviour, then there is the mind, mentalization, and, clearly, one is only complete and accomplished once one has "mentalized". And this is why we say "psychosomatic", in that order, and not the contrary.

Automation and programming, then: when he turns towards the unconscious, Marty speaks of a primal, fragmented unconscious, the first mosaic. In other words, little bits will come together to form a whole. It is a conception that implies a sort of embryologism, but it is pure hypothesis. It is somewhat reminiscent of Glover's famous conception of *ego-nuclei*, which come together to form the constituted ego. But, here, the inspiration is perhaps less clearly psychical. We take for granted the idea that there is the baby who lives in a state of fragmentation. This is a received idea, accepted by everyone, the Kleinians included. What is the depressive position if not the formation of an object in the process of becoming whole? It seems to me, though, that it is a bit more complicated than that. This sort of evolutive grouping-together is again an effect of "Martyan" programming, of which I think one can say that it is innate. These are ideas that have their weight in biology, but which are more debatable when we are referring to the mind.

A new distinction—again, one of major importance—is proposed between *regression and disorganization*. This distinction is at the basis of a clinical differentiation. In disorganization, it is true that we get the impression that the individual is "coming apart", and that the way that this happens is quite different from a regression. Clinically, this explains a reality that is not accounted for by other theories. Although, for Freud, Schreber's regression was not comparable with that of hebephrenic/catatonic schizophrenics in psychiatric hospitals, here, too, we can speak of psychical disorganization. This means we must give a great deal of thought to the question of the forms of mental or somatic disorganization.

It is by no means easy to conciliate the views of Marty and Freud. When I read Marty, I get the impression of a "biological imagination working beyond Freudian biologism". For example, he writes:

> . . . at each level of organization, the new functional ensembles include a certain number of pre-existing, as it were constitutive functions, at the same time as a new evolving ensemble gives the functions that constitute it a new form of life; it subordinates them by withdrawing certain qualities which formerly guaranteed them a relative independence. The new evolving ensemble thus seems only to leave in place a kind of management which takes on a hierarchical role of great importance. [Marty, 1976, p. 119]

However, the principal component of the organizing power goes still further. In order for the essential movement of the evolving organization that has just been described to be executed properly, functional elements constituting an evolving association must be assembled, etc. We are not accustomed to this language in psychoanalysis; it is a biologically-inspired style that is very interesting, but much closer to the way we may think about the integration of the digestive, respiratory, and immune functions than the way things that concern the mind present themselves. Can we say that what is involved here is the pre-psychic, in so far as it is prior to the psychic? I do not know. in any case, the usual referents of psychoanalytic theory are not present.

I can understand that Marty's patients posed these problems for him, but what does the solution that he adopted mean? He tries to imagine, in his theorization, how psychical functioning occurs according to the somatic model much more than how psychical functioning occurs with the referents of psychoanalysis. Or, alternatively, he seems to unify them in favour of the somatic. I am simplifying here for the needs of discussion. It could be said that we are dealing here with psychophysiological functions rooted in two models: the somatic model and the psychical model, without it being possible to see a common level emerging from the transition from one to the other. In the description I have just given, I search in vain for the so-called unity of monism. Likewise, the mechanisms Marty refers to are mechanisms that obey a causality to which he gives a name and tries to present to us as a working hypothesis, but the economic pole, on which he rightly insists, takes prominence while the semantic pole is progressively evacuated. This is evident with regard to regressions: I note, in passing, expressions designating excessive excitations at the psycho-affective level, a mental disorganization with a minor depression, a psychic regression with a somatic disorganization, etc. One gets the impression that Marty reasons essentially in terms of excess, insufficiency, non-integration, and disorganization, thus, in terms of references which, in my view, are much more reminiscent of those we come across when we are studying a biological function. And this is at a level of clinical theorization which belongs to phenomenology but where, in fact, it is excess, deficiency, and deviation which are in question: *hyper, hypo, dys.* What becomes of the major aspects of psychoanalytic theory? Of pleasure, for example? And of the psychical disorganization which threatens the psychical apparatus, but against which a repression sets in which is likely subsequently to produce a return of the repressed. And of the danger of tipping over into psychosis? All these basic significant organizations, which can be made more complex with the theories of Winnicott or Bion, do not have their place because somatic thinking has absorbed psychical thinking. That is how things happen, you will tell me. I would like

to see the evidence.

Marty's model of thinking lacks a general theory of representation, although he constantly refers to it. In the relations between mentalization and somatization, we cannot make do with the quantitative reference: well mentalized, moderately, poorly mentalized! Tell me what they do with their mentalization; do not tell me that it is simply "a bit too much" or "a bit less" or even an "uncertain mentalization". In Marty's model, we get the impression, in spite of the insistent reference to monism, that there is basically a soma and, at the other extreme, a mental life, and what stands there in the middle? As he describes it, there is a field marked by characteristics which are more biological than psychical, where psychical phenomena are accounted for in terms of excess, insufficiency, deficiency, defect, a lack of organization, disorganization, etc. But according to which model? Neither normality nor neurosis can be described in these terms. We have passed over to the other side of the mind. This is apparent, for example, in his *La Psychosomatique de l'adulte* (1990). The notion of quantity becomes linked to the notion of discharge. If there is too much, it must be evacuated . . . how, then, is it evacuated?

These are questions that Marty asks himself:

> The obstacles to the necessary evacuation of stimuli usually occur at the heart of the mental apparatus, either because of a fundamental insufficiency of the preconscious system of representations or because of a psychical disorganization owing to the fragility of this system, or inhibition, avoidance, or a repression of representations, or the precedence of an "ideal Ego", etc. [Marty, 1990, p. 51]

In fact, this mental apparatus is rudimentary. It does not tell me anything about how a mental apparatus functions generally, and this is where I come back to the question of *L'Investigation psychosomatique*: "Where is the humanity of these subjects?" Are these subjects deprived of humanity? Are they even subjects, or, rather, sophisticated robots?

I am far from being hostile to the biological reference. I have even proposed that it would be interesting to argue in favour of the existence of a *metabiological* point of view to characterize certain aspects of the psychical process present in borderline-cases or in those "on the limits of the analysable". The reference to the economic point of view, recommended by Freud, should not be applied to the letter.

It was necessary for someone to describe things as Marty described them, that is, by adopting the standpoint of a sort of biological reference or causality in order to envisage the functions of this elementary mind that I call "pre-psychic". This vague term applies to a mythical state where the only element in play is the psychical representative of the drive dissociated from (or before) the encounter with the thing- or object-presentation. This component of representation always pulls it towards the soma. Here, the two components are dissociated. Having said this, I think that there is also room for another approach in psychosomatics, which is concerned with questions that equally concern psychoanalysis. We know that Marty is not the only one, and that there are other psychosomatic theories. I am not speaking about non-psychoanalytic theories. In the field of psychoanalysis, McDougall has proposed theorizations with which Marty was in almost total disagreement, but once again there was no debate. On the other side of the Channel, are Winnicott's contributions negligible?

When I was President of the Paris Psychoanalytic Society, I let Marty know that we were ready to give him a whole evening during which he could develop his ideas, even an entire day if he thought a scientific session was too short! He refused. I do not understand very well why, because, really, Marty's theory enjoyed total success; one cannot say that he was an accursed psychoanalyst; everyone referred to his work, his articles and his ideas were cited, so why this withdrawal?

A different version of clinical practice

I am now going to look at things in a different way. I am referring to the article by Colette Jeanson-Tzanck (1993): "Une intervention réorganisatrice dans la psychothérapie d'une vie opératoire" [A reorganizing intervention in the psychotherapy of an operational life]. Why have I chosen this article from the abundant literature that exists on the subject? Because I had the privilege of listening to the exposition of this case in a work group that I ran at the beginning of the 1980s, of which Jeanson-Tzanck was a member. She waited until 1993 to publish this article, which I find remarkable and a rich source of food for thought. It shows that psychosomatic psychopathology cannot be reduced to the conception that is proposed to us. At the time of the experience related, Jeanson-Tzanck was a young colleague, in her third year of analysis. She took part in psychosomatic consultations. One day she was given a case of haemorrhagic proctocolitis in a young woman, and she was told,

"No interpretations, but apart from that feel free to follow your intuitions . . ." A real *double bind*! What sort of countertransferential position does one find oneself in when one is inexperienced and you are told, "You are going to take on a serious case; above all, don't make use of what you know, but apart from that let your feelings guide you." Jeanson-Tzanck found a certain number of traits in her patient which corresponded to what Marty had described. The patient arrived, had nothing to say; no, everything was all right. She lived with her parents and her sister and slept with them in the same room. She simply commented, "It's not at all practical." It is not practical for four people to have to sleep in one room, and the proctocolitis is not practical either, because you have to go to the toilet on the landing very, very quickly. She had practically no memories; yes, a big fright at the age of five when she saw her mother fall into a sewer hole one evening when there were fireworks. In other words, there was a double attraction, from below and from above. She did not ask herself if it was a real or false memory. She was asked about her dreams, and she said, "My dreams are always about stories at the office, which is annoying; it's enough to experience them during the day." The mother was someone who was overly present, guessing everything and, thus, intrusive, presenting rather particular symbiotic modes of communication: "I sometimes have strange fears for my mother's body, when she's expecting her period; I don't know how that affects me." In terms of preconscious impermeability, this is rather remarkable.

Katia, since this was her name, had episodes of nervousness and probably used self-calming procedures. Jeanson-Tzanck's attention was drawn to the strange relations between the outside and the inside in her patient. Katia had insatiable curiosity concerning the outside. She needed to explore the space around her. One could say that the less she had internal space to use, the more she felt obliged to explore external space; but this space was not neutral, it was perfectly clear that there were many demands on her to investigate silently. She presented signs that suggested a malaise in her self-image; she dressed in a way that the therapist found striking. Her clothes never fitted her, they were either too large or too tight. Her relationship to her body was strange. For example, if she broke a nail, she would put it aside and stick it back on later, out of coquetry, she said. She was absolutely incapable of being on time, though this did not prevent her at the office from asking for her status to be given more recognition. She was categorized as a typist and wanted to have the title of secretary.

Jeanson-Tzanck employs colourful images, speaking of a "violent presence of emptiness" in her patient. Yes, you must take interest in the void when working with psychosomatic patients; if you do not, you cannot understand them because that is what psychical space consists of. She gives the impression there is a sort of reality, brimming to the full (the hypercathexis of reality of which Marty speaks). The therapist adopted an attitude that consisted in adopting a technique of binding, in linking ideas together. At a certain moment, the patient began to dream abundantly. The dreams were highly charged, indicating a very important level of instinctual violence, with signs reading "danger of death" in the manifest content. Jeanson-Tzanck says, "I had the impression that there was a second, malevolent or absurd reality in this patient's life". This observation is of considerable theoretical interest. In other words, instead of having a conscious mind and an unconscious mind, we have two realities: a neutral reality and a malevolent or absurd reality. This shows that projection is indeed operating, but in a diffuse and barely identifiable way as such.

This leads me to put forward the hypothesis once again that psychosomatic patients are capable of "normal" delusions. I will explain what I mean by *normal delusions*. The distinction between reality and the imaginary is not well established, but this is not at all because they project their fantasies into reality, as one would say of a psychotic. For example, Katia dreams that someone reproaches her for having violently slammed the door shut, and she adds, switching abruptly into the register of reality, "You know, I shut the door very gently!" In other words, she defends herself against an accusation in reality, as if the dream were the extension of a reality conveying a hostile parental superego. There seems to be a sort of confusion between perception and representation. Jeanson-Tzanck notes, in the dream narratives, the insistent presence of *white*. Everything is very white, the white makes everything seem larger, there are no walls, there are columns, and it is as if there were mirrors reflecting everything endlessly, *mirrors which reflect nothing but white*. This representation of the absence of representations is indicative of the considerable field occupied by negative hallucination, which Jeanson-Tzanck notes in passing. I think that it is absolutely impossible to understand the functioning of a psychosomatic structure if one does not make use of the notion of negative hallucination.

As for the "putting outside", Jeanson-Tzanck reports an astounding event of great semantic richness. It was Christmas time, and Katia's boss had given a small gift to each of the members of his staff: hers was a silk scarf. When she spoke to her therapist about it, she blushed with pleasure. She left the office late and, to celebrate the event, she went off to buy some camembert. Pleasure = silk + camembert. She was very proud of knowing how to choose camembert well. She caught the bus and went home—the journey was rather long. While she was on the bus, she could not stop thinking about the scarf and the camembert. Then she arrived home and noticed that she no longer had the bag in which she had put both these precious objects; she had lost it. It was a violent shock, a trauma. She decided immediately to set off in search of the bag by retracing her journey, but this time on foot, imagining that the bag might have fallen on to the floor of the bus, before being trampled on by the passengers and dragged out onto the pavement. From this moment on, she acted like a sleepwalker, the notions of time and space disappearing on the way. So she went along questioning one *concierge* after the other, as well as shopkeepers, who, she said, still feeling very upset, did not understand anything of what she was saying and answered her disagreeably. For the therapist who was listening, there was a strange conjunction between her increasingly unreal wanderings around and the "operational" (*opératoire*) discourse expressing them. Katia's account of the position of the buildings, everyone's respective attitudes, the polite questions that she had asked them, and the off-putting replies she had received before she finally got to the street where she had caught the bus, was extremely detailed. Coming in the opposition direction, she noticed an elderly couple who looked friendly; she went up to them and asked them the same question, to which they gave a curt reply. Feeling exhausted and nervous, she was about to get into the bus when she saw at her feet, *in the gutter*, the paper bag . . . but empty. It is hardly possible to overlook the implicit symbolism of this pseudo-recognition, in the flow of water carrying contents towards the drain, of a container emptied of its precious contents. Feeling relieved, surprisingly, she picked it up and put it in her handbag. "Of course," she said, "I was upset not to have found the scarf, but it was important to have found the place where I lost it."

If someone speaks to me about uncertain mentalization, I will reply that, for me, it is *over-mentalization.* But it is a mentalization that is only interpretable on condition that a grid of interpretation is applied to it which has nothing to do with that of neurosis, nothing to do with fantasy in forms that we are familiar with, and which implies the existence of other references that are closer to the delusional organization.

Finally, things evolved, a bedroom became available on the same landing, her parents managed to acquire it, and they began to get the premises in order. The therapist was spared no details concerning the material process of rearranging the home, the cleaning up, the bookshelves that would have to be arranged differently, the paint chosen, the wallpaper: this rather than that . . . Then things suddenly came to a standstill, and, after a month and a half, there was still no movement. And yet, the patient had changed. But, from a certain moment on, she no longer knew what was happening, she could not co-ordinate her movements any more, there were surprising gaps, holes . . . In one session, she was in disarray, she could not see what was missing at all, did not know where objects were any more. Everything was blank, and the date when they were due to move in had faded into the distance. Katia asked herself what was missing. Jeanson-Tzanck said to her: *I think the bottom shelf in the cupboard is missing and that the hammer is still on the windowsill; the paintwork also needs touching up.* And Katia replied, her face lighting up, "Goodness." That was my reaction, too . . . "Goodness . . ." I thought this interpretation was brilliant! Because the configuration of the domestic space had been conserved and the place of the objects had not been negativized.

It is clear that the fundamental experience is the alteration of a sort of mnemic ego capable not only of registering events, but of conserving them, of linking them together by giving them a meaning. This mnemic ego is blocked, frozen, immobilized; otherwise, it would guarantee the movement of continuity. It is the experience of temporal and spatial continuity that is at stake. This absence of a frame for conscious experience explains why representation is not operative. It is not supported by the maintenance of the stages of temporal and spatial succession, both at the level of the integration of perceptions and of the transition from perception to representation. Consequently, the place of objects and the constitution of external space as a reflection of internal space create a spatial equivalence without discrimination. Because if we think that a plank is a plank and a hammer a hammer, we are lost! Of course, it is not appropriate to give an interpretation in terms of hammer–penis, but we have to realize that a level of symbolization is concealed which we need to get in touch with by trying first to establish the conditions of this continuity and of the differences between the two spaces.

One week later, everything was finished. Katia was going to have a house-warming party. Jeanson-Tzanck says that from that point on, the patient was able to say, "That makes me think of . . ."; "I think that . . ."; "What do you think about . . .?"

Some personal examples

I would now like to make a succinct presentation of a few personal cases. This experience is much less detailed because the memory I have of it is imprecise, since it belongs to a distant period of my psychoanalytic practice. I am going to present two theses: in the first, I will show that there can be a significant degree of mentalization in patients suffering from psychosomatic disorders; in the second, I will show the absence of somatization in patients with whom I expected, given their mode of functioning, that it would be present.

A was twenty-three years old; she was sent to me by a university assistant, a Lacanian psychoanalyst, who told me that if she had help, she would be quite capable of achieving something later on (from her university point of view). The reason for the consultation was an attack of anxiety following a narcissistic wound: failing an exam. The teacher who had failed her had a terrible reputation for being an authoritarian and intolerant man. I linked this up later with the image of a grandfather who terrorized her mother, but with whom she had had a good relationship as a child. I realized that I was dealing with a sort of noisy hysteria, beyond what we are used to seeing! It was the first patient I had seen for a consultation—there have not been any since—who, having decided to smoke during the interview, got up to take the ashtray that was on my table, beside the armchair, even though there was one near her. This seemed to be a particular kind of impudent provocation, but it was already a mark of envy). . . . I worked with this person for twenty years, before concluding with a therapeutic failure. I learnt, as time went on, that when she was preparing for an exam during the period prior to the consultation with me, she would go to bed to do her revision; she would stop eating and her mother would spoon-feed her. She had a strange hairstyle that made me think of a crown on her head, standing up like a tower. Her anxiety was very apparent; she was nervously excited and spoke in an agitated manner. As I have said, I thought it was a severe case of hysteria, and no more; moreover, the first stages of the analysis were marked by typical hysterical behaviour. She shut herself away at home and would not let her parents in; they were terrified that she was going to commit suicide, especially as she herself threatened to do so all the time. She never put her threats into action, but, at the time, I received phone calls from her father, her mother, and her sister, who in turn threatened to denounce me to the medical association for not assisting a person in danger. The family was organized in a very particular way, with a father who, in his view, was devalued (whereas I think, in fact, he was a good man who had seemingly fulfilled his paternal duties suitably), and a mother who got on well with her husband but maintained an oozing homosexual relationship with her two daughters and occupied a dominating role in the family group. The elder daughter recognized the father's existence, while the younger, my patient, showed little manifest attachment towards him. She presented a total refusal to take into account her positive Oedipal complex, the fusional relationship with her mother being the only one that was admitted. After the beginning of the analysis, once she had taken and passed her exams, she made plans to spend her summer holidays at a university holiday camp, with the obvious aim of meeting young people—a first separation from the family. This turned into a big family issue! They prepared a fiancée's *trousseau* for the occasion, as if she was obviously going to meet her Prince Charming! Of course, nothing happened. Her relations with the young people were marked by an unmistakeable phobic position. The homosexual fixation was too important. She preferred the mother of a fiancé who had been attributed to her to this young man with whom she had no affinity.

Her friendships with women took up a considerable place in her life that was jealously guarded by her mother, who had been very touched by the influence that a teacher had had on her. It was a female teacher, of course. Any kind of anxiety strengthened the tie of dependency on her mother. Thereafter, I had the feeling that the analysis was not leading to much, that there was no notable change. At the beginning of the analysis, she had said that her plan was to finish her studies. So she finished her philosophy degree and then decided she would study psychology, which meant moving closer to psychoanalysis. This programme, at least, had been accomplished. At the end of four years, I spoke about interrupting the analysis at the end of the year. During the summer vacation she had a sudden, unforeseen attack of proctocolitis. On the couch, she had remained silent about her symptoms. She had belly pains but did not say so! This was probably because it would have meant introducing her body into the analysis in a way that she did not want to. I was extremely surprised by this bout of proctocolitis, and wrote to my friend Michel de M'Uzan to ask him what he thought about it. He replied giving me two or three indications, speaking to me about the narcissism of these subjects and of the affects of greed and envy in them. This helped me a bit, because I could recognize my patient in what he was saying. This situation seemed to me at once tragic and significant. The gastroenterologist who had given her a proctoscopy said to her, "Your intestines are crying with blood." The image was striking, but she had not presented phenomena of psychical pain. Rage, desire for mastery, and isolation of the transference were there. I questioned myself as to my eventual errors and blind spots. At that time, I was not familiar with the experience of borderline cases. Faced with this new situation, I started backpedalling. I said we would continue the analysis, and I was even imprudent enough to say that we would continue it for as long as was necessary. After her bout of proctocolitis, she said, "I will never ever have proctocolitis again", and she has never had it since! I was somewhat astonished by this omnipotent position she adopted towards her body and by her mastery of bodily functions, which she carried to great lengths. Her sexuality, which was inaugurated during the treatment, was always partial. Even if she had some sexual relationships, she never fell in love or never admitted to having done so. She spoke to me at length about her dreams, and every time a dream presented elements of sexual seduction, she always ended by saying, "There was no penetration."

Later, she began to complain of swelling in her breasts. This gave rise to a nightmarish analytic phase. In fact, she had Reclus' disease, or polycystic breasts, for which she had consulted various gynaecologists. She felt sensations of breast swelling which seemed to me to correspond more to a change in her bodily experience than to objective variations of volume. It was only an impression, but a strong one, none the less. She gradually shut herself away within an incurable sense of pain, saying, "It hurts me." All the doctors she consulted said, "It's strange, it shouldn't hurt you!" She repeated, "It hurts!" She called her mother and said, "It hurts!" Her mother replied, "Yes, it hurts you, but what can I do about it?" "I don't know, you're the mother!" This was reproduced on the couch. Another narcissistic wound occurred. Since the death of her maternal grandmother, with whom she had got on very well, unlike her mother, the latter had become somewhat distant towards her and had ceased to play the manipulatory and fusional games to which they had hitherto abandoned themselves, in order to devote herself to bridge. This was a catastrophe for my patient, because she experienced it as an abandonment and a betrayal. Retrospectively, she had the feeling she had been used as a weapon in her mother's conflicts with her own mother. Once the grandmother had died, she felt she was of no interest any more to her mother. As for her mother's attachment towards her father, it was erased from her mind. There was reason to suppose, however, that penis envy in her was based on the fact that the father possessed what enabled him to keep the mother with him. The only tie with her father took the form of a wish to take his place. Coming back to her relationship with her mother, not everything was positive there. She sometimes experienced it in terms of intrusive omnipotence (psychically and physically during episodes when she would refuse to eat certain dishes prepared by her mother). At certain periods, there were episodes in which she would persecute me with the telephone, to the point even of calling me anonymously forty times a day. At the end, I was subject to uncontrollable and overwhelming countertransferential reactions—I did not hit her, but it was not for lack of desire to do so! I often thought that her father ought to have spanked her a few times to sanction her unbearably disturbed attitude. I witnessed phenomena that I call normal delusions. For example, she would say, "It's dreadful, my ceiling is damaged; water from my neighbour's bathroom is leaking into my apartment." This sort of thing, which all of us may experience occasionally with displeasure, would turn into a nightmare for her. It is no longer just a disagreeable event, giving us the impression, as we look at the ceiling, that it really does look bad, and that we have to do something about it such as telephone the householder's association and then have things repaired quickly. For her, it became a barely symbolic anal penetration, a rape, a forced enema, as if the event was experienced in her body. And when I would give an interpretation and compare this with some episode in the past when her mother forced her to eat, she would reply, "But it's obvious!" The symbolic equation was not symbolized, in the sense that it did not lead to much associatively and, in particular, to a deduction.

Finally, one day, in view of the overwhelming nature of the transferential and countertransferential experience—the interminable telephone conversations outside the sessions which led to nothing, and sometimes sterile eruptions of anger on my part—and having reached a stage where I felt caught up in a pathological countertransference, feeling powerless and without any further hope, I decided to put an end to the relationship. I set a time limit, diminished the number of sessions, giving her time to adjust, but the end of the analysis was very distressing. She enjoined me to give her an explanation: "I want you to tell me why it hasn't worked!" Which meant, "What has happened in your countertransference to explain why it hasn't worked? Because, on my side, everything was normal in my transference. I am your failed child!" And this was accompanied, at a certain moment, by fantasizing of a critical nature, making me fear a psychotic breakdown that never, in fact, occurred, but I could, none the less, sense the delusional aura of the fantasy!

Her condition required her to be followed by a psychiatrist whom she saw, then she went to see seven or eight colleagues, telling them that I was an awful analyst who did not understand her, who assaulted her, etc. She finally found an analyst who accepted taking her on: this was unhoped for and, of course, she did not turn up on the appointed day, she did not follow it up, and chose another without any more success.

She had a demand: "I refuse to do any other form of therapy apart from analysis. If I am told that I cannot do analysis, it's an unacceptable wound." As she read a lot, she knew that we meant that, in short, she was poorly mentalized! A colleague whom she had seen told me that for him it was clear: she was a psychotic who imagined she could do analysis when in fact she could not.

To conclude, I have to say that she taught me a lot and she inspired all my descriptions of the "double limit" (1982). A long time after she had finished with me, she lost her mother and I thought that she was going to collapse, but this is not, in fact, what happened. On the other hand, she fell out with her whole family because her sister and her father accused her of having killed her mother by her attitude. I propose this for your consideration. (I have been informed by a colleague who met her and identified her, having read a paper I had written about her, that he proposed that she should continue an analysis with him. She rejected his proposal. Her somatic condition was now that of a precancerous state. Reading the newspaper some years after, I was informed that she had died at the age of fifty-four.)

B. A case of severe asthma, with eczema, the patient had an elder brother who suffered from polio and had developed a liking for transvestites. He himself was in a position of homosexual and masochistic submission towards this elder brother. He indulged in masturbatory and masochistic practices, which went as far as pushing a knitting needle into the urethra.

This man was extremely moving owing to his intense suffering, which made him, quite literally, extremely "irritable", since he suffered from a very invasive skin allergy. During the analysis he had a delirious episode. At the time, I used to live in a street where there were many art galleries. On his way to where I lived, he began to become delirious in connection with a painting that he had seen in the gallery that was situated at the foot of my building. He developed a delirious episode, which cleared up in a few days. Thereafter, I continued to see him face-to-face while he was having crises verging on states of asthmatic suffering. I managed to stop the bouts of asthma during the session, by interpreting them. However, he had begun overdoing things at the masochistic level. The whole family was pressuring him, saying, "You must stop this analysis." One day he said to me, "I hit the security barrier on the motorway!"

Well, I must confess, I was afraid this was a failed suicide attempt, so I found a way to bring our work to an end gradually. Since then, he has been followed from time to time by a colleague who is a psychiatrist and psychoanalyst. He is doing well on both the somatic and psychic levels.

These were both patients, then, who presented major somatic symptoms: the first during the analysis, and the second since childhood. Both seemed to me to have a "rich" mentalization. Patient A had highly rigid defences and was definitely fragile narcissistically, but her psychical life was far from impoverished. Patient B was psychologically very sharp. His almost permanent physical pain did not prevent him from having an intrapsychic fantasy life, accompanied by fruitful associations that made these sessions full of interest.

I am now going to discuss cases where, on the contrary, all the elements were present to favour the emergence of somatic illnesses, even though these never developed.

Of all the cases I have presented in this paper, this patient, C, is the one that poses me the most insoluble problems. I am the third analyst to have treated this woman, who has been in the hands of colleagues for at least twenty years. Why did I accept her into psychotherapy? Perhaps because I had the feeling I understood something about her, whereas I had the impression, rightly or wrongly, that nothing of her had been heard up until then—a sin of pride which is always paid for very dearly. I cannot go into the details of this treatment, and will confine myself to mentioning only what is relevant to the discussion. I have never observed with more intensity in any other patient phenomena involving blocked associative activity, the paralysis of fantasy life, and psychic sterilization. In addition, thought disturbances manifest themselves with incredible force in intellectual work, which is a source of conflicts. The patient presents marked characteristics of the structure that I have described as *primal anality*. Her narcissism is in tatters, she is immensely isolated, extremely destructive, and her psychical pain is permanent. Moreover, the transference is expressed in exclusive and exaggerated forms in such a way that analytical psychotherapy has become a substitute for her life. Her relationships are poor, her erotic life non-existent, and her libidinal anaemia allows—extremely rarely—very crude dreams to explode which are not elaborated or explored in terms of their meaning. Defences of rationalization and intellectualization are intermittent and employed characteropathically. She imposes a double bind situation. If one does not respond to this, one creates in her the idea that she is the object of intolerable scorn, and if one attempts to interpret, one meets with a wall of obtuse incomprehension: "I don't understand anything, please explain yourself, explain to me what you mean." I have wondered many times why this patient did not present psychosomatic illnesses—she had everything that was needed to do so. What is more, I asked myself if my interventions, which attempted to break through the dam and her resistances, did not in fact risk provoking them. She always enjoys perfect health.

The second case, D, for whom I was the third analyst, presented an enormous sense of guilt and strategic cunning in his associations, which I found astonishing. This patient made a marked use of unbinding, as well as tactics of subjective disengagement, with regard to which one could not help wondering why they did not lead to somatizations. She suffered from a concealed and permanent depression, with a constant low sense of self-worth, seeking repeated evidence for her uselessness and systematically annulling the narcissistic gratifications that she could receive. The narcissistic wound caused by diverse failures in her professional or sentimental life seemed incurable. It is true that her fantasy life was not inexistent, but, in any case, she mistrusted intensely any thoughts that were connected with what was not real. The transference, albeit very intense in my view, was barely analysable owing to the way she rationalized and, thereby, distanced the affects she felt towards me. The only ones that she allowed herself to acknowledge were those that expressed hostile feelings or nourished a sadistic image of me. But, above all, I was sensitive to the processes of associative rupture and sterilization of thought processes. The analysis was a hard ordeal, soliciting intense masochism and perilously calling into question the idealization of her objects and her self-idealization. I often wondered why this patient did not somatize. The fact is that it did not happen. I have to say that this analysis, which was often distressing, ended in a very positive way and led to very satisfying analytic work during the last year. This was a fortunate outcome, but what are we to think of this tenacious mental functioning, which may be explained, moreover, by the existence of the long-term after-effects of a childhood trauma which had been isolated? The analysand did not realize how her present symptoms could reflect the unconscious guilt that was associated with it.

These clinical cases seem to me worthy of discussion. I am hoping that my colleagues from the Paris Institute of Psychosomatics (IPSO) or from the Geneva Association of Psychosomatics (AGEPSO) will shed light on their obscurities for me. During the discussion, I will propose an alternative to Marty's position, which is based on a general theory of representation that is not limited to the pair word-presentations–thing-presentations. It is a grave error to consider that Freud's psychoanalytic theory of representation is limited to word-presentations–thing-presentations. Let me remind you that the drive is the *psychical representative of a state of excitation originating from within the organism* and, furthermore, we know that a drive has psychical representatives that cannot be reduced to what are called thing-presentations. It is from this position that we can seek to communicate with the psychosomaticians, not so much in order to contest what they have described, but *to offer a stepping stone to psychoanalytic theory*, which, it seems to me, still has to be conceptualized.

A general theory of representation

The last work by Marty (1991) is titled *Mentalisation et psychosomatique*. "Mentalization" is a term which he practically invented. In this short and welcome work, whose clarity of exposition is very useful, Marty poses the question: "What does mentalizing mean?" This deserved to be elucidated. He arrives at the conclusion that mentalizing means to appreciate the quantity and quality of psychical representations. This leads us to a question that is not self-evident: "What does to represent mean?"

What does to represent mean? The question of time

To represent is to "make present", in the absence of what is perceivable and which thus has to be formed by the psyche again. Making present is to be taken literally, in relation to the moment when it occurs, when something is evoked which was, but is no longer present, but which I make present once again differently, by re-presenting it; at the present instant, in the absence of what I am speaking about, I represent. To represent is also, I believe, as Marty shows, to associate. To associate is to establish a certain number of relations between representations, so it involves binding. The whole dimension of the past joins up with the dimension of the present, since these associations also concern pre-existing represen-tations. This means that there is a link between what is made present and what the psyche has already conserved, and, perhaps, bound (in the unconscious) in one form or another. This brings us back to the relations between representation, memory, imagination, associations, etc.

Another dimension to consider is that to represent is to project. But projecting always involves conceiving of a dimension in rela-tion to what is possible, to virtuality, depending on the future. So, past–present–future are "represented" in the activity of representa-tion.

Representation is also the activity of a subjectivity that takes up a position. An individual who projects or who represents, decides. He reveals himself through his positive and negative choices. He always implicates himself in relation to his representations: "I agree to that or I don't want to". Sometimes, this manifests itself in sessions by: "There is something, but I don't feel like talking to you about it . . .", which is the minimal form of "I don't want to"; the maximal form is the foreclosing form, "I don't even want to hear anything about it", or "I have a blank".

Finally, when we reconstruct the activity of representation, we will discover that there is an evident problematic of time, but there is also a spatial problematic of representation. In fact, when one considers the field of representation, one can see that it includes different spaces. This can be the body, the world, or the other: these are the three fundamental dimensions of representation. The body, the world, and the other are places that are not only different, but radically heterogeneous. These are not philosophical categories that I am proposing, but simply a classification in the order of represen-tations. It is clear that the analyst will not treat these representations in the same way. The field of bodily representation ranges from the most fundamental bodily experiences to its appearance. It will involve a mode of carnal representativity which will be different from that of the representation of the world. The representation of the world covers the thing- or object-presentation. As for the representation of the other, language will have a prevalent role in it.

Drive and psychical representation

The model of wish-fulfilment

When we draw up an inventory of the question of representation, we cannot content ourselves with its restriction to the duality word-presentation–thing-presentation (ideational representative and affect representative are just a subdivision of the thing- or object-presentation). It is here that we need to recall Freud's definitions of the drive. Freud says, "If now we apply ourselves to considering mental life from a biological point of view . . ." (see below), a part of the statement that is always left out. Yet, it is impossible to disregard it, as it is really an absolutely fundamental Freudian predicate; it means, "If we situate ourselves theoretically from the biological point of view, that is, of human life, we will say that . . ." What is said has no meaning outside a biological point of view. Bion would speak of a "vertex".

So,

> If now we apply ourselves to considering mental life from a biological point of view, the "instinct" appears to us as a concept on the frontier between the mental and the somatic, as the psychical representation of the stimuli originating from within the organism and reaching the mind. [Freud, 1915c, pp. 121–22]

We really have difficulty in understanding what the term "frontier concept" means. It is a concept that does not only concern that which is at the frontier between the somatic and the psychic; it may also be a concept on the frontier of what is conceptualisable. If you consider things from a biological point of view, and not from the standpoint of the mind, is this conceptualizable? The formula "psychical representation of the stimuli originating from within the organism and reaching the mind" refers to an extremely complex reality, of a nature that is at once topographical (the spaces crossed) and dynamic (the movement conveying the stimuli which are also a source of information). Freud then refers to the question of the measure of the demand made upon the mind for work, something the psychosomaticians are very familiar with and which relates to a qualitative and quantitative function. This definition of the drive thus comprises the three dimensions of metapsychology: dynamic, topographical, and economic. The economic dimension is designated here through the demand for work; the dynamic dimension is the excitation originating from within the body and transported, *transferred*, to the mind, a trajectory that originates in the depths of the body and enters the psychical domain. In another context, Freud said that on its path from the source to the object, the drive becomes psychically active, which means that the drive is divided between an organic source and an object that is not organic, but that, in the end, it is its relation to the object which gives it its psychical quality. The topographical dimension is due to the territorial division, the stimuli originating within the body and reaching the mind, that is, entering another territory. Later on, in the *Papers on Metapsychology* (1915), Freud uses the term psychical representative of the drive. This provokes a state of uncertainty because we are not sure what he means: the psychical representative of the drive is confused with what is referred to in Anglo-Saxon terminology as the "ideational representative" (*représentant-représentation*, in French terminology): a regrettable confusion. I think that the psychical representative of the drive is the representative of what these bodily stimuli that represent the dynamic force of the body, that reach the mind, and that are thus represented within it in a non figurative form, become. This dynamic force of the body is the basis for a meeting between this psychical representative and the memory trace of the thing- or object-presentation left by an earlier experience of satisfaction.

The experience of satisfaction has left a trace, a trace of the satisfying object, and, when a wish reappears later on, the wish for the breast, for example, this will manifest itself as a demand for satisfaction originating in the body. What is this "demand for the breast" going to do? Failing immediate satisfaction, it will call up, among the available representations, the representation of an earlier experience of satisfaction, and of the object that caused it, that is to say, the breast, and will put its trust in it, in other words "suck" the representation of the breast. The child will be no further on for that, but from this moment on, an internal link will be created between the psychical representative of the drive (bodily demand for the breast) and the imaginary dimension of the thing- or object-presentation (the experience of the breast providing satisfaction). We will then have a complex dynamic representation, which will itself subsequently divide into ideational representative and affect representative. Affect is the result of what remains of the drive when a work of representation has taken place in respect of the object-presentation. The affect that invests this object is a manifestation of the subject's affect, for affect is distributed—in my opinion—throughout the psychical apparatus and energizes it.

Recalling this Freudian model, which I have returned to and commented on many times and for diverse purposes, is of particular interest here. If we postulate that there are relations, in both directions, between somatic and psychic, which requires us to distinguish these two entities first, considering somatic pathology from the angle of its relations with the mind can lead us to particularly fruitful hypotheses. If, clinically, we can observe the weak permeability of the preconscious and the irregularity of mental functioning, from a more speculative point of view, and addressing a more unconscious level, somatic-psychic relations can appear in an entirely new light on the basis of this model. When we are dealing with a somatic pathology concerning which there is reason to suppose that it is sensitive to psychic influences, several eventualities may be envisaged. It might be the case, for unknown reasons, that the stimuli originating within the organism never reach the mind, because the described apparatus is unable to "hear" the call of the somatic stimuli, and because their demand expresses a demand for work that must be interpreted by the mind. Or, alternatively, it could be that the somatic, having succeeded in crossing the somato-psychic barrier, finds it is refused access to the mind and sent back to its source, in the same way as Freud speaks of access to the conscious mind being refused to an instinctual impulse or an unconscious idea. Here, it is a question of repression. In the case I am describing, it would probably be more appropriate to speak of a suppression. But what is the distinctive feature of this case? It may be that the demand that has reached the mind contains a very strong destructive charge. Thus, to protect itself, or perhaps to protect the ego or the object to which the demand for work is addressed, the equivalent of foreclosure occurs, a sort of repressive

deafness of the mind which leaves the subject prey to this destructivity, which then finds expression at the somatic level itself. The
subject is totally unaware of this destructivity, which, moreover, is
not noticeable at the psychical level; but he will, none the less,
suffer the consequences of it in the severity of his somatic illness.
Here, we have an example, then, of an enlightening application of
the model of the drive in the psychosomatic field, provided, that is,
the soma is seen as playing an equivalent role to that which is
played by foreclosure for the mind.

Three forms of representation

This theorization reveals the contradiction concerning representation. When Freud says, "psychical representation of the stimuli
originating from within the organism and reaching the mind", the
stimulus that reaches the mind bears no relation to the stimulus
originating from within the body. Let me explain: if I am thirsty, this
is a mechanism that biologists describe as the result of intra- and
extra-cellular dehydration. Freud would say, "You are experiencing
a tingling sensation in your throat, which has absolutely nothing to
do with the earlier biological perspective. The tingling sensation
occurs at the psychical level, whereas dehydration occurs at the
biological level!" The proof that the two aspects do not coincide is
that this is only true for average values. In other words, if you are
thirsty under ordinary conditions, and you drink something, you
are satisfied and feel well again. But if you are in the desert and you
are very thirsty after days and days of drinking nothing, and you
then drink without restriction as soon as water is available, you will
die if you do not take some salt at the same time. But your body
sends you no sign to tell you that you must take some salt! We are
at the level of the psychical representative of the drive, which
expresses the need to recover well-being again by satisfying thirst.

    There is a second aspect of representation: it can be conceived as
the image of a real object in the mode of a copy of the latter. This is
representation as illusion, as with the image of the candle in the
mirror in as much as it reflects the object that is outside the mirror
in reality. There is a relation between the image and object, as is
implied by the thing- or object-presentation. The difficulty lies in
condensing the two forms into one, which is of another type. This

is how the nature of the ideational representative is to be understood. In the first topography, because the model is founded on optics, it is the first conception, namely, the psychical representative, which is sacrificed. The drive is outside the apparatus. In the second topography, it is the contrary, because, with the id, the apparatus now includes the drives.

The third type of representation, word-presentation, involves language. It, too, has strictly nothing to do with the thing! There is no relation between the word "tree" and the thing "tree". And even less with the psychical representative of the drive. What is important is to recognize that the latter sustains the investment of representations. Representations must be invested if they are to be transformed. If I refuse to give value to these representations, if these representations are too painful, if I am unable to suppress them, and if I cannot free myself from the sway they have over me, I destroy them. This outcome is completely different from repression. We end up with a theory of representation that has to be pushed to the paradoxical point of abolishing the distinction between representation and perception, for what is abolished is the possibility of "perceiving" these representations, as the perceptions are abolished in negative hallucination. In this sense, perception can be considered as a sort of representation, that is, of external reality, in the same way as unconscious representation makes it possible to perceive psychical reality. But there is a huge gap. The image perceived is supposed to give a representation of reality, but reality is never reflected neutrally. So, when Marty speaks of the insufficiency or unavailability of representations, we are obliged to interpret this by asking ourselves if this insufficiency or this unavailability is due to a deficiency or to a refusal of the type: "I don't want to know about it . . .". The paradox is that the factual is hypercathected, just as the positive hallucination covers a negative hallucination.

Bodily configurations

Another aspect concerns an issue that, contrary to appearances, has not been discussed today. We have spoken about the soma and about somatizations, but we have forgotten the body. Now, in my view, it is not possible to reflect on psychosomatics without taking into account the structural differences between the soma and the body. Let us consider briefly what are known as *functional disorders*. In the "Wolf Man" (1918b), Freud says that the patient's bowel began to "join in the conversation". Clearly, at that moment, Freud was giving meaningful and even representative value to this bodily manifestation that served as a sort of reminder of the patient's anality and was expressing itself in the patient's relation to his body, almost in the mode of conversion.

A great deal of discussion has been given to the relations between *conversion* and *somatization*. This subject was considered by Marty: it raises the whole problem of symbolization or non-symbolization. Compared with the recognized mystery of psychosomatics, conversion is at least just as great a mystery for me! The explanation that we give for conversion is an explanation that is worth what it is worth, but it loses nothing of its depth and opaqueness, in spite of its relations with symbolization.

Another aspect we need to consider is the *actual neuroses*. If neurasthenia is sometimes reminiscent of depression, and if anxiety neurosis evokes diffuse anxieties, there is one, however, that poses much more complicated problems, and that is *hypochondria*, which is rarely discussed in psychosomatics. Hypochondria, the first stage of psychosis according to Freud, involves the setting-up of a persecutory relationship, of an object inside the body which breaks away and speaks in its own way. It is clear that the model of actual neurosis obliges us to take into account a sort of destructive auto-erotism which arises from a segregation, and installs, via an organ, the voice of a whole object, a quasi-person.

And that is what is crazy: how can you speak about the body without speaking about the *delusions of bodily transformation*? I wonder why the psychosomaticians seem to have so little interest in this form of psychical elaboration of bodily experience compared with the non-elaboration by somatic patients of their psychical conflicts.

Finally, psychosomatics. It is very clear that we have spoken about organizations that are meaningful in very different and unequal ways. Marty wanted to distance psychosomatics from a certain image surrounding it. He wanted to jettison certain theorizations that described particularities of character corresponding to diverse types of psychosomatic illnesses, and I think he was right. That does not spare us the necessity of comparing these different configurations, which will lead us to clarify the distinctions between the soma and the body.

The "body" is the libidinal body, in the broad sense (erotic libido, aggressive libido, narcissistic libido), whereas the soma refers to what is known of the biological organization. It is quite conceivable, moreover, that the latter can cut itself off from the libido and the unconscious, as Marty maintains. Generally speaking, in analysis, it may be considered that we are *always* dealing with the body, even when there is a somatic disorganization! Can we deal with the soma directly? For my part, it seems scarcely possible.

In analysis, that is, when we approach problems from a psychical point of view, we only have indirect relations to the soma. This is illustrated by the case I have just presented. Essentially, we never touch the soma, we are in the position of observers in relation to it; we take into consideration what is happening, but we can only speak to it through the voice of the body. On the contrary, we can speak to the body; even when faced with somatic symptomatology, we can speak to the bodily aspect of this somatic symptomatology. But the bodily aspect is not the somatic aspect, since the latter is transformed by its relations with the psychical, to the point that it is as if the body can "go crazy" with regard to the expressions of the somatic, and it is this "delusion" alone which is of concern to us.

Meaning and non-meaning

These remarks lead on to the question of the relations between meaning and non-meaning. When, in psychoanalysis, we discover the existence of an unconscious causality which makes the patient say, "I didn't do it on purpose . . . it was a slip of the tongue, don't put words into my mouth . . .", well, in respect of the double meaning of words, we infer a different causality from conscious causality. We, none the less, claim that it is psychical; so, at this point we are dealing with two causalities, one of which wants to say something and depends on conscious causality, while the other, on the face of it, does not want to say anything (it is stupid!), and the whole work of analysis consists in showing that the manner in which the tongue slipped was not pure coincidence and that, in fact, what was apparently in the order of non-meaning does acquire a meaning, but within an organization which is not the same as the first one. And so there is a causality that concerns the passage from non-meaning to meaning.

This phenomenon can be extended much further, as far as the frontiers of what is analysable. Here, too, we are can find another meaning, so we are always able to place two causalities in mutually conflicting relations without evoking the slip of the tongue: "This is perhaps want you want to say, this is what you are in fact saying, which suggests that something else is expressing itself in you which you refuse to say. I am proposing that we try to see together how we can throw light on another dimension which is not observable."

When you are faced with a psychosomatic structure, you have the conscious organization and the psychosomatic illness. What is between the two is a shagreen or rough skin. This is what Marty says: what he theorizes is precisely this effect of the shrinking of the preconscious, the reduction of the quantity and quality of its properties, particularly its representative properties, of its layers (thickness, layering), of the problem of affects, etc. We find ourselves faced with a situation in which the conscious discourse and the somatic structure are face to face. Everything that would be needed to form a buffer between the two or to reveal what is going on under the surface is extremely precarious, highly fragile, and even, perhaps, potentially dangerous to mobilize. This creates within the psychical structure relations with non-meaning of which we have little idea. The somatic illness continues to remain stubbornly on the side of non-meaning, not in the sense of absurdity or by treating someone who puts forward such an interpretation as crazy (an interpretation which hypothesizes an unconscious meaning), but as a rejection of a possible relation (with the psychical) because it leads to no reaction and falls into a void (Figure 1).

The zones with dotted lines represent respectively: the somato-psychic frontier (unconscious mind), the barrier of the preconscious (and the representative which is coextensive with it), and finally the stimulus barrier.

It is easy to transform this schema, which refers to the first topography, into the terms of the second topography: id anchored in the somatic, devoid of representations; unconscious and conscious ego; superego anchored in the id, and opening on to the territories of the unconscious and conscious ego, topping the whole structure.

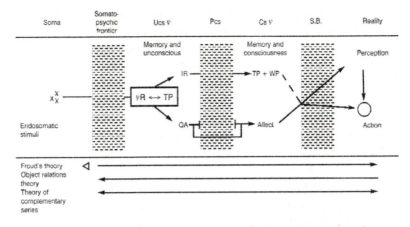

Figure 1. Key: ψR = psychical representative of the drive; IR = ideational representative; QA = quota of affect; TP= thing- or object-presentation (unconscious or conscious); WP = word presentation; O = object.

In the best of cases, what we will be able to do is to lead the subject to give a meaning to what is happening in him or with us, with great caution; to detach a part which has been included in non-meaning and to consider it differently with a view to making it meaningful; but the non-meaning of the somatic illness remains, though it does not remain intact. We approach it indirectly without being able to imagine or conceive of the paths by which the relations between meaning and non-meaning will be influenced by it. And yet, it continues. Smadja has said as much with regard to the somatic symptom: there is no meaning as such, but there is a meaning within somatic pathology. Evidence for this can be found in the way somatic events are interconnected. All this is a meaningful sequence in the order of a natural causality which has nothing to do with what we call "meaning" at the psychical level. There is an aporia in psychosomatic medicine that is the problem of non-meaning whose frontiers can be pushed back but never suppressed. I would like to help you appreciate what I have said with a summary.

The four territories

I am going to return to the points set out above and attempt an enumeration that will entail certain repetitions. Four territories need to be distinguished: the soma, the unconscious mind, the conscious mind, and external reality. These territories help us to sort out our ideas, but they also correspond to a certain reality (see Green, 1995). Earlier, in giving a definition of the drive, I spoke about stimuli originating from within the soma: this is the moorings of the somatic. Freud speaks here of "body", but elsewhere he says the "soma" whose excitations reach the mind. Here, there is a first zone of transition, which I consider to be absolutely fundamental, which is the somato–psychic barrier: no one speaks about it, but it is of cardinal importance.

These stimuli that reach the mind are precisely what is meant by the drive, and it is considered that it is these stimuli that reach the "edge" of the mind, that is, which can eventually acquire meaning. This formulation is metaphorical, more or less mythical. What is important is to consider the drive in this position; it designates the "psychical representation of the stimuli within the body".

The psychical will become associated with the trace of the object-representation, that is, the representation of the breast, arising from an earlier experience of satisfaction, and, under these circumstances, a new psychical bloc is created. In other words, the trace of the breast, a libidinal object, is carried by a dynamic force. Imagine a sort of internal dialogue that would go like this: "Things are not going very well with the soma, there is a need for nourishment, a need for milk, something is needed . . . You must do whatever is necessary to make it happen." The soma poses a problem and it is up to the psychical structure to resolve it. How does the infant make this breast come? He begins by returning to the traces of the earlier satisfaction: this is hallucinatory wish-fulfilment. This provides momentary relief, but it does not remedy the situation. He then expresses his dissatisfaction and protest, even his anxiety, distress, and pain: he gets agitated, he cries, etc. The mother comes as soon as she hears the signs of distress, the breast arrives with her and the demand is satisfied *a minima*. But the combination of the demand and the response will represent a dynamic force. It is in this sense that the psychoanalytic structure of representation has nothing to do with the representations of philosophy.

The representations of the philosophers do not concern us, because our reference is to what happens in the transference. There is a demand as above. Likewise, the patient will say to the analyst,

"Things are not working out in my life; things don't work with my wife (or my husband) or in my job, do something!" The analyst listens, tries to imagine what is happening through the transferential discourse and proposes an interpretation based on the discourse of the demand that is addressed to him. This is not what is going to modify the situation, but in the session something will have been heard and reflected back. At this moment, the initial demand changes: it becomes a demand to be heard, even if one is unable to provide a solution to the problem. But to be heard and understood changes the person who makes the demand and changes the demand as well, which becomes a demand to be heard.

This occurs at the unconscious level and it is here, I think, that this complex of matricial representation divides into what the Anglo-Saxons call the *ideational representative* (the content) and the *quota of affect*. We can see how the affect becomes charged with the dynamism that existed at the level of the psychical representative. What happens now? The two representatives will try to cross the barrier into consciousness. Here, the second zone of passage is encountered which is different from the somato–psychic barrier: it is the *preconscious*. Those who come from the field of psychosomatics say to me, when they see this schema, "Isn't it possible to spread out the preconscious more?" In any case, it is a territory and not a frontier. What is important to realize is that the preconscious is also a barrier or a filter. *It is a censor, a filter, a passageway, and a space of psychic transformations*. And it is at the level of these transformations that we have thoughts, properly speaking; because the preconscious gives room to word-presentations. In consciousness, we are dealing with thing-presentations associated with corresponding word-presentations, as Freud points out. To this may be added affects that are expressed here in a qualitative manner.

And, finally, the zone of transition: this separates the psyche from external reality and is called the *stimulus barrier*. Hence, the use psychosomaticians make of stimulus barriers and the importance they give them in relation to the object. It is worth recalling here that, according to Freud, reality is represented in the ego by ideas and judgements related to reality, to use his own terms.

The usual Freudian schema consists in travelling from the soma along the entire chain. In the modern schema of so-called object-relations, the schema goes in the opposite direction. That is, it starts out from the object and arrives at soma. In the first direction, it is the intrapsychic that prevails; in the second, it is the object-relation or even the intersubjective relation. In my view, we do not have to choose between the two. It is, rather, a permanent to-and-fro situation. Sometimes, stimuli originate in the subject. They can originate in any of the four territories: the soma, the unconscious mind, the conscious mind, or external reality, that is, in the external object and in the relationship with the object. Sometimes, they are emitted in the vicinity of the object and affect more or less each of the territories, sometimes exhausting themselves in one of them.

In these territories of investment, the activated area sets the structure on fire. From then on, the direction in which the fire spreads is extremely interesting, but it is not predetermined. It can originate in the soma, the unconscious, the conscious, or in reality, but from whatever point it starts, it is the direction followed by the course of excitations that is important, whether progressive or regressive or alternating each direction while mobilizing the capacity for absorption and elaboration of each of the territories traversed.

Marty speaks of the flow and the obstacle to the flow. This is certainly one of the dimensions of the problem. We must beware of falling into unidirectionality. The psychical structure, faced with the problem of flow, or of retention, must decide whether to maintain excitation in the nascent state or, on the contrary, to transform it. The psychical apparatus is, first and foremost, an apparatus of transformation, which is what we call *psychical elaboration*. In the field of reality, perception and action must be linked up, while including a detour via the outside. It will be seen that the object-relations perspective will be interested in looking for traces of the object right down into the depths of the unconscious mind. Beyond, in the soma, there is no object relation. Traces may be found in approaching the somato–psychic frontier, but, at the level of the soma, we fall into the sphere of non-meaning, which does not permit us to speak of an object relation. We cannot distinguish the investment of soma from the process of somatic excitation itself. What is important is the presence of the object, whose influence extends into the deepest depths of psychic structure. By the same token, the subject is everywhere, but his precursor is the drive.

The drive is the pre-subjective state that in itself implies the potentiality of a subject. A subject is indeed a person whom psychoanalysis will help to assume responsibility for a certain degree of instinctual freedom. Instinctual freedom does not mean satisfying the drives directly, but elaborating them, not only in the internal world, but also in relation to the object. When one values one's objects, one is obliged to take them into account and to take care of them! It is clear, then, that it is not appropriate to speak of the drive alone, nor of the object alone. What we must speak of is the drive–object pair and of the relations between this pair. The drive will always bring the dynamic element with it. This is what keeps people alive, what makes them move, run after, etc., and what gives meaning to their undertakings, for no psychical structure can satisfy itself alone entirely. On the other hand, if the drive is not entirely sufficient unto itself, it can only satisfy itself through an object, the lack of which reveals to the subject his nature as a desiring being. Of course, this lack can be pushed very far, as far as essential depression, a state in which a subject feels devitalized or already dead.

As we have a general theory of representation, since it includes perception and the drive, we can perhaps move in Marty's direction by imagining that there is room for intermediate positions between the Freudian model and the model that he proposes. This is the position I shall take, while drawing on the contributions of Winnicott and Bion. From Winnicott, I shall borrow the notion of an intermediate area, a locus of transitional processes which makes it possible to form the hypothesis of the potential space of union, a precious notion for psychosomatic patients for whom the separation psyche–soma seems to be without mediation. I shall refer to Bion in respect of everything that concerns the problem of thinking, so neglected by Freud, and impossible to ignore in non-neurotic structures. Contradictions exist around the notion of operational functioning, which was initially linked to thinking, and then, strangely, to life, as if there was hesitation in front of the choice between *psycho* and *soma*. However that may be, one thing seems certain, especially after presenting the clinical material: it is not on the side of the model of neurosis, as Freud theorized it, that elucidation is to be sought for understanding, even in terms of a negative comparison, the psychic functioning of patients suffering from somatization.

Notes

1. I have tried, in transcribing the papers' discussions, to conserve something of the oral style of the exchanges that took place.
2. This conference was designed to stage a debate between Pierre Marty and André Green. But as Marty had passed away in the meantime, it took place with his pupils and was organized by the Geneva Association of Psychosomatics. The present paper was first published as a Monograph of the Paris Psychoanalytic Society, in "Interrogations psychosomatiques", in the collection. "Débats de psychanalyse", *Revue française de psychanalyse*, February 1998.
3. Translator's note: Marie Besnard (1896–1980), nicknamed "la Bonne Dame de Loudun", was suspected of being a serial killer and was at the centre of one of the French judicial enigmas of the twentieth century.

References

Freud, S. (1915c). Instincts and their vicissitudes. *S.E.*, *14*: 111–140. London: Hogarth.

Freud, S. (1915). *Papers on Metapsychology*. *S.E.*, *14*. London: Hogarth.

Freud, S. (1918b). *From A History of an Infantile Neurosis*. *S.E.*, *17*: 3–122. London: Hogarth.

Freud, S. (1938). *An Outline of Psycho-Analysis*. *S.E.*, *23*: 141–207. London: Hogarth.

Green, A. (1982). La double limite. In: *La Folie privée*. Paris: Gallimard, 1990.

Green, A. (1995). La représentation de chose, entre pulsion et langage. In: *Propédeutique. La métapsychologie revisitée*. Paris: Champ Vallon.

Green, A. (2000). *Chains of Eros: The Sexual in Psychoanalysis*, L. Thurston (Trans.). London: Rebus Press [*Les chaînes d'Éros*, Paris: O. Jacob, 1997].

Jeanson-Tzanck, C. (1993). Une intervention réorganisatrice dans la psychothérapie d'une vie opératoire [A reorganizing intervention in the psychotherapy of an operational life]. *Revue Française de Psychanalyse*, *57*(1): 135–146.

Marty, P. (1976). *Les Mouvements individuels de vie et de mort*. Paris: Payot.

Marty, P. (1990). *La Psychosomatique de l'adulte*. Paris: Presses Universitaires de France. Coll. Que sais-je?.

Marty, P. (1991). *Mentalisation et psychosomatique* [Mentalization and Psychosomatics]. Paris: Synthélabo. Coll. Empêcheurs de tourner en rond.

Marty, P., & Fain, M. (1955). Importance du rôle de la motricité dans la relation d'objet [Importance of the role of motricity in the object-relation]. *Revue de psychanalyse française, XIX*: 1–2.

Marty, P., M'Uzan, M., & David, C. (1963). *L'Investigation psychosomatique* [Psychosomatic Investigation]. Paris: Presses Universitaires de France.

CHAPTER TWO

The mysterious leap of the somatic into the psyche*

Marilia Aisenstein

I n this chapter I shall argue that the Paris Psychosomatic School is strictly Freudian and rooted in concepts such as the drive, representation, and transference.

Referring to the psychosomatic phenomenon and the link between psyche and soma poses the problem of the drive head-on. Already in 1899, in "Screen memories", Freud mentions "two most powerful motive forces"—the term used in the original is *Trieb-federn* (1899), "drive springs"—hunger and love (1899a, p. 316). But the German term *Trieb* as a metapsychological category only appears in his writings in 1905, in *Three Essays on the Theory of Sexuality*:

> By an "instinct" is provisionally to be understood the psychical representative of an endosomatic, continuously flowing source of stimulation, as differentiated from a "stimulus", which is set up by single excitations coming from *without*. [1905d, p. 168]

---

*Translated by Steven Jaron.

The drive is, thus, exclusively the psychic representative of continuous internal excitation. Freud, however, qualifies this initial affirmation, adding,

> The concept of instinct is thus one of those lying on the frontier between the mental and the physical. . . . [T]he instinct is without quality, and, so far as mental life is concerned, is only to be regarded as a measure of the demand made upon the mind for work. [1905d, p. 168]

The *Three Essays* is a text in which Freud seeks to think through human sexuality, and it is in this context that the conception of the drive was born. The psychoneuroses must, therefore, be related to drive force, and he adds,

> By this I do not merely mean that the energy of the sexual instinct makes a contribution to the forces that maintain the pathological manifestations (the symptoms). I mean expressly to assert that the contribution is the most important and only constant source of energy of the neurosis . . . [*ibid.*, p. 163]

Freud is seeking a better understanding of the drive among subjects close to the norm, the neurotics, through the psychoanalytic method.

This is, for all psychoanalysts, the experienced and the trainees, quite banal. I wish, however, to note two points immediately.

In my reading, it seems that Freud sees a drive force, or, rather, a force of the alloy of two drives, which, by its excess, paves the way for pathological psychic manifestations. Freud does not know just why this excess occurs; it is biological. Thus, I think that one must see it as constitutional, or constituent: it is, and we must take it into consideration.

My second remark touches on the notion of continuity. The drive thrust (in French, the term used is *poussée*) is continuous, or, rather, it ought to be. In fact, one of the major contributions of the Paris Psychosomatic School is to have brought to the attention of the psychoanalytic world the discontinuities in mental functioning. The initial reply that comes to mind is to relate the failure of the "demand of representation" to the defusion of the two drives altering the alloy. In 1924, in "The economic problem of masochism"

(1924c), Freud makes primary, erotogenic masochism the guarantor of drive fusion.

If the notions of source, object, and aim are defined and differentiated in 1905, one must wait until 1915 for Freud to bring them together through the idea of thrust, a quantitative economic factor, in order to give the drive a comprehensive definition. I must further emphasize, in this context, the enigmatic, paradoxical character of the alliance between two opposed terms: an economic factor, the thrust; and a non-economic and qualitative factor, the "demand of representation". "The characteristic of exercising pressure"—their thrusting character—"is common to all instincts; it is in fact their very essence" (1915c, p. 122). Freud relates the constancy of the thrust to the demands of representing. This explains the title of my chapter: from the body comes a demand to represent, but the representation itself has its demands.

Where should we should we place the demand in topographical terms? Must we see it as a principle that transcends the agencies? My tendency would be to think of it in such a way. In order to think this through, I shall look into two fundamental texts, "The unconscious" (1915e) and *The Ego and the Id* (1923b). An attentive reading shows a change from one topography to the other: in the first, the emphasis is placed on unconscious representations that are always combined with the "thrust", whereas in the second, topography with the id, the reservoir of the drives, one sees force win out over representation.

The conception of the drive as the foundation of a somatic psychoanalytic theory of the human

Psychoanalysis existed before the definition of the drives, and yet I would say that the notions of excitation and the drive do not enter into a relationship of continuity. One may see "a radical caesura" in Freud's thought before and after.

In an article dating from several years ago, Smadja (1992) retraced the construction of the conception of the drive in Freud's writings from 1890 to 1905. At the time, Freud shared with Breuer and others a psychophysical conception of the psychic apparatus founded on the notion of excitation, the affect being its subjective side.

In "Psychical treatment", the article in which Freud defined "psychical treatment" as "treatment (whether of mental or physical disorders) by measures which operate in the first instance and immediately upon the human mind" (1890a, p. 283), one reads,

> The affects in the narrower sense are, it is true, characterized by a quite special connection with somatic processes; but, strictly speaking, all mental states, including those that we usually regard as "processes of thought", are to some degree "affective", and not one of them is without its physical manifestations or is incapable of modifying somatic processes. Even when a person is engaged in quietly thinking in a string of "ideas", there are a constant series of excitations, corresponding to the content of these ideas, which are discharged into the smooth or striated muscles. [*ibid.*, p. 288]

I understand in this statement, which is, however, drawn from an early article, that the elaboration of the somato–psychic concept of the drive is ineluctable. It is already at work.

In 1895, Freud wrote the "Project for a scientific psychology" and, in the same year, *Studies on Hysteria* (with Breuer, 1895d). Then, in 1896, "The aetiology of hysteria" appeared, in which he demonstrated the specifically sexual origin of hysterical symptoms.

I think it of some interest to examine this development, which leads Freud to describe excitation little by little; it becomes "sexual" and no longer somatic and diffuse, then he gives it a vectoring, and finally arrives at a model of psychic work and of its strictly sexual source. Thus, he defines "psycho-sexuality". We must keep in mind that, at the time, Freud still believed in the reality of a traumatic seduction, and that, at the same time, his conception of repression imposed itself on him through the cures of hysterical patients. Repression, then (in 1896) covers the entirety of the unconscious.

In September 1897, Freud wrote his famous letter to Fliess: ". . . I no longer believe in my *neurotica* . . . I have no idea now where I have got to, since I have not achieved a theoretical understanding of repression and its interplay of force" (Letter 67, *S.E.* 1, pp. 259–260). It is beginning with this that he will apply himself to the task of forming a notion of infantile sexuality and, thus, of the drive as a dynamic psychic process that is organized and vectorized, and anchored in the body and desperately in search of an object.

The year 1915

In March 1915, Freud devoted himself to writing a series of articles about which he noted his intention "to clarify and carry deeper the theoretical assumptions on which a psychoanalytic system could be founded" (1917d, p. 222, n. 1). The five articles comprising this group that we call "Papers on Metapsychology" are "Instincts and their vicissitudes", "Repression", "The unconscious", "A metapsychological complement to the theory of dreams", and "Mourning and melancholia" (1917e). They are all major texts and were written one after another, which is important to bear in mind. In order to show that the approach of the Paris Psychosomatic School, which we practise, is derived from the Freudian conception of the drive, I will focus on "Instincts and their vicissitudes" and "The Unconscious".

Once Freud has emphasized how the concept of the drive is fundamental, he will try to give it content by approaching it from different angles, first, from a physiological viewpoint. What is the relationship between the drive and excitation? The drive is not a psychic excitation; it is not a physiological excitation acting on the psyche like light striking the eye, since it may only arise out of the interior of the organism and never acts like a momentary force of impact, but always as a constant force.

Freud imagines "an almost entirely helpless living organism, as yet unorientated in the world, which is receiving stimuli in its nervous substance" (1915c, p. 119). The small being

> will very soon be in a position to make a first distinction and a first orientation. On the one hand, it will be aware of stimuli which can be avoided by muscular action (flight); these it ascribes to an external world. On the other hand, it will also be aware of stimuli against which such action is of no avail and whose character of constant pressure persists in spite of it; these stimuli are the signs of an internal world, the evidence of instinctual needs. [*ibid.*]

In my view, the question must be asked whether these excitations, which are acknowledged as internal, are already "rudiments of representation". The essence of the drive is defined by its origin in the sources of internal excitation manifesting themselves as a constant force. Freud's presupposition is that it is "biological".

The second presupposition, which is no less important, is that the drives force the human nervous system to renounce its ideal intention of keeping the excitation away.

> We may therefore well conclude that instincts and not external stimuli are the true motive forces behind the advances that have led the nervous system, with its unlimited capacities, to its present high level of development. [*ibid.*, p. 120]

It is with this statement that Freud introduces the presupposition of the demand of representation and foreshadows the entire problem of sublimation.

I am intentionally leaving aside the phylogenic reflections that follow, as well as mentioning the pleasure–unpleasure principle, seen in this context only according to a quantitative principle and which Freud will be led to revise in 1924, when he was obliged to admit, in "The economic problem of masochism", that there also exists pleasure in the pain of the tension of excitation. This revision of the pleasure–unpleasure principle and the introduction of primary, erotogenic masochism is fundamental, since the latter is the guarantor of a retention of the libido that I consider as the basis of all mentalization.

I now come to the celebrated definition of the concept:

> If now we apply ourselves to considering mental life from a *biological* point of view, an "instinct" appears to us as a concept on the frontier between the mental and the somatic, as the psychical representative of the stimuli originating from within the organism and reaching the mind, as a measure of the demand made upon the mind for work in consequence of its connection with the body. [*ibid.*, pp. 121–122]

The demand thus comes from the body which imposes on the psyche a measurable "amount of work" and, I would add, indispensable to its perfection and thus to its survival. André Green puts it well: "The psyche is, so to speak, worked by the body, worked in the body" (1973, p. 170). *The body requires labour from the psyche (elaboration arises out of labour).* And he continues:

> But this demand for work cannot be accepted in its raw state. It must be decoded if the psyche is to respond to the body's demands

which, in the absence of any response, will increase its demands (in force and in number). [*ibid.*]

This view seems to clarify rather differently the somatic disorganizations, which may then be understood as consequences of an impossibility of the psyche to decode or translate the exigent demands of the body.

Last, the few words of Freud's definition of the drive are crucial and contain nested within it the entire psychoanalytic theory, as well as the psychosomatic corpus. In my view, this elementary definition ought to be axiomatic.

Drives and topographies

"Instincts and their vicissitudes", "Repression", and "The unconscious" were written between 15th March and 23rd April. The origins of Freud's preoccupations are found in the necessity of supplying content and giving a definition to the drive. The drive destiny of repression follows naturally. Freud is familiar with repression through its effects in the cure. He will try to deduce a theory from this experience. The essence of repression consists in pushing the conscious aside and keeping it at a distance. Repression is correlative of the pleasure–unpleasure principle from which it draws its existence. That which is provoked by unpleasure is repressed. Repression and the unconscious are, thus, correlative; in order to deepen one's knowledge of repression, it is necessary to learn more "about the structure of the succession of psychical agencies and about what is unconscious and conscious" (Freud, 1915d, p. 148).

I wish to reread attentively Freud's description of the unconscious of the first topography. This text is particularly important to us for several reasons. It is fundamental in itself, but above all a large number of "difficult" non-neurotic patients—limit cases, somatic cases—are described as patients among whom free association is non-existent, which makes the access to unconscious material problematic. It is customary to say that they present failures in preconscious functioning. I should like to understand this assertion better by basing myself on the text of 1915.

The essence of repression is to impede representations representing the drive from becoming conscious, but its specific aim is the repression of the development of *affect*: "the work of repression is incomplete if this aim is not achieved" (1915e, p. 178). The affect cannot be repressed, but its repression is the aim of the repression. There is, thus, not, strictly speaking, unconscious affects, but formations charged with energy which seek to break through the barrier of the preconscious.

Freud will, moreover, compare the affect to motility: the two are governed by the conscious and are synonymous with discharge. Freud writes,

> Affectivity manifests itself essentially in motor (secretory and vaso-motor) discharge resulting in an (internal) alteration of the subject's own body without reference to the external world; motility, in actions designed to effect changes in the external world. [*ibid.*, p. 179, n. 1]

In my view, this indicates the importance of the active presence of the body of the two protagonists in the cure.

Thus, the psychoanalyst's preconscious affects may be perceived by the patient and encounter in them an unconscious "rudiment" seeking to break through. This may only be qualitifed in the transferential–countertransferential process in which the treatment by the analyst's preconscious gives it its status as an affect.

However, additionally, in part six of "The unconscious", Freud studies the "Communication between the two systems". Any passage from one system to another implies that *it paralyses the first system and isolates the other—a counter-cathexis I imagine as a kind of massive mechanism of suppression*. We should not forget that the unconscious is naturally alive: it communicates with the other systems and remains subject to the influences of the preconscious and of external perception. This, then, is perception, about which Freud does not say that it is unconscious. Freud, in fact, never theorized about unconscious perception, even if it underpins the complete dream theory (without it Chapter Seven becomes unintelligible). Bollas (2007) shows this clearly in *The Freudian Moment*, Chapter Two.

Eight years later, in *The Ego and the Id*, we are given tremendously complex and interesting answers which I will not summarize here because they merit a discussion specifically dedicated to them, so critical are their implications.

The second topography gives us an anthropomorphic and psychodynamic vision of a less demarcated ego that is also a repressing agency whose defensive operations are, in large measure, unconscious. The ego wrestles with the id, or what Freud calls, in the *New Introductory Lectures*, a "chaos" (1933a, p. 73): "It is filled with energy reaching it from the instincts", he writes, "but it has no organization, produces no collective will . . ." (*ibid.*). The subject is an unknown and unconscious psychic id on whose surface is formed an ego, which is the part of the id modified by the influences of the external world, that is, the sensorial perceptions originating in the outside. Very different from the first topography, the second topography moves from the qualitative to the structural and privileges force, the drive motions, to the detriment of representations-contents. This seems to reflect a change correlative of the introduction of the second drive theory, conceived in order to account for a destructiveness that, up to that point, had been left aside. This is the essential difference between the unconscious and the id: whereas the unconscious of the first topography remains in the register of pleasure, the id is inhabited by *contradictory drive motions, including destructive ones,* it is a chaos. In this context, one must pose the question of representation. Should it be included in the drive motion? It seems to me that the drive motion, in fact, contains the thing-presentation or the memory trace charged with energy. The energy comes from the body; the representation comes from the perception. The meeting of the two, and the fusion of these two elements, is, thus, necessary. However, even this answer does not resolve the fundamental ambiguity of the origin of representation.

If the demand comes from the body, which imposes it on the psyche (as I would tend to think of it in my psychosomatic perspective), it would be the drive pressure that, in its quest, engenders the representation of the object. Its origin would, thus, be an economic imperative. But, then, where does the qualitative passage occur? In Chapter Five of *The Fabric of Affect*, André Green very clearly states the alternative: an economic origin or rather a symbolic origin. I quote:

> the "origin" of the representations would have to be sought in the symbolic order as endopsychical equivalents of external perceptions, ghosts of perceptions, that is "phantasy traces". Freud does

not choose clearly between either of these two conceptions. [1973, p. 170]

In my view, we must envisage a mix, which I would formulate thus: an economic order and a quest in the symbolic order. One might imagine a series of *mutative operations*, from "decoding and translation", moving from the most organic to the most psychic, with the most psychic being the word-presentation.

I relate this to what Pierre Marty called the "quality of mentalization". This quality must be appreciated according to three axes: its thickness, its fluidity, and its permanence (Aisenstein, 2006).

The change of the topography in 1923 thus poses, in relation to representation and, consequently, the "demands of representation", a crucial question. In fact, we are seeing a waning of the concept of representation in favour of the notion of drive motion. Now, this turning towards the economic implies a *new preference in Freud's thought for, namely, affect.*

This change in emphasis, which shifts from representation to affect, is far-reaching and its clinical implications are immense. In fact, with certain patients, including but not limited to somatic patients, any analytic work will be centred on the access to affects and on metabolizing them.

Affects and anxiety

In the analysis of the psychoneuroses, the guiding principle that will give us access to the unconscious material is that of free association. In analytic work with non-neurotic patients, actual neuroses, limit cases, and somatic patients, we are frequently confronted with "non-associativity". The discourse is not, or is no longer, "living"; psychic functioning turns out to be mechanical and the affects are, apparently, absent. There is a non-elaboration of psychic energy that is expressed more by acts or, as we are arguing, through the body. We detect neither resistances nor derivatives of the repressed, nor compromise-formations; everything occurs as if there were no conflict between the opposing psychic forces. Often, the guiding principle is that of anxiety, or affect anxiety, as Freud called it. In this context, I wish to recall very briefly the radical opposition between anxiety neurosis and hysteria. In anxiety neurosis, we observe a symmetric and opposite mechanism from that of conversion hysteria: the conversion would be a leap of the psychic sexual into the soma; it conserves the link with symbolization. In anxiety neurosis, this leap is produced from the psychical sexual into the somatic. "The leap from the physical sexual to the somatic brought about by anxiety has no links with symbolization" (Green, 1973, p. 61).

As an affect of unpleasure, the anxiety is an avoidance in the face of the libido, of which it is at once an outcome and an impairment. I will not enter into the complex question of the relations of anxiety to the agencies, but I will simply say that the place of the anxiety, like the affect, is the preconscious and then, in principle, the ego. A rudiment of unconscious affect seeking to break through may, thus, appear in the preconscious transformed into anxiety. The work of the cure and the transferential–countertransferential play may qualify and give it, or, perhaps, give it back, the status of a veritable affect.

Here then are two brief clinical vignettes illustrating this kind of work.

A patient whose operational (or mechanical) functioning was patent and exemplary had the habit of telling me the facts and events of the week in a chronological order. There were neither affects nor anxiety in his discourse. One morning he sat down, looked at me, and remained silent. He twisted his body like a terrorized child. I asked him what was happening. "I'm afraid," he told me. I asked him, "Afraid right here and now? . . . So you're afraid of me?" "Yes," the patient told me, "I feel that you're not the same, you're angry." That morning, I had had a nightmare whose mad rage was tugging at me—a furious anger that was badly damned up and poorly elucidated when I awakened, but it was, nevertheless, set aside. It was from that point on that the memories of his childhood terror in the hands of a psychotic and sadistic mother could arise.

The second patient was a young woman forty years of age. She had severe asthma, an illness that prevented her from working. She was single and had no children. She was eight months into a twice weekly, face-to-face treatment in a hospital setting. Her psychic organization was typically borderline, but with long, very mechanical (operational) periods.

For months she closely fixed her gaze on me and threw herself into either factual descriptions of her life or furious diatribes against the weather or government, Social Security or doctors, and so on. She was one of those distressing patients with whom I have learnt to be silent and wait. She was in the present; she did not recount her history and recalled nothing of the past. One cannot speak of classic transference, but of a massive, undifferentiated cathexis.

One day, after the patient had complained about her allergist, the secretary, and my silence, she began to describe at length a new, violent intercostal pain she had been experiencing since the weekend. She told me that a rib fracture had been diagnosed, secondary to her coughing fits and the high dosages of corticosteriods.

I then thought about a very dear friend who had died of an embolism. This friend had not seen a doctor for the pain that she, herself a doctor, had thought was an intercostal fracture. I was seized by a powerful affect of sadness. A few seconds later, the patient moved and breathed loudly—an asthmatic fit was beginning. She got up as if she was going to leave. She cried and screamed at me, "There, it's your fault! You let go of me!"

I asked her to sit back down and then I spoke to her at length.

I told her that she was correct; in my mind I *had* let go of her. I had thought about somebody else whom *she* made me think of. Still, we had to consider together her intolerance of not controlling an entirely different person's thinking.

At that moment, the patient, who was still standing, sat down. She breathed more easily and I suggested a construction by telling her that it was probable that she had made me experience an invasion and thought control from which she had most likely suffered in the distant past. She cried for the first time.

This was a powerful moment. Based on the introduction of a third party and history, analytic work could begin (see also Aisenstein, 2009).

The patients' discourse, in these two cases, is actual and factual. For each, it is a matter of a rare moment in which an anxiety affect appears suddenly. These moments will be, as in these two cures, fecund moments in which the anxiety affect may be qualified and become an object of construction or interpretation thanks to the transferential–countertransferential work. It is a matter here of countertransference widened to the mental functioning of the psychoanalyst in the session, as André Green defines it. But there is the transference, even if it is not a matter of a classic transference interpretable as transference neurosis. Now, some of our patients affected by a somatic illness and who consult at the Paris Psychosomatic Institute arrive having been "prescribed". They affirm that they are interested neither by the "psychic" nor by introspection, but frequently continue to come, often for years on end.

For a long time, I thought that this submission to the rule was quite enigmatic. The classic reply, according to which they pursue their treatment because it would be, for them, "a-conflicting", has never been very convincing to me.

I believe they come and return because *there exists within the human psyche a "transference compulsion"*. Small children fall in love with a doll or a truck; these are already transferences. Classical transference would be the most sophisticated, but includes transference into language, and the first form of transference: from the somatic to the psychic. *The drive's demand of representation is an obligation to transfer from the somatic to the psychic.*

Freud adopted two successive theories of the transference. The first dates from 1895, with *Studies on Hysteria,* and the second from 1920, with *Beyond the Pleasure Principle.* The latter covers the period of 1920 until the end of his work. The former has often been named the "libidinal theory of transference", a term we think slightly obsolete, but which he clearly explains in "The dynamics of transference" (1912b). The motor of the transference is the eternally renewed need of instinctual satisfactions, and these in the frame of the pleasure–unpleasure principle.

The seeds of the second, in my view, were already present in 1914, when Freud termed the repetition compulsion, but they did not fully develop before 1920, when he saw in the transference a fundamental tendency for repetition that would be "beyond the pleasure principle". In the chapter on transference in *La cure psychanalytique classique,* Maurice Bouvet writes,

> Since the traumatic situation, or the experience responsible for the complex, has led to unbearable tension, it cannot be under the sign of the search for pleasure that the subject transfers, but rather in function of an innate tendency to repeat. [1958–1959, p. 227]

These two conceptions of the transference are not contradictory and may coexist; nevertheless, they imposed themselves based on different clinical experiences, since it was the failure in clinical practice that led Freud to reconceptualize the drive opposition, the topography, anxiety, masochism, and so on. It is, however, a conviction which Freud never desisted from, beginning in 1895 and going all the way through to 1938.

The transference is an "odd" phenomenon. It is the most powerful spring in the cure; the decisive part of the work depends on it. This striking phenomenon, an expression of the unconscious and the id, is also the only tool we possess to access it.

If Freud never argued with this idea, it is because the transference remains the only means of accessing the unconscious, though it must be thought of differently.

The first period. The reference, or matrix, for Freud's entire clinical practice and the theory he develops out of it are the psychoneuroses of defence, which he will likewise call the "transference neuroses" and whose first model is hysteria. The work of the cure essentially aims at the access of latent material through mechanisms such as displacement and decondensation.

Transference, the process by which drive motions and unconscious desires are "updated" on to the object, is "classic": what occurs is the displacement of the affect of one representation on to another, and then of an object on to another. Transferential expressions are symbolic equivalents of unconscious desire and fantasies.

The second period. Freud is confronted with clinical work in which negative narcissism, destructiveness, the act, and discharge reigns. The transference is no longer "libidinal", and remains under the aegis of a pure repetition compulsion. What, then, is its texture? It is a matter of a compulsion, of the appetence towards the object, which condenses a tendency towards inertia and regulatory mechanisms aiming at the relief of instinctual charges through fragmentation. In my view *this kind of transference functions like traumatic dreams.*

I believe that it is necessary to account for it on several levels: the transference of the somatic on to the psychic; and the transference into language and then on to language so that a transference with displacements of one object on to another may arise, which will update the history and, thus, make regression possible.

Now, the affect, which is the drive representative *par excellence*, is at once the sole access to the id, but, above all, *the means of fusing these strata of the transference.*

One of my patients came to me following two cerebrovascular accidents and confessed three years later that she had never mentioned, exactly as she was concealing it from her doctors, the occurrence of frequent paroxystic tachycardia. I expressed my stupefaction and anxiety, which was tinted with anger. She then explained that telling me about it would have meant losing it because, were she to put it into words, she would have shared a bodily experience that made her feel alive. It was only later on, and *après-coup* that I could finally make the interpretation that, by speaking to me about it she would have directed her *battements de cœur*—"the beatings of her heart", or "heartbeats"—to me; and that, since she was dramatically disappointed by the primary object, she systematically wished to give the other short shrift. I would say that she met me and cathected me with a transference compulsion, which functioned like a traumatic dream but changed texture at the moment when, having pulled herself together, I could show her that keeping her somatic symptom "unenunciated" was equivalent to a defence. This example shows what I call the different levels of transference.

In conclusion

The foundations of contemporary psychosomatics must be sought in Freud's metapsychology. The concepts of the drive, transference, affect, and representation are indispensable in order to face this new and rich clinical work with patients suffering in their bodies and expressing their suffering through it.

References

Aisenstein, M. (2006). The indissociable unity of psyche and soma: a view from the Paris Psychosomatic School. *International Journal of Psychoanalysis, 87*: 667–680.

Aisenstein, M. (2009). Discussion of Sander M. Abend's "Freud, Trans-ference, and Therapeutic Action". *Psychoanalytic Quarterly, 78*(3): 893–901.

Bollas, C. (2007). *The Freudian Moment,* Chapter Two. London: Karnac.

Bouvet, M. (1958–1959). "Le Transfert", *La cure psychanalytique classique.* Paris: Presses universitaires de France, 2007.

Freud, S. (1890a). Psychical (or mental) treatment. *S.E., 7:* 283–302.

Freud, S. (1895). *Project for a Scientific Psychology. S.E., 1:* 295–343. London: Hogarth.

Freud, S. (1896). The aetiology of hysteria. *S.E., 3:* 191–221. London: Hogarth.

Freud, S. (1897). Letter 69 to W. Fliess (September 21, 1897). *S.E., 1:* 259–260. London: Hogarth.

Freud, S. (1899). Über Deckerinnerungen. *Gessamelte Werke,* 1: 531–544. Frakfurt and Main: Fisher Verlag, 1999.

Freud, S. (1899a). Screen memories. *S.E., 3:* 303–322. London: Hogarth.

Freud, S. (1905d). *Three Essays on the Theory of Sexuality. S.E., 7:* 130–243. London: Hogarth.

Freud, S. (1912b). The dynamics of transference. *S.E., 12:* 99–108. London: Hogarth.

Freud, S. (1915c). Instincts and their vicissitudes. *S.E., 14:* 117–140. London: Hogarth.

Freud, S. (1915d). Repression. *S.E., 14:* 146–158. London: Hogarth.

Freud, S. (1915e). The unconscious. *S.E., 14:* 167–204. London: Hogarth.

Freud, S. (1917d). A metapsychological supplement to the theory of dreams. *S.E., 14:* 222–235. London: Hogarth.

Freud, S. (1917e). Mourning and melancholia. *S.E., 14:* 243–258. London: Hogarth.

Freud, S. (1920g). *Beyond the Pleasure Principle. S.E., 18:* 7–64. London: Hogarth.

Freud, S. (1923b). *The Ego and the Id. S.E., 19:* 12–59. London: Hogarth.

Freud, S. (1924c). The economic problem of masochism. *S.E., 19:* 159–170. London: Hogarth.

Freud, S. (1933a). The dissection of the psychical personality (lecture 31). *New Introductory Lectures. S.E., 22:* 57–80. London: Hogarth.

Freud, S., & Breuer, J. (1895d). *Studies on Hysteria. S.E., 2:* 1–305. London: Hogarth.

Green, A. (1973). *The Fabric of Affect in the Psychoanalytic Discourse,* A. Sheridan (Trans.). Routledge: London, 1999.

Smadja, C. (1992). Les pulsions, excitation et pulsion. *Les Cahiers du Centre de Psychanalyse,* 25: 19–35.

CHAPTER THREE

Psychosomatics: the role of unconscious phantasy

Catalina Bronstein

"To have a 'mummy', to be a 'mummy'"

Introduction

I n this chapter, I would like to convey my thinking about working with patients who present psychosomatic disorders. I
would like to address in particular how a primitive psychically
unprocessed conflict is relived in the transference relationship via
the psychosomatic symptom. As analysts, we occupy a particular
and specific position from where we can explore and study the relationship that patients establish with their bodies and with their
illnesses. From the many different perspectives that aim to explain
psychosomatic disorders, we can broadly distinguish two main
approaches: one that sees the symptom as a product of psychic
conflict (with its underlying unconscious phantasies) and another
that places the accent on a deficiency or deficit in the patient's
psychic structure and on the lack of a capacity to function symbolically. The lack of a capacity to symbolize (even in a primitive way)
has been extensively explored and written about by authors from

the Paris School of Psychosomatics (Marty, De M'Uzan, Fain, and Aisenstein, among others). These authors propose that the somatic manifestation replaces a conflictive situation and that psychosomatic illnesses act as a point of fixation in a move towards a more general mental and progressive disorganization. This is seen to go together with the anarchic destruction of mental functions and the cancellation of libidinal activity, and leads to a state of "essential depression" where the organizing of mental functions (such as identification, projection, association of ideas, symbolization) disappear and the "death instinct asserts itself" (Marty, 1968, p. 248; see also Marty, 1967). The relationship between patient and clinician cannot be described as a proper relationship, and would constitute what Marty called a "relation blanche", lacking in real emotional involvement. The idea is that patients bring to analysis their "soma" rather than their libidinal body (Fine, 1998).

From the perspective of psychoanalytic schools of thought that follow the model of psychic conflict, the Kleinian school addresses the issue of psychosomatic illnesses by exploring the potential unconscious phantasies and psychic conflicts that might underlie psychosomatic symptoms, as well as the different defence mechanisms, such as splitting and projective identification, that give way to this process (Garma (1959); Klein (1958), Rosenfeld (2001), among others). The process of splitting and projective identification can adopt very complex forms in that, in phantasy, unprocessed aspects of the self can be projected not only into external objects but also into parts of the subject's body. This notion was developed by Rosenfeld, who saw psychosomatic symptoms as the result of projective identification that create what he called "psychotic islands" (Rosenfeld, 2001).

Klein (1958) regards phantasy as a basic mental activity, rooted in the body and present in rudimentary form from birth onwards. Isaacs described it as "the primary content of unconscious mental processes", the psychic representative of instinct (Isaacs, 1948). Isaac's and Klein's definitions of phantasy is much wider than Freud's, and there is an assumption that the earliest phantasies have an omnipotent quality and are experienced as mainly visceral sensations and urges. These early phantasies are based on early sensory experiences and feelings and have attributes that Freud thought as characteristic of primary processes (Bronstein, 2001;

Isaacs, 1948; Spillius, 2001). Unconscious phantasies range from those that are very primitive, of the type described by Segal as symbolic equations and akin to what Kristeva called "metaphors incarnate" (Kristeva, 2000), to those carrying proper symbolic significance. Via their connection to unconscious phantasies, psychosomatic disorders are seen to be anchored in the mind and, therefore, available to analytical exploration (Bronstein, 2009a).

These two ways of understanding psychosomatic disorders work on different basic assumptions that stem from a different conceptualization of what constitutes the death drive, as well as to the role that affect and representation occupy in early development. I think that when thinking about psychosomatic processes, Bion's contribution to the study of early psychic organization and of the development of the capacity to think is extremely valuable and might help to bridge the gap between a theory that stresses the lack of psychic representation of the symptom and a theory that sees it as it being always linked to an unconscious representation of conflict.

Bion's notion of the role of maternal containment had a profound theoretical and clinical impact. Early unprocessed raw impressions related to emotional experience (*beta* elements) need to be transformed into *alpha* elements in order to be able to be used to create dream-thoughts . If they cannot be processed, they will be evacuated. One of the possible routes for evacuation is via psychosomatic disorders (Bion, 1962; Meltzer, 1986). Bion's ideas on the role of splitting, evacuation, and projective identification are complementary with Segal's ideas of symbolic equation, by which unconscious phantasies are seen not to represent the object (as a proper symbol would do) and are seen instead as an equation between the subject and the object to be represented (Segal, 1957). In his later works, Bion placed greater importance on the degree of quantity of excitation experienced by the archaic state of mind and the possibility that some intense inchoate feelings might be experienced as physiological ("sub-thalamic") (Bion, 1979). The body can thus give rise to new thoughts that have not been thought before (Lombardi, 2008). These later developments share some similarities with the explanations sustained by the Paris School, though, for Bion, splitting, dissociation, and disintegration are part of an active defensive stance (however early in life) (Bronstein, 2009a,b). However concrete the patient's symbolic capacity is, I think that in analysis we are always dealing with a libidinal body. Psychosomatic disorders can pose a challenge to our therapeutic technique but, for me, this should not preclude the possibility of working analytically, trying to understand the unconscious meaning and the place the symptom occupies in the transference relationship, as it manifests itself in the *here and now*.

From evacuation to internalization

A fifteen-year-old girl, whom I will call Martha, sat looking at me while she busily talked about her daily activities. There never seemed to be any space for thinking and there was no space for me to say anything. This evacuative discourse, which did not allow for any silence and for any possible introspection, was accompanied by her constant scratching. Her arms, her head, her face, her abdomen were all victims of this intense activity. I felt that I was meant to be a silent and impotent onlooker that had to be kept at a distance and be entertained while at the same time I had to passively observe what felt to be a furious (or maybe passionate?) self-harming activity. In my countertransference, I often felt the wish to hold her hands to make her stop scratching. While at the same time that space and time were cancelled out by an excited, rather manic detailed account of her comings and goings, every three or four minutes Martha turned round to look at my clock. Her quite palpable claustrophobic anxiety was momentarily eased by feeling reassured that the clock was working, that it was marking the passage of time, and that she would be able to leave. The alternative possibility, one in which she was perhaps anxious because she "had" to leave at the end of the session was not consciously available. There was no apparent register of separation anxiety.

Martha came to see me because she could not settle at school, she was playing truant, had numerous fights with her parents, and seemed restless and anxious. Martha had eczema since birth, but this became much worse after the sudden death of her mother, when she was three years old. At this point, she developed such a serious generalized eczema that she had to be admitted to hospital. Martha could not remember her mother and did not have many feelings about her death. But she held on to an idealized picture of her mother and of how her life—and her skin—would have been should her mother still be alive. There was a longing for this idealized mother, but there was also great fear of the dead mother. She reported that she feared that her mother would pull her into a hole (sometimes felt to be under Martha's bed) where mother was buried; she was dead, but somehow still alive. This sometimes appeared as a dream and sometimes it had the quality of a hallucinatory experience. At times, she also felt that people could read her thoughts. Throughout her childhood, Martha had numerous hospitalizations and she had a memory of herself completely bandaged. This made her often say that she felt she was a "mummy" (like an Egyptian mummy). I think that anxiety stirred up by her identification with a "mummy" that turned her into a "mummified" girl was accentuated by her pubertal development. This was lived out in her relation to her own body. Her constant preoccupation with her skin was contrasted by her neglect of her body and by her reluctance to take care of it. Equally, I think that her scratching became the embodiment of this conflict, as the experience of an "alive" body was matched by her sense that she was also carrying a partially dead body (after one of my interpretations when I mentioned her body, she said, "I don't have a body. Just bits of dry, dead, rotten pieces of skin").

When I first met her, Martha appeared to be intensely anxious to please me and, I thought, to appease me. She felt that her family forced her to come to therapy and that she did not want to come, but even though she frequently played truant at school, she never missed any sessions. Her difficulties were increased by the fact that she was struggling with her evolving sexuality, difficulties at school and at socializing, and she had to contend with a changing image of herself. Martha was rather unruly and often got into trouble both at home and at school. She found it very difficult to concentrate and silences were absolutely unbearable. I also felt that there was pressure from the family that she should be a happy child, and the fear for Martha's life probably accentuated the family's need to see her as never feeling unhappy.

In her sessions, Martha could not keep her hands still. There was also an intense oral activity as her talk was more like an evacuative action than a medium for communication and to express thoughts. She sometimes sucked a bottle of water, biting off little pieces of paper that she then swallowed. But most of the time she scratched herself. When my interpretations were felt to be dangerous or to address issues that she was trying to avoid, essentially, when she felt she could not control me, the scratching became more intense. I sometimes felt that my interpretations could trigger a dangerous acute inflammatory reaction and that I should be extra careful. Martha alternated the scratching with the application of creams. I was meant to listen to her verbal outpouring while I also seemed to have to witness how she was engaged in this erotized pleasurable and painful activity that was apparently done in a mechanical way and was meant to be ignored by both of us.

Very slowly, her anxiety about the threat posed by my thoughts diminished, and she became more able to think with me about her feelings and about what she was doing in the sessions. Her manic activity sometimes diminished, allowing for some moments of reflection and insight. The session I will describe started with her showing some sense of panic, as she said she could not think what to talk about. This was highly unusual, as she used to launch into a torrent of words before even sitting down. She then spoke about a number of subjects that I later found very difficult to recall as they were enumerated very fast and I felt that they did not mean anything much to her: books she or somebody else had been reading, possible outings, clothes, TV programmes, schoolwork.

All of this was initially said while sucking and biting a plastic bottle and eating bits of paper from the label. I made a remark about her words coming out of her mouth while she was placing the "bottle" in her mouth. She said that as a child she ate paper when she got bored.

This reminded me that in the previous session she had been licking and biting her skin instead of scratching. I made this connection now.

She said that she remembered that, as a child, she thought that if she ate her skin it would turn into something else inside her and make her of a different species

She then mentioned a character, "Supergirl", who was very powerful. She said that she used to love this character because it made her feel good. As a child, she liked wearing the Supergirl costume and she once lost the "Supergirl eye mask" and got desperate, but her Nan later found it.

I said she was grateful to her Nan to have found her "eye-I mask" that made her feel so good about herself. I also said that while she tells me this she is eating bits of paper—like bits of skin—that make her feel good and powerful in the session. This seems to be cancelling out the anxiety she felt at the beginning of the session when she felt bored and anxious and made her start sucking and biting the bottle.

She had now stopped eating paper and was by now scratching again. She excitedly told me an episode when, as a child, an aunt had been given her some sweet that made her suffer a terrible reaction. The ambulance had to be called and they put a tube into her throat as she could not breathe. "It was great. I had never before been in an ambulance!"

I said that I thought she became frightened of me, that she felt I had taken away the mask that made her feel like a powerful Super-girl and given her instead something that made her ill, could even kill her, the opposite of being powerful! Instead of feeling fear, she makes it into an exciting trip in an ambulance.

For the first time in the session, her activities diminished and she stopped scratching and said that she felt that the sessions were "worse than hell", but that she actually likes coming here. She said, "Before, when I left the sessions, I collapsed in the lift. Now I can stay up."

I thought that by the end of the session she felt that, despite her fear of me and of what I was giving her and feeding her with (potentially deadly hellish stuff), she felt that there was a me who was trying to help her. She felt I was also helping her to be able to have some more real strength to stand up and not to collapse on the floor of the lift. The combination of going high/collapsing gave way to the possibility of having her feet on the ground and to be more in touch with reality, diminishing her identification with a dead mother who she was carrying in her skin.

In the next session, she told me that after the session she asked her father many questions about her mother's death. She had never been able to do this before. She said, "I want to live long." I thought that this showed a growing capacity to be able to think and to be curious about her mother's death. I think this was enabled by a lessening of her being in a state of projective identification with her dead mother's body. With time, Martha became more able to look after her body and to take care of her medication. Her eczema and the scratching became also far less intense.

The role of the skin in the early mother–baby relationship

Anzieu (1980) stressed the enormous importance that early skin contact between baby and mother has in the constitution of the ego. Among the functions of the skin, he counted the function of providing support, containment, protection against stimuli, support for sexual excitation, integration, and interconnection of different sensations (Anzieu, 1995; Ulnik, 2007). The early experiences of feeling and holding to the mother's body would be at the base of both attachment and separation. Anzieu (1995) agrees with Angelergues (1975) that the "body image would be a representation of a boundary that functions as a 'stabilizing image' and a protective envelope" (Anzieu, 1980, p. 54). The body image would fall "within the category of fantasy and secondary elaboration, a representation affecting the body" (*ibid.*). Anzieu, as well as Esther Bick, gave great importance to the early bodily experience between mothers and their infants, both in actuality and in phantasy. The physical contact would not only provide an experience of boundary between outside and inside, but also help achieve "confidence for progressive mastery of the orifices" (*ibid.*, p. 29).

For Anzieu,

> By skin ego I mean an image that the child's ego uses during the early stages of development to represent itself on the basis of the child's experience with the surface of the body. That phase corresponds to the period when the psychic ego is becoming differentiated from the body ego on the functional level but remains confounded with it on the figurative level. [*ibid.*]

From a different perspective, Esther Bick addressed a similar process,

> The thesis is that in its most primitive form the parts of the personality are felt to have no binding force amongst themselves and must therefore be held together in a way that is experienced by them passively, by the skin functioning as a boundary. But this internal

function of containing the parts of the self is dependent initially on the introjection of an external object, experienced as capable of fulfilling this function. Later, identification with this function of the object supersedes the unintegrated state and gives rise to the fantasy of internal and external spaces. [Bick, 1968, p. 484]

The early sensation-based contact between mother and infant, where mother functions like a skin, provides a necessary physical containment and support to early, unintegrated aspects of the self. I think that mother's capacity to lend her "skin" to the baby can be also seen as a part of mother's alpha functioning role as described by Bion, by which unprocessed raw beta elements are evacuated (projected) into the mother who, through her capacity for reverie and alpha function, will be able to process the baby's inchoate feelings and anxieties and give meaning to them. What is then introjected by the baby is the capacity to process thoughts, that is, a capacity to think.

Bick's concept of "second skin formation" describes the creation of a substitute formation that would provide the indispensable sense of cohesiveness of the skin's surface. When there are difficulties that impinge on this containing process, the infant can become imprisoned in a close system of bodily sensations (Ogden, 1989). These early stages of unorganized experience that are lived through the body are sensations that also carry some primitive form of representations ("phantasies encarnated") and via the introjection (internalization) of the mother's skin/containing function provide the basis for ego functioning that will slowly enable the discrimination between internal and external.

Among the ego's first activities are the defences against anxiety (experienced initially as persecutory anxiety) via the use of processes of splitting, projection, and introjection. These processes are fundamental to the structuring of the ego and to the organization of its experience. Projective identification corresponds to an unconscious phantasy in which aspects of the self are located in other objects. Aspects of other objects can also be seen to be part of the self. Splitting and projective identification are necessary to minimize the anxieties stemming from the death drive; essentially, anxieties about fragmentation and annihilation of life (Klein, 1952). Projective identification has mainly two motives: communication and evacuation. Bion described the role of projective identification as communication in his theory of containment.

The role of defence mechanisms (such as early splitting) in psychosomatic disorders has been recounted by Aisenstein in her description of patients who treat their bodies like a "foreign land" (Aisenstein, 2006). Rosenfeld describes how, through projective identification, the body can be felt to be a potential persecuting object that has to be controlled and appeased (Rosenfeld, 2001).

The skin can then become both a vehicle for the expression of raw, unprocessed emotions and acquire a separate life of its own when, in phantasy, it is felt to be the recipient of the infant's projections, the embodiment of the object that the child is identified with. While itching is a way of relating to this object-skin, it also serves the purpose of resolving the impossible primitive love/hate relationship that has not been mediated by thoughts.

Anzieu stressed that the relationship between the pruritus, the compulsion to scratch, in the dermatoses and in generalized eczema expressed the fragility of the ego-skin as a circularity between auto-erotic and self-punitive mechanisms, partly trying to reverse the displeasure into pleasure. He reminds us of Spitz's question as to whether the child with eczema is demanding to be touched by the mother or whether what it shows is his narcissistic isolation, where the child provides what the mother has not (Anzieu, 1995). I think that scratching is the embodiment of a conflict that cannot be yet represented in a symbolic way. It is a way of keeping both the sense of union as well as an attempt at separating from the object that the skin has been identified with. It is both imprisoning and liberating.

The psychosomatic symptom in the session

I think that what Martha enacted in her sessions was the living out of a passionate love–hate and pleasure–pain relationship at the level of her skin while, *at the same time*, there was a rather precarious, dangerous internal object that had to be appeased and controlled. The body–mind split perhaps should be examined here in a more detailed way, as I think it encompassed a number of different processes that operated jointly. I think that through her skin, in phantasy, Martha was identified with her mother's body. The masturbatory pleasure–pain of caressing and scratching provided both confirmation that she carried her mother within herself (whose hands were the ones that she used to scratch herself with?) as well as the proof that she was not her mother, that she was still alive. The skin—her skin—was an object of both love and hatred, of passionate need and persecution, of cancelling of absence and loss and of claustrophobic anxiety (Bronstein, 2009b).

The claustrophobic anxiety was, I think, produced by this suffocating experience of carrying the object under/in her skin. Mason described a connection between paranoid anxieties, claustrophobia, and psychosomatic symptoms in asthmatic patients, where he thinks there is a projection of a suffocating part of the self linked to strong oral fixations (Mason, 1981)

I felt that Martha's orality carried some of these same aspects, but that it was also a point of contact with external objects. I think that the process of oral incorporation allowed for some more discrimination between self and object. She used her talk to prevent me from penetrating her with my voice, with my thoughts, while she fed herself pieces of paper (of idealized bits of skin that would make her powerful and protect her from my potentially dangerous feed). I think that while her oral activities also expressed a projection of her paranoid phantasies and anxieties into me, these were also linked to an object that was somehow more separate and therefore more available for exploration. Still, the feeding could also prove to be very dangerous.

The surface of the body allows us to distinguish excitations that are of external origin from those that come from within (Anzieu, 1990). But if this surface is felt to carry the projections of phantasies about the object, it stops being able to function as a surface that can help distinguish where the excitations come from. I think that in Martha, the eczema "was" the embodiment, the incarnation of an intense conflict with the lost mother, conflict that could not gain proper psychic representation, but that existed in and via the body.

There is a question as to whether this evacuation, which can be effected via projective identification, can be also effected by a banishment from the psychic that would leave a hole with no traces, as described by Green in his work on the negative. I am more inclined to think that, rather than a "hole", we find here the embodiment of the absent object that makes itself present in a persecuting way (Bronstein, 2009b).

In a previous work with patients with atypical facial neuralgias, we showed that the pain experienced by these patients, pain that was always present, was linked to the loss of a loved object, but that the pain did not represent the loss and its unresolved mourning, but that the dead object became the pain (Carpinacci, Bronstein, Palleja, & Edelstein, 1979). We came to the conclusion that the atypical neuralgias suffered by many patients encapsulated an unconscious link with a loved dead object, and that in the resurrection of the pain there was an imaginary resurrection of the dead loved object that continued to be alive in and through the pain. I think that, through her eczema, Martha kept herself—and her mother—alive, a mother who had been mummified and could not yet be properly mourned.

We can speculate about the possible reasons that might have made Martha react in such a way to the death of her mother, when her rather mild eczema became a death threat. It is probable that she felt she had caused her mother's disappearance, as well as feeling bombarded by a combination of very intense feelings that could not be contained by her grieving family. Hatred, guilt, and a desperate longing for the absent mother, perhaps an anxious waiting to see when she was going to reappear, the anxious looking at the clock without knowing the time, but knowing that it indicates her mother's comings and goings.

References

Aisenstein, M. (2006). The indissociable unity of psyche and soma: a view from the Paris Psychosomatic School. *International Journal of Psychoanalysis, 87*: 667–680.

Angelergues, R. (1975). Reflexions critiques sur la notion de schema corporel. In: *Psychologie de la connaissance de soi, Actes du symposium de Paris*, PUF.

Anzieu, D. (1980). *Le Moi Peau*. Paris: Dunod [first edition 1985; reprinted 1995].

Anzieu, D. (1990). *A Skin for Thought. Interviews with Gilbert Tarrab on Psychology and Psychoanalysis*. London: Karnac.

Anzieu, D. (1995). *The Skin Ego. A Psychoanalytic Approach to the Self*, C. Turner (Trans.). New Haven and London: Yale University Press, 1989.

Bick, E. (1968). The experience of the skin in early object-relations. *International Journal of Psychoanalsis*, *49*: 484–486.

Bion, W. R. (1962). A theory of thinking. In: *Second Thoughts*. New York: Basic Books.

Bion, W. R. (1979). The dawn of oblivion. In: *A Memoir of the Future* (pp. 429–576). London: Karnac, 1991.

Bronstein, C. (2001). What are internal objects? In: C. Bronstein (Ed.), *Kleinian Theory, a Contemporary Perspective* (pp. 108–124). London: Wiley.

Bronstein, C. (2009a). On psychosomatics: the search for meaning. *International Journal of Psychoanalsis*, accepted for publication.

Bronstein, C. (2009b). *Annie and the Hollow Object*. Lecture, unpublished.

Carpinacci, J., Bronstein, C., Palleja, O., & Edelstein, C. (1979). Neuralgias facials. Algunas consideraciones sobre sus determinantes psicologicos. Consecuencias terapeuticas. *Rev. Neurologica argentina*, *5*(2–3): 83–87.

Fine, A. (1998). *Interrogations Psychosomatiques*, A. Fine & J. Schaeffer (Eds.). Paris: PUF.

Garma, E. (1959). The predisposing situation to peptic ulcer in children. *International Journal of Psychoanalysis*, *40*: 130–133.

Isaacs, S. (1948). The nature and function of phantasy. *International Journal of Psychoanalysis*, *29*: 73–97.

Klein, M. (1952). The mutual influences in the development of ego and id. In: *Envy and Gratitude and Other Works 1946–1963: the Writings of Melanie Klein, Vol. 3* (pp. 57–60). London: Hogarth Press, 1975.

Klein, M. (1958). On the development of mental functioning. In: *Envy and Gratitude and other Works 1946–1963: the Writings of Melanie Klein, Vol. 3* (pp. 236–246). London: Hogarth Press.

Kristeva, J. (2000). Le genie feminine. *Tome II: Melanie Klein*. Paris: Editions Fayard.

Lombardi, R. (2008). The body in the analytic session: focusing on the body-mind link. *International Journal of Psychoanalysis*, *89*: 89–110.

Marty, P. (1967). Regression et Instinct de Mort. Hypothese a propos de l'observation psychsosomatique *Revue francaise de psychanalysis*, *31*(5–6): 1113–1133.

Marty, P. (1968). A major process of somatization: the progressive disorganization. *International Journal of Psychoanalysis*, *49*: 246–249.

Mason, A. (1981). The suffocating super-ego: psychotic break and claus-trophobia. In: J. Grotstein (Ed.), *Do I Dare Disturb the Universe?* (pp. 140–165). London: Karnac.

Meltzer, D. (1986). *Studies in Extended Metapsychology*. London: The Roland Harris Ed. Trust [reprinted London: Karnac, 2009].

Ogden, T. H. (1989). I on the concept of an autistic–contiguous position. *International Journal of Psychoanalysis, 70*: 127–140.

Rosenfeld, H. (2001). The relationship between psychosomatic symptoms and latent psychotic states. In: F. de Masi (Ed.), *Herbert Rosenfeld at Work—the Italian Seminars* (pp. 24–44). London: Karnac.

Segal, H. (1957). Notes on symbol formation. In: *The Work of Hanna Segal* (pp. 49–65). Northvale, NJ: Jason Aronson, 1981.

Spillius, E. B. (2001). Freud and Klein on the concept of phantasy. In: C. Bronstein (Ed.), *Kleinian Theory, A Contemporary Perspective* (pp. 17–31). London: Wiley.

Ulnik, J. (2007). *Skin in Psychoanalysis*. London: Karnac.

CHAPTER FOUR

A rash of a different colour: somatopsychic eruptions from the other side

Lila J. Kalinich

> "Nature teaches me by these sensations of pain, hunger, thirst and so on that I am not only lodged in my body as a pilot in his ship, but that I am closely united to it, and so to speak so intermingled with it that I seem to compose with it one whole"
>
> (Descartes, Sixth Meditation, 1641)

T he late Herbert Weiner, for decades one of the foremost American theorists of psychosomatic medicine, begins a recently written chapter on that subject with the preceding epigraph. In that chapter, he wonders why medical practitioners have not yet found a way out of Cartesianism in order to develop a comprehensive approach that treats sick *persons* rather than specific diseases. For Descartes, the "thinking I" only "seems" at one with the sensible soma; a gap remains between the two. The legacy of this gap, for medicine, Weiner writes, has been two approaches to the patient where there should have been one. We are left with one medicine for mindless bodies and another for disembodied minds (Weiner, 2008, p. 485).

Historical antecedents

Descartes believed that only mathematical entities were objective facts, constituting something like eternal truths. In contrast, the existence of the body and the physical world were subject to doubt. Such a mechanical theory could not account for mental phenomena such as problem solving, speech and language, and other forms of human creativity. His theory, therefore, demanded that he consider mind a "second substance". Though even his contemporaries criticized this notion, Descartes's dualism destined the course of virtually all of subsequent western philosophy. (Augustine actually introduced the dilemma centuries before Descartes. At first following the dualism of the Manicheans, he eventually came to believe in something like a unity of body and soul [Burns, 1981, p. 12]. Employing the methodology of doubt, he, with Descartes, concluded that one cannot doubt unless he exists [see Augustine's *Against the Academicians*, 386 AD].) Freud himself was trapped in dualism, despite his commitment to the idea that one day the physical basis for the mental would be understood.

Putting aside the interesting work of more recent philosophers and neuroscientists, such as Dennet, Edelman, and Damasio, who have grappled with Cartesianism, Weiner provides his own elegant analysis. He argues that the mind–body problem is insoluble because it is essentially based on a category error. The problem, he says, is a *metaphysical* one, not a scientific one, and, therefore, beyond solution. He adds, however, that the traditional medical approach to diagnosis has added to the predicament. Anatomy and pathology, the study of diseased structures, has been the study of the dead. The dead yield little information about the *function* of living persons, both healthy and unhealthy, in their milieu. Structure and function are different kettles of fish. Says Weiner,

> Quite apart from the conceptual inadequacies of the static, reductionistic, structural view, the medical sciences have eschewed a broad organismic view of biology—how complex organisms interact with each other and the environment with an irreducible individuality. [2008, pp. 485–486]

An integrated medicine for a whole person: contemporary psychosomatics very much embraces this aim.

Although Descartes's emphasis on the individual's capacity for rational thought helped to bring his era out of the darkness of magic and witchcraft, it also pushed theological anthropology toward the discourse of the "body and soul" and away from the more holistic view of the person present in the theology of the ancient Christian church. While the Gnostics longed for escape from the material body to the purity of the spiritual, the traditional early Christians embraced the more Judaic Pauline view. For Paul, the body is "ensouled" (Breck & Breck, 2005, p. 201). I find this reminiscent of Winnicott's notion of the "'indwelling' of the psyche in the soma" (Winnicott, 1966, p. 514). New Testament exegetes within the Greek tradition understand *soma* to signify "the entire composition of the created human being, including flesh, soul, mind, and spirit" (Breck & Breck, 2005, p. 200). *Soma*, a richly complex concept, therefore differs from the material, biologic body that dies and decomposes. The flesh, *sarx*, together with the soul, *psyche*, and spirit, *pneuma*, constitute *soma* (*ibid.*, p. 197). In that these terms often are not used systematically in Patristic tradition, *sarx*, the flesh, can also refer to the soul and the mind, *nous*, all transfigured by *psyche*, spirit. The theology and view of man implicit in these notions remain alive in Eastern Christianity, where Descartes had less influence.

Touch

I first became interested in "psychosomatic medicine" when, as a young adolescent, I worked in our family physician's office when the nurse–receptionist was on vacation. Since I believed I was headed for medical school, I was thrilled to be brought into the universe of patient care. Dr Mildred Bowen was one of those heroic women who were graduated from medical school in the 1920s. Her patients had serious illnesses, but many of them came for a different kind of healing as well. After getting to know the regulars, I concluded that most unconsciously used somatic complaints to gain access to her. They came to the office for Dr Bowen's warm smile and patient attention. She met human needs that were otherwise unmet in her patients' lives. And the touch of the physical examination seemed to have been essential.

I particularly recall Mrs B. Obese, diabetic, and hypertensive, she also had six children and an alcoholic, abusive husband. She made the case for a "broad organismic" medical approach if anyone did. It seemed obvious that her physical condition mirrored her entire life situation. But for her visits to the doctor, she was likely to be touched only when beaten. Were Mrs B a patient today, she would be treated by an internist for her medical conditions, referred to a psychiatrist for depression, and sent to social services to evaluate her home life. Her care fragmented, she would avoid most of her appointments, remaining effectively "untouched" by the entire system. Were Mrs B wealthy, however, she might seek "therapeutic massage" in order to compensate for what was missing in her care. A growing literature suggests that touch might offer Mrs B substantial medical benefit (Ornish, 1998, p. 140).

I will now describe two patients for whom touch was a complex, conflict-laden issue. Despite vastly different life histories, a part of that history came to write itself on to their skins. In one case, the absence of touch, and in the other, its complicated presence, seemed to be particularly related to skin diseases that surfaced during the course of their psychoanalytic treatments.

Joseph

At age thirty-five, Joseph was a very frustrated young man. By his own estimation, he had done everything right all of his life and still did. He had been a well-behaved, attentive first-born son in an immigrant family. A stellar student, he had attended an excellent college, where he played lacrosse and was a member of a rowing crew. He participated in weekend sports to maintain his trim, handsome physique. He had kept his job at an investment bank despite the recent global financial turmoil. He thought that his six-figure salary made his rugged good looks even more attractive to most of the women he met. Yet, despite his assets and wanting to marry and to have children, he never really had a long-term relationship. Realizing that he was nearing forty with no prospects in sight made him feel depressed and desperate.

Believing that "something must be wrong" with him, Joseph came to me for a psychoanalytic consultation. He said he wanted psychoanalysis because he had heard that it was the treatment of choice for "deep problems". "My surface is fine!" he said. "I'm smart, good-looking and successful, yet I can't seem to attract a woman I like for more than a few dates." Recently doing on-line dating, he was often seeing and having sex with several women a week. He was becoming increasingly bored. Bored and passionless, he complained, "I just want to have that feeling back that I had a couple of times in my life. It's too bad Janna had a boyfriend and that Jackie was planning to move. I was really crazy about them."

When I agreed to take him on as a patient, Joseph practically leapt on to the couch. He was relieved not to have me looking at him; he thought he would speak more freely. He began enthusiastically recounting his family story. His parents met in Bari, Italy, on the steps just outside of the Basilica of St Nicholas. It was "love at first sight". They married after a short courtship and found their way to New York City and to a small apartment in Queens. Father got a job as a taxi driver, despite his poor English. He worked hard to support his wife, who was soon pregnant with Joseph. Eventually, he saved enough to buy his own limousine. In a few short years, he organized a fleet of fellow drivers into a limousine service that became very profitable. Eventually, Father moved the family to a town in Connecticut with outstanding schools. Both the business and the family thrived, with Joseph paving the way for his younger brothers to gain entrance into private schools and prestigious universities. He reported that everyone seemed to be doing well, though his brothers, in their twenties, were, like him, still unmarried.

After telling his story, Joseph fell silent. Often with little to say, he used his analytic hours to complain about the daily frustrations of dealing with other people, whom he saw as either "stupid" or "unfair". He railed against friends who treated him poorly. "I call them and it takes them days to call me back. Andrew owes me a phone call for weeks already! When he needed advice about an investment I got back to him right away!" Joseph's outrage was almost palpable. When I tried to explore the depth of his reaction, Joseph exclaimed that I was just like his mother, who never let him express his anger. "'Don't be angry' was all she could ever say!" (Readers in the New York/New England area will recall the

NYNEX telephone company that was bought by Bell Atlantic in 1997. Its popular television advertising campaign for many years featured the phrase "Reach out and touch someone" for many years. Bell Atlantic later merged with GTE to form Verizon. Though few would have reason to recall this business history, the NYNEX slogan is almost slang for "to make a phone call".)

He talked about the women who were too short or too tall, too fat or too thin, too quiet or too loud, too this or too that. They got "under his skin". Occasionally, one would capture his curiosity. Melanie was one of them. They had common interests. She was as athletic, competitive, and witty as he and in a similar field. Joseph was immensely attracted to her nearly perfect body and porcelain skin. Melanie remained involved for several dates, but then something changed. Melanie distanced herself after Joseph did not match her efforts to move things along sexually. They both noticed that Joseph did not become aroused when they kissed. Eventually, Melanie stopped returning his phone calls. Something similar happened about a year later. Blonde, beautiful Natalie seduced Joseph on their first date. He reported that the "sex was great" until they discussed dating each other exclusively. Soon thereafter, Natalie abruptly broke off their relationship, saying that Joseph no longer seemed sexually interested in her. He was "less hard" and less attentive to her sexual needs than he had been. She promised to call him in a few days, but never did again.

While I felt sympathetic to this young man, I found myself to be unmoved most of the time. Sometimes I was rather put off, actually relieved when he left. Despite his having actively sought psychoanalysis, he disparaged what he knew of its ideas and me for my embrace of them. He often dismissed my efforts to explore the significance of what he talked about. He treated his dreams concretely, finding it amusing to think that I might believe that they had unconscious meaning. "Wasn't Freudian dream theory disproved long ago?" He took anything that verged on a transference interpretation as "more evidence that analysts are self-centred". He complained that the time of his hour did not precisely match his own wristwatch, set by satellite clocks. He felt shortchanged and upset if he believed that I ended his session a minute or two early. He slammed the door when he arrived at the office and slammed it again when he left. He denied being angry.

Joseph was not nasty exactly. His derision did not seem intended really to hurt me. Nothing cut too deeply. Joseph was actually just tedious. He seemed determined not to let me do the kind of analytic work that would touch him in a meaningful way. I inferred from his regular four times per week attendance that our work was important to him, but he challenged even that by talking about quitting each time we anticipated my vacation. I wondered to myself if he were working to stay "hard" for fear that I would abandon him if he went "soft" with emotion.

I knew that Joseph was in pain, but the first glimpse I actually had of it was the spot of blood that he left behind on the analytic napkin.

The following day, I saw the bloody lesion on Joseph's scalp as he lay on the couch. Joseph then told me that he had been getting patches of rash on his elbows and knees and in his scalp. The lesions were reminiscent of something he'd had as an adolescent that had remitted after a few weeks. The skin problem had added to his nightmare of trying to get a date for the prom. His parents circumvented the issue by forbidding him to attend.

Later that week, Joseph consulted a dermatologist, who diagnosed "psoriasis". The physician explained that "stress" often worsens the problem, conjecturing that the financial crisis and the threat of job loss might have precipitated a recurrence of the psoriasis he had had as a teenager. (For a discussion of the relationship between psoriasis and "stress", see, for example, Farber and Nall [1993]. The extant literature debates whether stress brings on the disease, or whether the disfiguration of the disease causes the stress.) The dermatologist advised Joseph to get away, to take a vacation if possible. On return, he would treat Joseph with a cytotoxic agent. Joseph agreed to heed the doctor's advice, but confided to me that me was not aware of having felt stressed. He was, none the less, happy to go on holiday and planned to leave the next week to visit a friend on the West Coast.

On return, Joseph reported having an experience while *en route* to the coast that had mystified him. His take-off had been delayed by some event on the runway. As he sat on the packed plane, he was surprised that he was not frustrated. Instead, he felt calm and reflective. His mind wandering to his parents, he felt something like affection or gratitude; he began to weep uncontrollably while imagining their deaths. They were in perfect health, so this made no sense to him. Then he wondered if this were somehow about his analyst. "I wondered whether I was missing you. Since I was leaving you, it was like I had killed you off." For the rest of his vacation, he had a vague feeling of longing to be back in the consulting room with me.

While Joseph was exploring his emotional experience on the plane, an ancient memory surfaced: "I was flying to Asia by myself in the fifth grade to visit my family. I was sitting next to a beautiful teenage girl who was very nice to me. I put my hand on her thigh. She drew away quickly from my unwanted touch. I felt very ashamed and alone for the rest of the trip." I was taken with the fact that he had travelled to Asia alone at such a young age. I wondered why this Italian family had sent their child to Asia. Though tempted to ask, I instead repeated his words: "unwanted touch". He continued, "I loved it when my Father played touch football with me. My Mother never touched me. She never hugged me. I was jealous of how she cared for my brothers when they were born. It was like she didn't want *me* to touch *her*. I watched a mother push her daughter in a swing in the park. I don't think she ever did that." He continued, "My Father once told me that her father died when I was little and then there was other trouble. 'Yusuf,' he said, 'She was depressed.' But I think it's just the way she is—something deep in her. Sometimes I wish that *you* would touch me, but that seems silly." (I had, in fact, noted an impulse to reach over and rumple his hair earlier in the week.) (For an interesting discussion of the usefulness of massage in the teatment of skin diseases, among others see Ornish [1998].)

"Yusuf?" I asked, unable to hide my surprise. "I know you think my name is Joseph, Joseph Mametto. (This, of course, is not Joseph's real name. It was, however, a juncture in the psychoanalysis where particular signifiers became crucial to the work. I have tried to approximate the quality of this moment.) Most people do. In Italian, it would actually be 'Giuseppe, Giuseppe Maometto'. That's Italian for 'Yusuf Mohammed'. I forget that that's my real name, my Father's name, too. My parents met in Bari, but they both came from Pakistan. It's a complicated story, but my Father came through Albania and my Mother from India to Europe. When they came to the USA, they decided to use the shortened name the

Italians gave them—Mametto. They thought it was better for business. And they did not care much for Islam. Our brown skin is actually pretty light. We easily pass for Southern Italians."

Later that week, Joseph revealed that his mother's extended family was Hindu. They were Dalits, the group once called the "Untouchables". The Hindu caste system has four groups. The fifth, the Untouchables, are "outcastes", so unworthy that they do not qualify to be called a caste. After human rights activism, they came to be called "Dalit", a self-description. See Mayell, 2003. His mother's mother had dared to attend her village school, where she was kidnapped by local Muslims and forced to convert to Islam. She worked in bondage to this family until she escaped and found her way to India.

Jeanette

Jeanette, a thirty-one-year-old recently married post-doctoral student in genetics, sought treatment because of her sexual discomfort. Her husband wished that she were more interested in sex, complaining that she seemed uninvolved when they were having intercourse. "He's right. I am not very involved. The truth is I mostly just tolerate it. I don't even much like being touched. I would like to enjoy it more myself," she said. The husband also claimed that Jeanette was angry too often. He had hoped for a more harmonious time. She was not sure that she agreed with him on that point. "He doesn't see the way he is aggravating. He wants me to be an old-fashioned woman, doing most of the chores. It's unjust. I want more equality in the relationship."

Jeanette was a feminist. The ideals of feminism were important to her, particularly given what she knew of her own mother's life. Her parents, comfortable middle-class Americans, had worked hard to give her opportunities that they had not had. Her mother was particularly ambitious for her, and struggled to protect her daughter from the burden of her one sibling, a brother three years younger, who had been severely brain-damaged by neonatal sepsis. Saddled with this child, the mother gave up her own career to give young Kevin care. Jeanette admired her parents for their dedication to keeping this boy at home; however, she was not sure it had been the best thing for the parents or for her. "I became very independent as a result. There wasn't a lot of time left to fuss over me. And that's a good thing I guess. We all love Kevin. But I think that he should have been placed. I know I wouldn't want that for my life."

Jeanette is passionate about the environment. She organized her department's recycling programme, later used as a model for the entire university. And she ardently embraced "zero population growth". In fact, she and her new sister-in-law, Jane, already close friends for many years, made a pact, swearing to one another that they would adopt children rather than conceive their own. "There are already too many children who need good homes. Why would we bring another into the world?" Jeanette took her commitment to this agreement with Jane very seriously.

A psychologically-minded and hard-working patient, Jeanette explored her phallic competitiveness, as well as the fear and envy of men that contributed both to her feminism and to her reluctance to be penetrated. It all seemed somewhat paradoxical to her, given the pathetic condition of her little brother. It was hard to see how he stood for something threatening. But an unexpected turn of events illuminated much of this for her.

"I am *furious*!" exclaimed Jeanette as she opened the session. "Jane is pregnant. She told me last night. I can't believe it! I just can't believe it! After all of discussions. I can't believe how irresponsible she is. This is stupid, just stupid. How could she have this *thing* growing inside her? Doesn't she understand that it can destroy her? Who knows what's growing inside her?" She continued in that tone, having difficulty finding the vocabulary to express her outrage. Jeanette fumed for most of the session, calming enough toward the end to wonder at the depth of her feeling. None the less. she believed her upset to be completely rational.

The next session was two days later. "You are not going to believe this! You are not going to believe what I have! I have shingles! I am a young healthy woman. I am not immune suppressed. I have no underlying physical problems and I have shingles!" As a geneticist, Jeanette had enough knowledge of the varicella-zoster virus to appreciate that the absence of risk factors in her case made the appearance of those vesicles over a dermatome on her belly extremely odd. Her anger during the previous session no longer mystified her. "I get it! I guess I have things growing inside of me too. I see pregnancy as a sexually transmitted disease! I must have seen Kevin as a disease. And he was diseased. I never knew where his infection came from. That infection almost killed all of us. Kevin's birth pretty much destroyed our lives." Yet, a certain irony about the herpes zoster intrigued Jeanette. "It's funny that I have round swollen things on my abdomen—like little pregnant bellies." Herself interpreting a compromise formation in the message, she saw both her desire to be pregnant and a defence against it. "I guess my body is telling me that I want to get pregnant. It's contagious! But I am terrified of what might happen if I do." Later she found humour in the notion that her symptom embodied what happens when "germ cells get together." (A group in Germany demonstrated that "psychosocial factors" can trigger oral herpes. A recurrence can be brought on by induced disgust [Buske-Kirschbaum, Geiben, Wermke, Pirke, & Hellhammer, 2001].)

Conclusion

The skin is an artful surface, both an organ to be represented and a canvas on which representations and messages can be painted. Few have appreciated the complexity of the skin's psycho-physiologic function better than Didier Anzieu. Grounding his imaginative and scholarly monograph, *The Skin Ego*, in the fact of the embryological relationship between skin and brain, Anzieu elaborates an extensive formulation of the skin ego's function. Since the skin ego's "reality is of the order of phantasy", it is, in effect, a bridge and an intermediary between mind, body, world, and other psyches. Therefore, it participates in all of life's aspects: in dreams, thought, speech, posture, etc., providing an imaginary screen or space on which "every form of psychopathological organization can be constituted" (Anzieu, 1989, p. 4).

Aspects of Joseph's and Jeanette's agonal life narratives, otherwise split off and unavailable, had to find their way to that imaginary screen, and then to the Real of the surface of the body. The destructive, non-neurotic elements from the deeply inaccessible unconscious painted themselves on the skin. These rashes, coloured by distinctly different psyches, shared a common push to the exterior. Once inserted into the psychoanalytic discourse, the unspeakable could be symbolized and spoken. Joyce McDougall's concept of an "archaic form of hysteria" captures the psychic struggles of these two patients, not directed "to preserving one's genital sexuality . . . but to protecting life itself" (McDougall, 1989, p. 169). However, Jeanette's own interpretation of her symptom reveals that it condensed the archaic with a less archaic, more neurotic organization. The important point is that in both patients, the appearance of disease seemed a necessary passage *en route* to psychological health. The communicative function of the skin disorder initiated the process of signification and structure building.

Jeanette unconsciously believed her skin's envelope, including the female genital pocket, to be overly porous and vulnerable to disease. Every penetration, every touch, aroused fear. Her rage at the offending intruder—organism, brother, mother, father/lover—deadened her desire. To be sure, there were straightforward neurotic conflicts in this talented young woman from a loving stable family. But these alone did not and could not account for her sexual difficulty. What looked at first like sexual inhibition was actually something more like annihilating sexual terror.

Joseph lived his family's split off, trans-generational trauma, but could not speak it. His depressed, remote mother transmitted and worsened the trauma that he embodied. Unable to integrate his intricate, painful history, he could not express much about himself with affective nuance. He raged at small slights, appearing aggressive, narcissistic, and alexithymic, unloving and unlovable (see Nemiah, Freyberger, & Sifneos, 1976; and also the French on "operative thinking": Marty & de M'Uzan, 1963). He was poorly equipped to negotiate the complexity of being brown-skinned in a white social situation. Despite his efforts to disavow his origins to live in someone else's skin, he unconsciously knew he was a marked man. The graphic bloody papules of psoriasis exposed a truth that Joseph himself could not touch.

In their comprehensive and valuable book, *Why People Get Sick*, Leader and Corfield describe the evolution of the concept of "stress" and describe its use in contemporary medical culture (Leader & Corfield, 2008, pp. 47–61). They make the point that bureaucratic systems have no room for individual human narratives. Using "stress" to account for the onset or exacerbation of a medical problem conveniently gets rid of the patient's personal and situational narrative (*ibid.*, p. 64). Recall that Joseph's doctor advised him to reduce his stress, so Joseph went on holiday. The physician's advice was not entirely unwise. However, it regarded the pathogenic part of the stress as *external* to the patient, as though it were something that Joseph could leave behind when he left town.

Although aspects of Joseph's worklife were difficult, his "stress" was mostly generated by events internal to him. And his narration of those events was crucial to his cure. Like Mrs B, he wanted to tell someone the story of his suffering. The saying of the unsaid was essential to the healing of the whole man. It was also vital that the listener tolerate *how* he told his story. Containing Joseph's aggression and using the countertransference to listen to the unsayable cleared a path for interpretation and reconstruction.

In contrast to their European and Latin counterparts, and the psychosomaticians in particular, American analysts have tended to be dismissive of Freud's concept of the death drive. (Kernberg is a clear exception; see Kernberg, 2009.) Contemporary American culture, however, seems to have accepted a version of the notion in the extreme in the form of widespread programmes in "wellness" and "stress management". In recent decades, self-help books in the USA were about themes like "self-actualization" and "self-affirmation". Assertiveness training programmes have been replaced by "wellness spas" that provide fitness programmes, yoga and meditation classes, massage, and guides to positive thinking. Extending life expectancy seems to be a major preoccupation. In other words, many Americans, particularly the younger generation, are actively working to modify destructive ways of thinking and living to keep the death drive at bay. Interestingly, they work through the *body* to the mind, embracing a very un-Cartesian but very Freudian unity of the two. (Aisenstein makes the point that Freud did not clearly distinguish between *psyche* and *soma* [Temple, 2002, p. 932].) Furthermore, they often do so by forming new communities, organized by a particular form of wellness practice. This is clearly a response to the dissolution of more traditional social matrices that were thought to play a role in maintaining both mental and physical health. And they work toward "spiritual" healing, too, often avid followers of individuals like spiritual teacher Eckhart Tolle. Tolle has captured millions worldwide with his idea of the (unconscious) "pain-body" that carries the past, creating negative, sometimes violent, emotion and thought (Tolle, 2006, pp. 129–160). (Leader and Corfield [2008, p. 159] describe Lacan's collaboration with Parisian internists and surgeons in the 1940s on the question of hypertension and heart disease. Anticipating more recent findings, Lacan concluded that an individual's relation to his social group was a more important predictor of heart disease than were risk factors such as diet and smoking.)

The point of the "wellness movement", then, seems to be to undo the split between mind and body that has been deeply entrenched in a Western way of thinking. It affirms, instead, the integration of *soma*: *sarx* and *nous*, transfigured by *psyche*, the "soma psychikon" (Breck & Breck, 2005, p. 190).

Editors Aisemberg and Aisenstein, with the contributors to this volume, most notably Andre Green, have used Freud's second drive theory, with its conflict between Eros and Thanatos, to expand contemporary thinking about the destructive aspects of the psyche. Their work has enlarged the practitioner's ability to work with both neurotic and non-neurotic forms of functioning simultaneously, especially in patients with serious physical illness. The profession of psychoanalysis is the better for it, as are patients with somatic illnesses like Joseph and Jeanette, whose stories have had happy endings.

References

Anzieu, D. (1989). *The Skin Ego*. New Haven, CT: Yale University Press.

Augustine (386 AD). *Against the Academicians*. M. P. Garvey (Trans.). Milwaukee, WI: Marquette University Press, 1957.

Breck, J., & Breck, L. (2005). *Stages on Life's Way: Orthodox Thinking on Bioethics*. Crestwood, NY: St Vladimir's Seminary Press.

Burns, J. P. (1981). *Theological Anthropology*. Philadelphia, PA: Fortress Press.

Buske-Kirschbaum, A., Geiben, A., Wermke, C., Pirke, K.-M., & Hellhammer, D. (2001). Preliminary evidence for herpes labialis recurrence following experimentally induced disgust. *Psychotherapy and Psychosomatics, 70*: 86–91.

Farber, E. M., & Nall, L. (1993). Psoriasis: a stress-related disease. *Cutis, 51*: 322–326.

Kernberg, O. (2009). The concept of the death drive: a clinical perspective. *International Journal of Psychoanalysis, 90*: 1009–1023.

Leader, D., & Corfield, D. (2008). *Why People Get Sick: Exploring the Mind–Body Connection*. New York: Pegasus Books.

Nemiah, J. C., Freyberger, H., & Sifneos, P. (1976). Alexithymia: a view of the psychosomatic process. In: O. Hill (Ed.), *Modern Trends in Psychosomatic Medicine* (pp. 430–439). London: Butterworth.

Marty, P., & de M'Uzan, M. (1963). La pensée opératoire. *Revue Française de psychanalyse, 27*: 345–356.

Mayell, H. (2003). India's untouchables face violent discrimination. http://news.nationalgeographic.com/news/pf/56390270.html.

McDougall, J. (1989). *Theaters of the Body*. New York: W. W. Norton.

Ornish, D. (1998). *Love & Survival*. New York: HarperCollins.

Temple, N. (2002). A critical enquiry into the psychoanalytic theories and approaches to psychosomatic conditions. *International Journal of Psychoanalysis, 83*: 931–934.

Tolle, E. (2006). *A New Earth: Awakening to Your Life's Purpose*. New York: Penguin.

Weiner, H. (2008). The concept of psychosomatic medicine. In: E. R. Wallace & J. Gach (Eds.), *History of Psychiatry and Medical Psychology: with an Epilogue on Psychiatry and the Mind–Body Relation* (pp. 485–516). New York: Springer.

Winnicott, D. W. (1966). Psycho-somatic illness in its positive and negative aspects. *International Journal of Psychoanalysis, 47*: 510–516.

CHAPTER FIVE

13 Brazil

Adolescence: the body as a scenario for non-symbolized dramas

Ruggero Levy

"Man should not be called "rational animal" but "symbol-icum animal""

(Cassirer, 1964)

Introduction

I intend to study the relations of the adolescent with the body, or, from the metapsychological standpoint, the mind–body link (Bion, 1962b) in the adolescent process. I propose that in this link, a container–contained relationship is established in which the body may become the *receptaculum* for non-mentalized emotions and/or the mind should develop a capacity of containing the body—and its pulsions—and symbolize it: a body that is initially strange to it.

I will focus on the symbolic reordering that takes place during this period of life, the anxieties deriving from this process, and their consequences. I intend to establish that, due to the "dismantling" of the representational system constructed throughout childhood, primitive anxieties come back into play, one especially, the annihilation anxiety. The more solid the internalizations of containing objects were, the easier the reworking-through of such anxieties. The more deficient those introjections and the symbolic network created throughout childhood, the stormier this process will be.

Due to this symbolic reordering, I suggest that mentalization insufficiencies (Marty, 1990, 1992) are inevitably created—to a greater or lesser degree—during adolescence, the body, therefore, playing a central role in the attempt to dominate the anxieties of this period. I will try to illustrate my ideas with a clinical vignette of an adolescent.

The symbolic reordering in adolescence and the mentalization insufficiencies

The large watershed between man and other animal species, according to Cassirer (1964), is the existence of a symbolic, intermediate system between the stimulation receptor system and the motor effector system, as Freud had already stated in "Two principles" (1911b).

Bion's great contribution to psychoanalytical metapsychology was to study the development of the mind from the vantage point of knowledge (K-link) (Meltzer, 1984). As we all know, his perspective is that the mind constructs itself pushed by its longings, being a true site of symbolizations (alpha elements) which represent the "truth" of the emotional experience (Bion, 1962b, 1965, 1970). Bion understands that the alpha elements are created by the transformation of beta elements (raw emotions, and sensations) through the alpha function. He understands that this occurs in a link, the K-link, in which X wants to know Y, where X and Y can be two subjects or two parts of the self (Bion, 1962b). This link establishes a container–contained relationship that may be creative, rendering growth to the pair, or destructive, favouring its involution.

On saying that the mind development only happens when L and H (*love* and *hate*) are subordinated to K, Bion elevates the search for knowledge, the demand for creating symbolizations of the internal and external world, almost to the status of a propelling force of development. This is very close to what Aisenstein (2009) calls, based on Freud, "a representation demand" of somatic into psychic, *imperative of human being complexity*. Green (1990) furthers this concept and states that we must understand psychism as an intermediate formation in the dialogue between the body and the world.

Concerning the adolescent process, it could not be any different. It is organized by the detachment from the previous representation systems organized by the self (Cahn, 1999) throughout childhood, and by the urge to create a new representation system that will cope with the new body, with the self in itself, the objects, and the world itself. We then witness, within the course of this painful process of deconstruction and reconstruction of a representation system, the emergence of a new subjectivity in the symbolic universe of the subject, transforming the adolescent in a great process of symbolization.

The new adolescent body emerges from puberty, with its new shapes, pulsions, and potentialities, placing an unprecedented work load on the mind. It confronts the adolescent with a *disquieting stranger* (Cahn, 1999) who must be internally represented to recreate a feeling of familiarity with oneself. To symbolize means to absorb a foreign body to a representations system (Castoriadis-Aulagnier, 1975). I, of course, refer to "foreign body" in a double meaning: as a strange element that has to be assimilated as well as a biologic body alien to the subject.

Besides the feelings of strangeness mentioned above, we will also be faced with deep annihilation anxieties, often a feeling of imminent death. The self—being a symbolic construction—feels threatened.

Winnicott himself (1951) said that the worst psychic suffering arises when one loses not the object, but its representation. At the end of the same publication, Winnicott introduces the issue of the negative in psychoanalysis, highlighting that when the representation is lost, sometimes the only reality possible for the object is its absence: the only presence of the object is its negative. Such people will cling to the void, the absence, and, therefore, to suffering as the only real thing. There are adolescents who, when faced with the loss of the representation of themselves and faced with the feeling of not existing, will often cling to the negative as the only tangible reality: suffering, feeling pain, and being destructive is the only way of being.

Besides, according to Aisenstein (2009), every object is invested by the two pulsions, that of life as well as that of death, and the imbrication of pulsions occurs *in* the object as well as *through* the object. Therefore, considering that in the mind, representation is an object of pulsional investment (Green, 1990), the loss of it leads to a pulsional de-fusion, flooding the mind with an excess of disconnected excitement. Such excess, potentially traumatic, will be evacuated in the soma or in behaviour.

Botella and Botella (2002) tell us how much the traumatic situation is installed due to the subject's incapacity of creating representations of an experience that connects emotions triggered by it. In this sense, we may predict that adolescence will be traumatic, since the subject is not able to recreate a representation system capable of dealing with this new experience, and, therefore, fails in the quest of constructing a new subjectivity over—and from—a pre-existing one.

Considering the above mentioned, we can infer that due to the very nature of the subjectivation process in adolescence, what Marty (1990, 1992) called "mentalization insufficiencies", referring to psychosomatic patients, are unavoidably created. Such insufficiency will be greater or lesser according to the quality of the symbolic network created in childhood and the consistency and solidity of the internalized objects. But there will always be a mind confronted with an amount of symbolizing work that has to be done, which exceeds its capacity at that point in time, generating fragilities during that period.

Self has many ways of expressing emotions. Speaking specifically of destructiveness, Jeammet (2001) suggests that it may express itself through the representational pathway, transforming destructiveness into aggression (Green, 1990), through the motor pathway of behaviour, and through the neuroendocrine, neurovegetative, neuroimmunologic, and psychosomatic pathways. I suggest that when facing emotions or pulsional motions which overflow the adolescent representation capacity, this excess will be evacuated in the somatic system, generating psychosomatic diseases, or through action (e.g., masochism, on which I will soon comment), there being the possibility of swinging from one to another form of expression in the evolution of analyses.

The body, destructiveness, and sense of existence

Considering the vicissitudes of the subjectivation process experienced during adolescence, the body is a privileged place (Jeammet, 2001) for the acting of the networks not contained in the mental sphere due to the mentalization insufficiencies mentioned above.

In the process of construction of the sense of existence through the creation of a clear image of oneself and one's body, libido is understood as having an important role (Blos, 1981; Cahn, 1999). Nevertheless, I would like to point out the core importance of destructiveness and the problems derived from it in situations in which, due to failures in the process of evolution, it interferes excessively. We could say that during this period of life, conditions similar to those of the beginning of life are recreated: the mind, with its insufficient symbolizing capacity, confronted with a new, strange body which presents to it a whole "representation demand". And, if erogenous masochism in the beginning of development is the "guardian of life" (Aisenstein, 2004, 2009; Freud, 1924c; Rosemberg, 1991), due to the fusion and intricateness of death pulsion to life pulsion, we will see that, in adolescence, masochism will also play a role.

Winnicott (1950) in his study on aggression and its role in the development of the individual, points out that it is aggression, rather than erotic experiences, that helps the most in establishing the *non-me*, which imposes itself in opposition to the *me*. The experiences of erotic gratification tend to be attributed to the *me*, due to the fact that the baby initially lives in a state of primary narcissism. He goes on to say that aggressiveness fused to the erotic experience is what enhances the feeling of reality. What is in accordance to Freud's formulations (1924c) on the importance of primary masochism at the beginning of life has been reaffirmed and emphasized by Aisenstein (2004) and Rosemberg (1991).

Therefore, Winnicott (1950) considers that aggressiveness will have an essential structuring role in constituting the objective object and the sense of reality. He elaborates on the role of destructiveness in development, specifically in adolescence (Winnicott, 1963b), emphasizing that during this stage of life, besides the possibility of realizing incest, there is the possibility of realizing parricide or even suicide. In adolescence, if libido has a central role, so does destructiveness. The emergence of the sexualized body of adolescence, capable of committing incest, differently from the erotic body of childhood, sets the adolescent in search of new objects that, at first, is the body itself, in this pulsional reorganization that moves from self-eroticism to object love. Therefore, over this background of narcissistic regression, destructiveness follows the same path. The frequent threats to the skin, ranging from tattoos to piercing to self-mutilations, illustrate how much this reorganization of the body investment is stained by destructiveness and aggression (Louppe, 2001). The initiation rites in adolescence usually involve risks to the physical integrity that often cause adolescents to pay for them with their own bodies. In this sense, the rites found in culture match the psychic movement of the adolescent and organize it.

Winnicott (1963a) describes the importance of aggressiveness in the constitution of the object, as the object survives the subject's attacks. In adolescence, as the body is taken as object again, aggressiveness once more plays an important role: the adolescent "plays" with the body, investing it sexually and aggressively. The "existence" of such a body begins, thus, to be constituted, as the body/object "survives". When disease prevails, the only way for the adolescent to feel real is often through self-mutilation or by exposing themselves to extremely dangerous situations that give them the feeling of being strong and alive enough to be able to have defeated death itself. The problem of such situations is the real risk of death often involved in them, which leaves us, as analysts, as repositories of a death anguish sometimes difficult to contain.

There is, therefore, in adolescence, a double process in which multiple anxieties potentiate one another: on one hand, the adolescent transformation leads to the failure of the representational system of the self and of objects, triggering the process of symbolic reordering with the dissolution anxieties already alluded to. On the other hand, the separation inherent to adolescence produces the fear of losing the object and its representation, especially intense when the process of infantile subjectivation was not successfully accomplished and the object was not created consistently in the internal world.

With the representations system at stake, the way out is through action and through the body. A narcissistic defensive system is set in motion. Through these lenses, we may have the following.

- In situations of less mentalization, or mental zones of poor symbolization, pulsions or raw emotions can be evacuated in the soma as beta elements (Bion, 1962b), generating psychosomatic disorganizations, or, as meeting the object cannot be coped with, there may be a sort of perversion where what is invested is excitement itself, generating deadly masochism (Rosemberg, 1991), a mental state of profound disobjectalization.

- In situations of intermediate mentalization, we may find a profound libidinal and/or aggressive catexia of the body, which renders the adolescent subject and object, denying the separate existence of the object, and having the experience of existing due to the body sensations lived, and experiencing the sensation of existing for being the subject of the action. Sadomasochistic situations in which the body is taken as object are created (*I inflicted pain! I exist!*) (Jeammet, 2001; Louppe, 2001), or fantasies of sadistic attacks on internal objects (Bronstein, 2008). Or, even more, to defend him/herself from the emotions triggered by the awareness of separation from the object and of the sensation of non-existence, the adolescent may, by projective identification, seize the object, install him/herself inside it, and become it (Meltzer, 1978, 1992; Steiner, 1993). Therefore, it seems to me that the separation anxiety, as well as the death anxiety, the anxiety of not existing, may lead to the construction of narcissistic refuges and blur the differences between the *me* and the other and between representation and act.

- In adolescents with good mentalization, there will be a larger possibility of oscillation between narcissistic defences and object relations, favouring introjective and identificatory processes mandatory for the construction of a subjectivity which will guarantee a narcissistic stability.

Bion (1959) introduced the concept of a neurotic and a psychotic part of personality. Marty (1990, 1992) defines mental structures according to their grade of mentalization: well mentalized neurosis, badly mentalized neurosis, and those of uncertain mentalization. Using these two concepts, we could assume that, besides people distributed in those three categories, it is possible to find in the self of a well mentalized person, badly mentalized and non-mentalized zones, and so on. Pure situations are rarely found, but, rather, maybe a dominance of one over the others.

Livio and his body

Livio always had an idealized relation with his mother. They mutually felt they were the ideal partner for one another. During childhood and the beginning of adolescence, they spent many hours together, eating, chatting, he massaging her back when she was tense, and, above all, speaking badly of the father, whom he found too aggressive and rude with his mother. The mother often told Livio that he had much more common sense and was much more understanding than his father, and that the father was very "rude".

At seventeen, he came to see me, because, after a "very wild" weekend during which he drugged himself heavily and took too much risk, his friends pushed him into looking for help. But he was very omnipotent and arrogant and believed all was well and that he did not need help.

He returned at nineteen, then attending college, curiously, the same course that would train him for his father's profession. The first sight of him had an impact on me, since Livio had many skin lesions that gave him a bad aspect. He came to me precisely because he had a "terrible psoriasis": desquamative lesions were all over his body; it was dramatic, since he was a handsome, attractive youngster, but at the same time repulsive as a consequence of the lesions. He was depressed. He would say, "I can't stand it any longer, besides itching all day, I'm ashamed of coming close to people. It seems to me that everybody looks at me on the streets . . ." He wanted help badly, and began his analysis immediately.

Psoriasis was the most intense symptom, along with his hatred and diffused whining. He thought what was happening to him was unfair. He was enraged at everything, but above all, of having to study: "I don't know whether I chose this course because I like it or if it is because of my father . . . All I know is I feel imprisoned. The whole of my life is attending college, I cannot live a free life, I hate this!" He entered the sessions almost dragging himself, and seemed to fall down on the couch, at the same time sighing as if that demanded much effort from him. He seemed numb, indolent, giving the impression that he made a huge effort to win over something that dragged him towards inertia.

Often, his discourse was a reverberant whining, generating sleepiness and confusion, which made me dizzy, lost, unable to understand which pathways we were following. He would recount dreams of repetition where he dived into, or swam in, dark waters, or walked in swamps, afraid of being entrapped in such situations. It was understood that those dreams were "narrating" (Ferro, 1995) what was going on in the analysis: the analytical relation was beginning to be seen as a dangerous place where he was afraid of getting lost, and that "swampy" environment was recreated through the form of his discourse. It is likely that this "swamp" lived in the environment of the analytical relation, was an experience of the same nature of the one that made him walk draggingly, as if something was holding him.

The dangerous, "swampy", shapeless environment gradually appeared more clearly. Something that happened later helped the understanding of this moment of the analytical process and his mental functioning. Livio's mother had to undergo a digestive endoscopy. He decided to attend the procedure. He said that, when he thought about watching the examination, he felt a "weird" feeling: "on the one hand I was curious and excited by the idea of getting to know the insides of my mother; on the other hand, I felt I was intruding, that it was not fair to Mum that I did that." It ended up that, when the examination began and the first images of the interior of the mother's body appeared, Livio started feeling an unbearable claustrophobic anxiety, a feeling of choking, of being about to faint, and that he should leave that place quickly. And, indeed, he got out of the room, feeling extremely bad. We analysed that, more than watching the mother's examination, Livio, in his fantasy, had introduced himself inside her, and that left him deeply frightened and invaded by a claustrophobic anxiety.

The pathophysiologic explanation for psoriasis is that it is excessive proliferation of the epithelium, resulting in crusts and desquamation. Aware of this, I often recalled McDougall's (1989) concept of "a body for two". Now we understood that Livio sometimes tried to enter inside the mother, to be the mother, and had the fantasy that they shared the same skin. We understood that what he was proposing in the analytical relation was to dive into the analysis, just as in his dreams—an almost fusional diving that frightened him. Nevertheless, from that resulted his fear of getting lost in the "swamp" of the analysis. This desire of entering the object and seizing its qualities was becoming delineated. He recalled that as a small child, when he was frightened, he soothed himself by putting his ear "against the soft skin of the mother's belly and stayed there listening to the sounds of her aorta". He then recalled the times he collected objects considered feminine (jewellery boxes and Hello Kitty stamps) and that he would stand in front of the mirror and hide his genitals between his legs, imagining himself a woman: he would soothe himself by means of a fantasy of penetration inside the body of the mother, and in his fantasy, he often became his mother.

Nevertheless, I imagine that parallel to the fantasies of fusion with the mother, there were non-symbolized engulfing and claustrophobic anxieties. This is evident in the episode of the endoscopy. He is conscious of his desire of intruding on the mother, but, on living the omnipotent fantasy that he was penetrating inside her, he probably experienced this unthinkable claustrophobic anxiety and lost consciousness. In this sense, can we think that it was the evacuation in the soma of this anxiety of engulfing that generated the uncontrolled epithelium proliferation and the psoriasis? Would this hyper proliferating epithelium be a barrier and, at the same time, a fusion with the mother? But this would be almost like proposing a symbolic meaning to these somatic manifestations, something I do not believe in.

Marty (1990) suggests that the "allergic" relational system would be a massive fixation to a pre-objectal state of primary indistinction with the mother. I believe that in adolescence, non-symbolized—and, therefore, traumatic—desires, anxieties, and primitive mental states ecloded again, probably due to the insufficient container capacity, as well as the scarce possibilities of transforming into alpha, that is, due to the few possibilities of mentalization of such primitive emotions, the somatic pathway was the site for evacuation. We may infer that those primitive emotions, protoemotions (Bion, 1965), or rudimentary emotions (Aisenstein, 2009), evacuated in the soma, could gain shape by being lived in the analytical field and in the relationship with the analyst. We obviously cannot rule out genetic, inherited, organic aspects of psoriasis. But we may presume that the psychological factors were important for its appearance and remission in this period of life (*ibid.*).

It is possible that, having been placed in a symbolic plane through our transformation work into alpha, this primitive mental state—made real through somatosis—of intrusion into, or fusion with, the maternal body and the anxieties derived from that, as well as the fantasies of intruding into the analyst, Livio's psoriasis entered into remission. The increase in the symbolization possibilities for primitive anxieties and states was leading to changes. But the broader acknowledgement of reality and dependency generated new anxieties. As he was not the analyst, there were many moments in which he felt alone and frustrated by it. Analysis generated frustration as it set boundaries through interpretations; it placed him in his reality.

Intense emotions, previously evacuated in the soma, were now expressed in behaviour. As I began to exist as object, and precisely because that frustrated him, hatred assumed a privileged space. He began to attack the analytical relationship and his own body: "Do I really have to go through all this anguish of analysis?" Livio started to skip sessions, attack the setting, and his own body.

He would come back from the weekends claiming he had "stoned" himself. He would drug himself heavily, with alcohol and marijuana, sometimes with cocaine. He talked about the pleasure he had when the moment of "being able to send everything sky-high, over the weekends, sleep as much as I want, drink as much as I want, get laid whenever I feel like it".

Having advanced in regard to his mentalization possibilities, I have the impression that, as the relationships with live and separate objects triggered intense anxieties, he got involved in addictive domain relationships (Jeammet, 2001) in which the emotions arising from the relation with the object are replaced by sensations. They give a feeling of existing as subject (*ibid.*), but by contouring the appropriate emotions of live and separated objects (Bion, 1962). I understand that in this moment there was a progress concerning his mental apparatus, since, instead of the concreteness of somatosis, there was here the construction of a narcissistic defence.

An addictive, promiscuous, and, at other times, masturbatory sexuality, intense drug use, and careless personal hygiene occupied the scene now. He masturbated many times a day. At weekends he would fall into a promiscuous sexuality with, for instance, four partners in five days, with no protection whatsoever against contamination. He gave the impression that erotization was almost addictive, and that, through sex and drugs, he intended to create an oniroid world of pure, idealized pleasure, with no boundaries where, in his fantasy, he was fused with an idealized object and avoided the frustrations of coming into contact with his internal and external reality.

As his acting out was signified, understanding the details of the narcissistic refuges into which he entered, the destructive aspect hidden behind this idealized universe started to be unveiled. Livio revealed that he had not brushed his teeth for years and he was proud of it, since it was clear to him that by doing so he did not give in to his father, who was "all tidy and meticulous". "Big deal to have decaying teeth!" He lived that with unmistakable pleasure and triumph. He felt strong and admired by his friends when he plunged from a hill between the rocks into the ocean, since nobody else would risk doing that; or even when he drank until falling unconscious, being recognized by all as the one who had drunk the most, then drove his car and woke up somewhere in town, not knowing how he had got there. It became evident that destructiveness was strongly present in those refuges idealized by Livio. Masochism became important then; through risky behaviour and attacks on the body he tried to feel strong, alive, and, narcissistically, subject and object.

At the same time, it triggered in me a sadistic countertransference of "putting him in his place", as a father disciplining a spoilt son. Sadomasochism was externalized in the analytical relationship. One day he came into the room, looked at a carpet glued to the wall, and said, "There is a large vagina there. For days it seems to me it is drawn there . . . I don't think it is quite possible, but I have the impression that you drew that on the wall . . . I can't stop looking at that drawing, I even get dizzy . . . I think you drew it to show me how I feel small close to women . . ." He felt the analyst had become an analyst/father who "offered" him the open, free maternal genital, yet sadistic, since he actively wished to make him feel small and intimidated. At the same time, he concretely showed me how much he felt effectively intimidated and small confronting the female genital, which he saw as gigantic, attractive, and engulfing.

Although the masochism and the self-destructive behaviours were an anguishing, risky, and difficult situation to manage, he had progressed from somatic into action, in the framework of a set of significances constructed within transference–countertransference. The self-destructive behaviour, the sadomasochistic relation in regard to himself and his internal objects were, nevertheless, an evolution. There was a higher degree of mentalization and objectalization, even if at the cost of attacking the body.

After many years of analysis, Livio established a tender relationship with a new girlfriend, graduated from the university, increased his capacity to tolerate frustration considerably, and, as a consequence, to symbolize. I would say that today, as an adult, he is a "good neurotic".

Final comments

Bion, in many papers (1962a,b, 1963, 1965), makes clear his viewpoint that protoemotions, sensations, and sensorial experiences are dependent on a positive container–contained relationship and on the work of the alpha function for them to be transformed into symbolic forms capable of being stored in the alpha reticule, or in the symbolic networks that constitute the human mind. When this transformation into alpha does not occur, these raw emotions are evacuated in the soma or in the behaviour.

When adolescence begins, as has already been described, the primitive scenario of the dawning of the human subject is reactivated, since again we encounter a relative symbolic insufficiency between the mind—made fragile due to the failure of the representations system—and a new body, a strange one, which places the demand of representation beyond its possibilities. Therefore, primitive anxieties—Oedipal and others—arise. Adolescents in whom the symbolic capacities and the introjections of containing objects (Bion, 1962b) have not been established firmly will refer to all kinds of defensive manoeuvres, from the most primitive ones, close to pulsion (Green, 1990), attacks on linking (Bion, 1959), generating an impairment of mentalization, or of the ability to think, according to Bion, to other, less regressive manoeuvres, closer to representation (Green, 1990), or neurotic, as Bion (1959) would put it.

Nevertheless, for the objectives of this chapter, the understanding of the psychosomatic manifestations in adolescence, I point out that we will find, in this period of life, from ephemerous manifestations (headaches, diarrhoeas, small allergies) to overt psychosomatic diseases connected to chronic or acute insufficiency of mentalizations. But we will also find attacks on the body, which, although not somatosis, are ways of expressing in the body some of those non-symbolized or badly symbolized dramas.

I believe that in Livio, as well as in many other adolescents in which somatosis appear, a negative container–contained relationship occurred. Lutenberg (2005) supposes that under such circumstances a hate link (H) is set to play between the mind and the body, which is the perpetuation of the sinister maternal–infant bond of a maternal primitive rejection to receive the massive projective identifications of the baby. He then repeats the primitive disaster of the impossibility of generating a thought, a symbolization, when faced with inominated emotions. A growing capacity of evacuating non-transformed feelings and emotions and aiming them at the body is then generated. The body now will have to "contain" the emotions and the primitive states not transformed in alpha, or, if we prefer, in representations.

I believe we can imagine a growing scale of thinkability, or mentalization, in which we are faced—either as dominant characteristics of an individual, or as synchronic aspects of the same individual—with raw emotions that could not be transformed and appeared as "things-in-themselves" (psychosomatic symptoms, self-destructive behaviour, and raw emotions in the psychoanalytic field), emerging thoughts which cannot be thought for the absence of a containing mind and will be split and projected in the analyst or in other objects, and, finally, a mind capable of thinking, containing its thoughts and operating with neurotic defence mechanisms, features of the classic psychoanalytic patients.

Besides the psoriasis, Livio presented in the analytic field (Baranger & Baranger, 1969) a quantum of raw emotions awaiting transformation or thinkability. Being "imprisoned", lost, disorientated, anguished, became "thing-in-itself" (Bion, 1962b) in the "here and now" of the analytical relation, felt by the patient or by myself.

The mind of the analyst, but more than that, the relational field (Baranger & Baranger, 1969; Ferro, 1997), currently becomes the great container and transforming element. In adolescence, the analyst's work of containing becomes even more important, since the failure of the representational system constructed in childhood releases a de-fused violence which the adolescent, specially the more fragile ones, will not be able to contain.

Winnicott (1963) comments that the mother–object should survive the attacks and the mother–environment should provide a stable environment during a long enough time gap to allow, after the attacks, the emergence of creative reparation. Especially in patients in whom destructiveness and evacuation have taken over an important role in their defensive systems, the mind of the analyst, the transformational capacity of the relation, and the analytical environment will be fundamental for the patient, throughout time, to be able to represent, contain, and work through emotions previously unthinkable.

References

Aisenstein, M. (2004). O doloroso enigma, enigma da dor. *Revista de Psicanálise da SPPA*, 11(1): 35–49.

Aisenstein, M. (2009). Les exigeances de la representation. *Rapport du XXX Congrés de langue française*.

Baranger, W., & Baranger, M. (1969). La situacion analitica como campo dinâmico. In: *Problemas del campo psicoanalitico*. Buenos Aires: Ed. Kargieman, 1969.

Bion, W. (1957). Diferenciação entre a personalidade psicótica e não-psicótica. In: *Estudos psicanalíticos revisados*. Rio de Janeiro: Imago Editora, 1988.

Bion, W. (1959). Ataques ao elo de ligação. In: *Estudos psicanalíticos revisados*. Rio de Janeiro: Imago Editora, 1988.

Bion, W. (1962a). Uma teoria sobre o processo de pensar. In: *Estudos psicanalíticos revisados*. Rio de Janeiro: Imago Editora, 1988.

Bion, W. (1962b). *Aprendiendo de la Experiência*. Mexico: Editorial Paidós, 1991.

Bion, W. (1963). *Elementos de Psicanálise*. Rio de Janeiro: Imago Editora, 2004.

Bion, W. (1965). *Transformações—Do aprendizado ao crescimento*. Rio de Janeiro: Imago Editora, 2004.

Bion, W. (1970). *Atenção e interpretação*. Rio de Janeiro: Imago Editora, 1973.

Blos, P. (1981). *La transicion adolescente*. Buenos Aires: Amorrortu.

Botella, C., & Botella, S. (2002). *Irrepresentável: mais além da representação.* Porto Alegre, Sociedade de Psicologia: Criação humana.

Bronstein, C. (2008). Duas modalidades de defesas maníacas—Sua função no colapso adolescente. *Conferência apresentada na SPPA*, maio de 2009.

Cahn, R. (1999). *O adolescente na psicanálise - a aventura da subjetivação*. Rio de Janeiro: Companhia de Freud.

Cassirer, E. (1964). *Ensaio Sobre o Homem*, M. Fontes (Ed.). São Paulo, 1997.

Castoriadis-Aulagnier, P. (1975). *La violência de la interpretación: del pictograma al enunciado*. Buenos Aires: Amorrortu, 2004.

Ferro, A. (1995). *A Técnica na Psicanálise Infantil*. Rio de Janeiro: Imago, 1995.

Ferro, A. (1997). *Na sala de análise*. Rio de Janeiro: Imago Editora, 1998.

Freud, S. (1911b). Formulations on the two principles of mental functioning. *S.E., 12*: 213–226. London: Hogarth.

Freud, S. (1924c). The economic problem of masochism. *S.E., 19*: 157–170. London: Hogarth.

Green, A. (1990). O trabalho do negativo. In: *Conferências Brasileiras de André Green—Metapsicologia dos limites*. Rio de Janeiro: Imago Editora.

Jeammet, P. (2001). Novas problemáticas da adolescência: evolução e manejo da dependência. In: *Casa do Psicólogo*. São Paulo, 2005.

Louppe, A. (2001). Automutilations transitoires a l'adolescence. *Revue Française de Psychanalyse, XLV*: 463–475.

Lutenberg, J. M. (2005). A criatividade negativa e as doenças psicossomáticas. *Rev. Psicanálise da SPPA, XII*(2): 329–351.

McDougall, J. (1989). *Teatros do Corpo--O Psicossoma em Psicanálise*. São Paulo: Livraria Martins Fontes Editora, 1991.

Marty, P. (1990). *La psicosomática del adulto*. Buenos Aires: Amorrortu Editora, 2003.

Marty, P. (1992). Mentalización y psicosomática. *Revista Psicoanálisis, 3*: 7–21.

Meltzer, D. (1978). Seminários de Novara. *Quaderni di Psicoterapia Infantile*. Roma: Bokla, 1978.

Meltzer, D. (1984). *Vida onírica*. Madrid: Tecnipublicaciones.

Meltzer, D. (1992). *The Claustrum—An Investigation of Claustrophobic Phenomena*. Strath Tay, Perthshire: The Clunie Press for The Roland Harris Trust Library.

Rosemberg, B. (1991). *Masoquismo mortífero e masoquismo guardião da vida*. São Paulo: Ed. Escuta, 2003.

Steiner, J. (1993). *Psychic Retreats—Pathological Organizations in Psychotic, Neurotic and Borderline Patients*. London: Routledge, 1993.

Winnicott, D. (1950). A agressão e sua relação com o desenvolvimento emocional. In: *Da pediatria à psicanálise*. Rio de Janeiro: Livraria Francisco Alves Editora, 1988.

Winnicott, D. W. (1951). Objetos transicionais e fenômenos transicionais. In: *O Brincar e a Realidade*. Rio de Janeiro: Imago Editora, 1975.

Winnicott, D. (1963). De la dependencia a la independencia en el desarollo de individuo. In: *El Processo de maduracion en el Niño*. Barcelona: Editorial Laia, 1975.

Winnicott, D. (1963a). El desarrollo para la capacidad de inquietud. In: *El proceso de maduración en el niño—Estudios para una teoría del desarrollo emocional*. Barcelona: Editorial Laia, 1979.

Winnicott, D. (1963b). O atendimento hospitalar como complemento de psicoterapia intensiva na adolescência. In: *O ambiente e os processos de maturação*. Porto Alegre: Editora Artes Médicas, 1982.

CHAPTER SIX

Psychosomatic conditions in contemporary psychoanalysis

Elsa Rappoport de Aisemberg

S ince Freud, psychosomatic symptoms have been considered as complementary elements to understand the patient, whereas nowadays those corporeal expressions are analysed to produce modifications. A large number of physicians have understood this, and, therefore, refer patients to psychotherapeutic or psychoanalytic treatment. This means a big change we have to account for, accepting the multi-factorial character of those symptoms.

To address this subject is an inspiring challenge to me, because, although the psychosomatic area has a history in the psychoanalysts' field, it has always been a little marginal within our general theoretical models. Challenge and marginality point to the fact that Freud never dealt explicitly with the psychosomatic issue, and, consequently, did not advance hypotheses in his theoretical body.

Nevertheless, I agree with many authors, such as Pierre Marty, Joyce McDougall, Jean Laplanche, and André Green, among others, that Freudian conceptualizations of actual neuroses and mixed neurosis, as well as the articulations of later Freudian theoretical models, the introduction of narcissism, mourning not worked through, early traumas, and Thanatos action, can now be used to understand psychosomatic phenomena.

Looking back in history

It all began in Chicago with Alexander (1950) in the field of psychosomatic medicine, which provided a more integrated perspective of the human being, stressing the relationship between emotions and somatic symptoms. It meant an extension of our field. Pollock's contributions (1970) about the anniversary reaction and the fragment of Engels' self-analysis (1975) are on this line.

Later there were further developments, especially in Paris with Marty (1990) and the Psychosomatic Institute of Paris that led psychoanalysts to focus on the somatic phenomenon. Moreover, there are McDougall's rich theoretical–clinical contributions (1978, 1982, 1989), based, among others, on Winnicott's concept of psyche–soma splitting (1967), and Green's theoretical advances about non-neurotic structures (1972–1986) and his formulations stated in Geneva (1998), where he describes a kind of psychic suppressive deafness which leaves the individual prey to destructiveness which then turns on his own soma, this being equivalent to what foreclosure is for the psyche. All of this placed somatosis at the core of the psychoanalytic field.

On the other hand, in Buenos Aires, since the beginning of the psychoanalytical movement, its founders made a point of including the body in their theoretical–clinical interests. Some, such as Rascovsky (1943, 1948), did so through psychosomatic medicine, while Garma (1954, 1958) approached somatosis as conversion or psychoneurosis. Finally, Rivière proposed that the expressions of the unconscious are manifested in three areas: mind, body, and the external world (Aisemberg, 2002). All this led to the inclusion of the corporeal and the soma in the training of many Argentine colleagues. Thus, one of them, Liberman et al. (1982), with colleagues, described over-adapted patients with a formulation close to McDougall's normopath, or the anti-analysand in analysis (1978).

I think that what contemporary psychoanalysis has gained through the inclusion of both psychoneurotic functioning and non-neurotic functioning, as well as classic cure and "enlarged" cure to deal with the extensions of psychoanalysis and which enables us to explore dark and unknown zones of the human psyche, lies at the core of our discipline. These extensions have been achieved through our broader listening, product of our personal analysis, of self-analysis, supervisions, and exchanges with colleagues.

I agree with Madeleine Baranger (2007) that the new becomes legitimized as psychoanalysis provided it is articulated with basic Freudian concepts: the unconscious, transference, infantile sexuality, the drive and its vicissitudes, if the hypotheses we construct from our clinical work can be articulated with Freudian theories and if creativity in the setting is related to the classic cure.

Two psychic functionings

One of the obstacles in the cure in current clinical practice is the emergence of the psychosomatic phenomenon that has compelled analysts to transform this problem into further knowledge. Thus, some of my ideas (Aisemberg, 1998–1999, 2001, 2003, 2005, 2007, 2008a) about the two psychic functionings, the neurotic and the non-neurotic one, are based on Freudian conceptualizations of mixed neuroses and actual neuroses.

This field, beyond the neurotic functioning that Freud (1895b, 1895f) discovered at the end of the nineteenth century, refers to the quantity of somatic excitation which has failed to transform into drive, which has no psychic inscription yet, and which short-circuits to the soma. Defence against this destructive excitation may be suppression of affect, mainly of aggression, and an equivalent to foreclosure of representation, as Green (1998) points out.

I have noted that in the clinical exploration of patients with somatic conditions, this psychoneurotic functioning may appear at the onset of the treatment and/or later, with the evolution of the analytic process. That is, both functionings coexist: the neurotic and the non-neurotic one.

Drawing on the ideas Freud set down in the Project (1895a), I understand that psychoneurotic functioning is built out of the memory traces left by the experience of satisfaction with the primary object, whereas the non-neurotic one derives from the sensorial traces left by the experience of pain which have not been transformed into psychic tissue, experiences of pain which have not been bound, that is, Rosemberg's (1991) lifeguard masochism as psychic survival.

Cure or treatment

I understand the psychosomatic phenomenon as a *mise en scène* of the investment of those sensorial traces that have not been processed, so the challenge in our clinical work consists in producing constructions that transform them into psychic tissue.

This is the field of repetition (Aisemberg, 2007, 2008a; Freud 1914g, 1920g; Green, 2000a; Marucco, 2007) beyond the pleasure principle, the evil compulsion, to follow Bolognini (2006), repetition compulsion of the archaic, traumatic perceptual traces that find expression in different short-circuits: (a) to the body, giving rise to somatosis; (b) to the act, with acting-outs and accidents; (c) to the mind, emerging as a hallucinatory episode in a non-psychotic person.

This field of repetition is related to Thanatos, to helplessness anxiety, to early traumas, or pre-psychic traumas, as Rousillon (1991) names them, which, not having been transformed into psychic structures, keep the primitive traces split, that is, proper unconscious (Aisemberg, 2005, 2007, 2008a). Such traces, once invested, come into the scene and become the object of exploration in contemporary psychoanalysis, thus enabling us to create something new between patient and analyst, similar to the artist who, by his/her work, can alone transform his/her primitive traumatic traces into figurations (Aisemberg, Bustamante, D'Aniello de Calderón, Eckell de Muscio, & O'Donnell, 2000).

Our present challenge is to be met in the exploration of the *mise en scène* of the sensorial primitive marks, previous to the word, archaic, of the genuine or absolute or proper unconscious with its roots in the soma: the id of the second topic, as Freud delineates it in 1933.

In the master's footsteps, we attempt to turn obstacles in the cure into new knowledge concerning our field of work. Our aim is the installation of transference, the functioning of the fundamental rule to reach the unconscious derivates.

In my experience with patients with predominance of non-neurotic structures (Aisemberg, 2003), mostly psychosomatic ones, who start with psychoanalytic therapy, that is, with some flexibility or creativity in the setting, while having in mind the active matrix, as Green (2003) calls it, the inner setting or the analytic thought, in many instances installation of the transference can be attained, and then a classic form of analytic treatment develops with transference, dreams, Oedipus, infantile sexuality, and the *report of a violence which is not suppressed as when it was in the soma.*

I have conceptualized this as the coexistence of two psychic functionings: the psychoneurotic and the non-neurotic. I think that the concept of mixed neurosis Freud advanced in 1895 is a significant antecedent to these ideas. Freud's concept refers to the simultaneous presence of two diverse functionings: one is associated with somatic sexual excitation, as in anxiety neurosis, while the other refers to psychic excitation, as in hysteria. So, there coexists in the same subject a psychoneurotic organization and a somatic one, with a deficit in the psychic linkage: actual neuroses.

The latter can find expression in anxiety as well as in somatic symptoms. There is suppression not only of what is sexual, but also especially of aggression, while the actual points to the event as well as to bodily symptoms.

I wonder whether this insufficient psychic linkage, as Freud formulates in "Draft E" in 1894, is so because it failed to construct a representation, leaving excitation on the pathway between soma and psyche, or because representation was foreclosed as the defence to surviving psychically when threatened by extremely painful or violent experiences. This last option has been McDougall's main thesis since her first works on the subject (1982). I believe both options may be possible.

On two unconsciouses: the repressed and the genuine, or proper, one

As I have already stated (Aisemberg, 1998–1999, 2001, 2003, 2005, 2007, 2008a), there is a structuring functioning stemming from endosomatic excitation, excitation that results from inner and external perceptions of the relationship with the object, which is transformed into drive, and this in turn is inscribed as psychic representation, this being the dynamics that prevails in the field of psychoneurosis.

Instead, when endosomatic excitation fails to transform, has no psychic representation, does not turn into drive, and is not translated into a psychic representative, it remains on the border between soma and psyche yielding primitive inscriptions. This non-structuring functioning may be the origin of somatic disorders, among others.

The structuring organization originates from the experience of satisfaction.

Need or self-preservative drive sets this circuit in motion. It is the perception of the experience of satisfaction with the primary object that will be the foundation of pleasure and sexuality and be inscribed as memory trace. This trace will, in turn, be invested by the drive psychic representative, eliciting a thing-representation. Anaclisis provides the functioning of the partial sexual drive and the structure of desire. Now the psychic representative is liable to repression: the ideational-representative on the one hand, and the quantum of affect on the other hand, will follow different pathways. The repressed unconscious (Freud, 1915c,d,e) is being constructed. Thing-representation is articulated with the drives and also with language, giving rise to word-representation. We are in the field of psychoneurosis.

Instead, if the experience of pain is not bound by lifeguard masochism, it leads to disinvestment, splitting, and short-circuits. This is endosomatic excitation that has no psychic resolution, that has no mental representation, and that is inscribed only as sensorial traces. This is the proper unconscious that never became conscious. This is the id of the second topic that Freud delineates in Lecture 31 in 1933. He says,

> It is certainly hard to say today how far the drawing is correct. In one respect it is undoubtedly not. The space occupied by the unconscious id ought to have been incomparably greater than that of the ego or the preconscious. I must ask you to correct it in your thoughts. [1933a, p. 79]

Later, in *Moses and Monotheism* (1939a), he says,

> The *repressed* is to be counted as belonging to the id and is subject to the same mechanism; it is distinguished from it only in respect to its genesis. The differentiation is accomplished in the earliest period of life, while the ego is developing out of the id. At that time a portion of the contents of the id is taken into the ego and raised to the preconscious state; another portion is not affected by this translation and remains behind in the id as the unconscious proper. [1939a p. 96]

To my mind, he highlights the id as a proper or genuine unconscious with roots in the soma, as the origin of life and chaos.

I would like to mention here an excellent work by Riolo (2006) in which, from a Freudian stance, he differentiates two unconsciouses: one repressed and the other non-repressed, which gives rise to actions.

On drives: differences between Eros and Thanatos

This excess of unbound endosomatic excitation that is not translated is a quantity that disorganizes, that disobjectivizes (Aisemberg, 2005, 2007, 2008a). It reminds me of Green's description (2000b) of the death drive, or destruction drive, as this author proposes, when it is orientated towards the interior.

In contrast, Eros organizes and objectivizes the psyche, starting from the memory trace of the experience of satisfaction, and builds the structuring circuit I have already mentioned.

In 1915, Freud describes the drive as formed by representation plus affect. This definition corresponds to the erotic drive formulated in 1920, or a mixture of both drives turned into sadomasochism in 1924(c).

But also, in 1915, Freud presented a formulation of the drive as a limit concept between psyche and soma, which originates in endosomatic excitation as a result of extero and intero perceptions in connection with the object, and this excitation will be translated into a psychic representative of the drive (1923b) eliciting the structuring of the apparatus and the psychoneurotic functioning.

On the other hand, when this amount of endosomatic excitation between soma and psyche fails to attain psychic transformation, in my opinion, it gives rise to actual neuroses as Freud formulated them at the beginning of his theories.

This quantity that has no representation, that is not bound, that is disobjectivized, seems to me closer to the idea of the death drive, death drive surely rather mixed, which will invest the pre-psychic traces, thus leading to evil repetition, somatosis being one of its destinies.

These reflections prompt me to think Eros and Thanatos are of different essence. Eros is an organized drive represented in the psyche, whereas Thanatos is a disorganized quantity, pre-psychic, or on the border between soma and psyche. The former undergoes the vicissitudes of psychoneurotic functioning, while the latter prevails in non-neurotic functionings.

Representation and affects

The drive defined by Freud as a frontier between soma and psyche is itself the *representative* of endosomatic excitations. And, in turn, as Laplanche (1987) points out, *by delegation*, the drive has its psychic representative or drive representative. The delegation of the soma in the psyche, or the "translation" of somatic excitation into psychic language, is an *intrasubjective* pathway, which articulates with another pathway, an *intersubjective* one, that of the infant–mother relationship, or the supporting object in initial helplessness. By anaclisis, the partial sexual drive and the structure of desire are set in action, yet, when there is deficit in the mother or primal object, resulting in failure to provide the protective barrier against excess of stimuli, there is the predominance of early traumatic structure, beyond the pleasure principle; there is disturbance in this pathway, and no construction or deconstruction of psychic representation. Then quantity arises, and this leads us to affects, which break into the scene when there is no representation to bind them.

I have described (Aisemberg, 1998–1999) three destinies for affects:

1. Affects bound to the repressed unconscious, the three destinies that Freud describes in 1915. They point to neurotic functioning and can be articulated with the patient's discourse.
2. The transformation into anxiety in actual neuroses, where quantity without binding prevails. That is why I agree with other authors that actual neuroses are Freudian anchorages in psychosomatics.
3. Affects expelled from the psyche, related to the split or genuine or proper unconscious.

This is the fourth destiny that McDougall (1982) terms disaffectation, or the short-circuit that Green proposes as passage to the act or to the soma. These are *split affects* (Green, 1972–1986, 1973, 1995). These affects can be captured in countertransference by the analyst and be useful, if previously transformed, in producing constructions.

On trauma

Sexuality is the Freudian axis that accounts theoretically for the structuring organization of the psyche and of psychoneurosis. Freud advances its most developed model in "Metapsychology" in 1915. But, in 1920, in *Beyond the Pleasure Principle*, the creator of psychoanalysis introduces another axis, which deals with the other psychic functioning, that of traumatic neuroses that come with repetition, quantity, pain, and Thanatos. By trauma, I mean the quantity that cannot be bound, which overwhelms the psychic apparatus. This definition "coincides", or "overlaps", with that of automatic anxiety, of acute psychic pain, and of actual neuroses.

I understand anxiety as a reaction to danger, to economic disturbance due to the increase of external or internal (drive charge) excitation that cannot be processed psychically, which overwhelms the psychic apparatus. It points to the *infans'* psychic helplessness, a correlate of biological helplessness. This primary economic dimension of anxiety, close to the concept of trauma, lies at the centre of the first theory of anxiety that Freud formulates between 1893 and 1895. It is characterized by the presence of excess of quantity, excess of somatic excitation that has no mental resolution, and, because of insufficient psychic linkage, cannot be transformed into libido, cannot be bound with representations, and, consequently, becomes anxiety. This is an explanatory theory of actual neuroses, mainly of anxiety neuroses.

In their paradigmatic work on pure trauma, Madeleine and Willy Baranger and Jorge Mom (1987) describe actual neuroses as those gaps that have not become part of history, present but unattainable, what is left of not worked through trauma. We are in the field of early trauma. In initial helplessness there is a predominance of the economic order together with a deficit of the supporting object not discriminated yet, the mother who is not able to fulfill satisfactorily either her role as a protective barrier against excess of stimuli or as decoding and nominating the *infans'* emotions. This lack of representation exposes him/her to helplessness, since he/she cannot bind the quantum of excitation, which contributes to a chaotic atmosphere.

Successive experiences of satisfaction with the object construct the memory trace and the representation of the object. This web of representations paves the way for binding quantity, but quite often it turns out to be insufficient, owing to infantile helplessness or because representations are swept away by anxiety or foreclosed as defence.

We have to single out the psychic trauma or sexual trauma or structuring trauma which will give rise to the Oedipal fantasmatic, to psychoneurosis, from early trauma or pure trauma described by the Barangers and Mom (1987), or pre-psychic trauma or lost trauma according to Rousillon (1991). In the latter case, although the experience is potentially traumatic, as there is not yet a consti-tuted subject, so it remains latent or frozen.

This highlights the importance of the relationship between trauma and representation. In psychic trauma, there is a represen-tation of the traumatic experience and a structuring transformation which organizes the psyche, whereas in the pre-psychic or early trauma, such experience has not been turned into representation yet, so it is only a sensorial mark, a remainder that could not become structure and that emerges with compulsion to repetition, seeking binding or meaning.

Actual traumas would be a third class, as those described in assessing the psychic consequences of the Holocaust among sur-vivors or their descendants, as well as other equivalent experiences: wars, social and family violence, sexual abuse, etc. Bohleber (2004) and Grubrich-Simitis (1979), among others, deal with this, and so do Krystal's works, quoted by McDougall (1982), with his state-ments about post-traumatic alexithymia, viewing psychosomatic outcome as result of these poignant traumas. Survival is achieved through the body. When a part of the psyche is devastated, only the soma remains as source of life and survival.

About transference

The analytic cure enables us to include all the dimensions of the past that are active in the depths, and these dimensions can emerge in transference in any of the three psychic/pre-psychic registers: drive, narcissism, and the archaic.

1. In the field of the drive it is expressed by transference to the word.
2. In the field of narcissism, of course secondary, it is manifested in the transference to the object, narcissism that turns into identifications and is manifested in transference to the object.
3. In the pre-psychic field of the archaic originated in early perceptive traces, it arises as passage to the act, to the soma, to the mind.

This last register, quasi-mythical, of the sensorial marks between soma and psyche lacks mental existence and only acquires it when it becomes psychic tissue through the construction of remembrance between patient and analyst in the transference–countertransference situation.

Repetition and memory

In regard to psychoneurotic functioning, our aim is to retrieve the forgotten or repressed memory of the Oedipal conflict, while our present challenge, contemporary psychoanalysis, includes the non-neurotic functioning which strives to "construct memory", to elucidate primitive experiences previous to words, which never became conscious, what Green (2000a) calls "amnesic memory".

In the field of somatosis, McDougall, in 1995, called the primitive marks "body memory", the origin of the short-circuit to the soma.

Besides, I would like to remember a master of my society, José Bleger, who, in 1967, referring to the primitive aspects deposited on the setting, pointed out that they are not repressed, but split, so interpretation "gives rise to the secondary process. It is not interpreted on amnesic gaps, but on what never was part of the memory" (p. 517). The value and relevance of this statement points to the preverbal primitive functioning, which has not turned into psychic tissue and which has to be constructed in the analytic situation.

On clinical work

The construction of remembrance in the analytic situation implies a further step in Freud's text of 1937 about constructions. This text enables us to approach shadowy areas in the clinical work as well as in the theory: it comprises the wide field of non-neurotic, borderline, psychosomatic pathologies, among others.

When we work with a patient's psychoneurotic functioning, we try through interpretation to elicit repressed memories. But when we do so with non-neurotic functioning, as happens with somatosis, we have to construct memories: this is broader remembrance. We try to achieve that from repetition in transference and in countertransference. This construction is accomplished in the analyst's mind, and this implies that we are able to transform experiences, emotions, preverbal or paraverbal elements into images and words, into figurations and representations.

This communication from unconscious to unconscious, which Freud (1912c, 1941d) had already announced, used as a tool, thanks to our own analysis or self-analysis, has expanded our listening and our capacity to understand the patient.

Naturally, the construction that occurs in the analyst's mind poses the problem of conviction in the patient and whether the formulation we offer corresponds to his/her truth, whether it belongs to him/her. This problem was already observed by Freud himself (1937d), although he stated that the hallucinatory conviction of reality of the memory originated in the analyst's psychic functioning has the same effect as that of the memory recovered by the patient.

I believe conviction has at least two sources of confirmation: one, the feeling of experiencing the repetition in the transference–countertransference, which the analyst, through his/her hypotheses, will try to turn into representation; the other, the appearance of dreams, indicators of the transformation of traumatic traces into an attempt to fulfil a desire, as Freud advances in Lecture 29, in 1933a. And, as Sara Botella recalls beautifully in her work "Isn't dreaming a form of remembering?", a paper I had the pleasure of discussing in the Paris Encounter of 2006.

This idea of two subjects or two psyches working together, although there is asymmetry in the setting, has been examined by well-known authors:

- Cesar and Sara Botella (1997, 2001), in their excellent conceptualizations on regredience, figurability, and the "work by double" in the session;
- de M'Uzan (1994), with his wonderful description of the chimera;
- Bion (1966), with his priceless concept of *reverie* to account for early mother–baby communication and which would be recreated in some situations of the analytic session;
- Madeleine and Willy Baranger, with their formulation of the analytic field, first advanced in 1961–1962, understood as a product of crossed projective identifications between patient and analyst. Later, they defined it as the meeting of two psyches that generates a common basic unconscious fantasy, in the manner Bion describes for groups. Recently, Madeleine Baranger (2004) conceives the field as a structure built by patient and analyst in the analytic situation, and this structure is a third one which has both a symbolic and a mythical dimension. That is to say, these marks of the past that are repeated or recreated in the analytic field and which have a mythical dimension can attain symbolic transformation in the interplay of the analytic situation.

It should be noted that in this model there is circulation from intrasubjectivity to intersubjectivity and from the latter to the former. I fully agree. This view differs from the intersubjective model in which interaction prevails instead of the meeting of two subjects with their unconscious.

All these models try to account for the communication from unconscious to unconscious, which would give rise to "perceived" experiences without being aware of it, which would function as day's residues that stimulate the use of the analyst's mind as well as that of the patient's. Thus, I think that corporeal perception is the origin of the unconscious to unconscious communication, which, of course, must be transformed by the analyst, who, in these cases, works as an "auxiliary", lending his/her mental capacity, as de M'Uzan pointed out in 1976, since the patient is not able yet to turn them into words or representations. In addition, this would throw light on figurability, or on the analyst's dreams aroused by the patient's clinical material, as a complementary remembrance activity in the analytic field.

About violence

Another important dimension to be taken into account is that in these patients with predominance of non-neurotic structures, when they evolve positively, the psychoneurotic functioning emerges and it is expressed in transference, infantile sexuality, Oedipus, drives, and mainly *the report of the violence* that was suppressed before and circulated through the soma or the act.

I understand violence as the clinical expression of the quantity of indiscriminate excitation that was suppressed and had no linkage to representation, or that representation was erased in order to survive. All this is characteristic of the non-neurotic functioning.

This violence is awakened by intense emotions both of love and hatred, positive and negative. I think this is close to McDougall's concept of archaic sexuality (1989), where primitive sexuality and violence emerge undifferentiated.

Somatic course of mourning

Exploring clinical work with patients who suffer from severe somatosis, we often find an unwritten history of early mourning and traumas that have not been processed, mourning and traumas of the patient and/or his/her objects of identification.

The difficulty these patients have in coping with psychic pain, as well as with emotions in general, may lead them to a somatic course of mourning, what I have called "a peculiar pathology of mourning" (Aisemberg, 1994). Sometimes, it is not only their own mourning or traumas that have not been processed, but also identifications with parents who could not work through theirs. This subject leads us to Faimberg's developments (2005) on the telescoping of generations.

Our task with these patients consists in transforming the suffering and pain of severe somatosis into psychic suffering and pain, creating an external–internal space for this purpose.

Juana

I will now introduce a clinical vignette of a patient who stimulated my research into somatosis. Juana came to my office some years ago, when I had under treatment only patients with a classic setting: four/five times a week and on the couch.

She was thirty-four, divorced, and had one daughter. She herself was an only child. She was a psychologist, but had difficulties in working at her profession and also in being part of a steady couple. She did not want the couch, but a face-to-face therapy, as she did with her patients. We began the interviews according to her demands.

Juana used to report very painful moments in her life with a smile on her face: she talked about her father's physical and mental decline, about his death, which had been very distressing, about her problems with her couple, and her physical complaints.

I pointed out the *dissociation* between her discourse and the almost daily *body pains*. As this situation did not change after several months, based on my countertransference concern, I decided to make a "wild" utterance: I warned her about the possibility of a serious illness in her body if she continued to be unaware of her *psychic pain.*

What emerged, in passing, as a matter of fact, was that she had had a nodule in her breast, as big as a ball, for two years.

I put as a condition to continuing with the treatment that she should consult a breast specialist. She did so. It was cancer; she was operated on, and received cobalt. Besides, I suggested starting a psychoanalytic treatment on the couch three times a week, which she underwent for five years. She finished both the medical and the psychoanalytic treatment at the same time.

Throughout the cure, she was confronted with her mourning not worked through for her father's illness and death and for the difficulties in childhood due to maternal lack. Her mother was a childish, depressed woman, with little holding capacity, and who changed roles with her only daughter. Her father was an immigrant without history, and, through the telescoping approach, we reconstructed the father's not worked through mourning. Juana travelled to her father's birthplace to recover her family background, a violent and painful situation from which her father had fled and tried to erase.

This disidentification enabled her to contact emotions such as psychic pain and violence so that they were not suppressed, but were circulated and were open to be worked through to bring about psychic change. I think that present traumas and mourning resignified the primitive traumas unconsciously transmitted by her father. During the post-analysis, ten years later, Juana wrote a book of great aesthetical and emotional impact, which contained an elaboration of this experience.

Metapsychology of the cure

The aim of the cure is the access to unconscious derivates. With psychoneuroses, it means to recover representations and affects linked to the Oedipal problematic which structure the repressed unconscious. With somatosis as non-neurotic functioning, the question lies in constructing something new on the primitive traces, as in art. To transform the non-neurotic functioning produced by the experience of pain and violence, through a patient–analyst positive encounter, into an equivalent to the experience of satisfaction, which initiates a structuring circuit that gives rise to inscriptions, will construct a repressed unconscious: memory traces, representations; where there was proper unconscious, now we may contribute to organizing repressed unconscious.

References

Aisemberg, E. R. (1994). *Modelos teóricos en psicosomática* [*Theoretical Models in Psychosomatics*]. Buenos Aires: Panel del I Diálogo Psicoanalítico sobre Psicosomática.

Aisemberg, E. R. (1998–1999). Más allá de la representación: los afectos [Beyond representation: affects]. *Revista de Psicoanálisis*, Número Especial Internacional, 6.

Aisemberg, E. R. (2001). Revisión crítica de las teorías y los abordajes de los estados psicosomáticos [Critical review of the theories and approaches to psychosomatic conditions]. *Revista de Psicoanálisis, 58*: 2 [reprinted in *Psicosomática*, Buenos Aires, Lugar, 2005].

Aisemberg, E. R. (2002) Psicosomática [Psychosomatics]. In: *60 años de Psicoanálisis en Argentina*. Buenos Aires: Lumen.

Aisemberg, E. R. (2003). Abordaje teórico-clínico a los trastornos somáticos: ¿Trabajo en las fronteras o trabajo psicoanalítico? *Revista de Psicoanálisis, 60*, 3 [reprinted: Theoretical approach to somatic conditions: work at the frontiers of psychoanalysis or psychoanalytical work? *International Journal of Psychoanalysis, 85*: 977–981, 2004].

Aisemberg, E. R. (2005). Trauma, pulsión y somatosis [Trauma, drive and somatosis]. *Revista de Psicoanálisis, 62*, 2.

Aisemberg, E. R. (2007). Repetición, transferencia y somatosis [Repetition, transference and somatosis]. *Revista de Psicoanálisis, 64*, 2.

Aisemberg, E. R. (2008a). La sombra de la herencia en el psicoanálisis contemporáneo. *Revista de Psicoanálisis, 65*(1) [reprinted: The shadow of heritage in contemporary psychoanalysis. *EPF Bulletin, 62*: 93–103].

Aisemberg, E. R., Bustamante, A., D'Aniello de Calderón, H., Eckell de Muscio, I., & O'Donnell, P. (2000). El autorretrato [Self-portrait]: la dimensión narcisista de la transferencia. *Revista de Psicoanálisis, 57*(3–4): 493–508.

Alexander, F. (1950). *Psychosomatic Medicine*. New York: Norton.

Baranger, M. (2004). La teoría del campo. In: *El Otro en la Trama Intersubjetiva*. Buenos Aires: Lugar-APA [reprinted: *Field Theory. Truth, Reality, and the Psychoanalyst*. London: IPA, 2005].

Baranger, M. (2007). Desarrollos y controversias en psicoanálisis: pasado, presente y futuro. *Revista de Psicoanálisis, 64*(2): 393–397.

Baranger, M., & Baranger, W. (1961–1962). *Problemas del Campo Psicoanalítico*. Buenos Aires: Kargieman, 1969 [reprinted: The analytic situation as a dynamic field. *International Journal of Psychoanalysis, 89*(4): 795–826, 2008].

Baranger, M., Baranger, W., & Mom, J. (1987). El trauma psíquico infantil, de nosotros a freíd. *Revista de Psicoanálisis, 44*, 4 [reprinted: The infantile psychic trauma from us to Freud: pure trauma, retroactivity and reconstruction. *International Journal of Psychoanalysis, 69*(1): 113–128, 1988].

Bion, W. (1966). *Learning from Experience*. London: Karnac.

Bleger, J. (1967). Psychoanalysis of the analytic frame. *International Journal of Psychoanalysis, 48*: 511–519 [reprinted: Psicoanálisis del encuadre psicoanalítico. *Revista de Psicoanálisis, 24*(2): 241–258].

Bohleber, W. (2004). Evolución de la teoría del trauma en psicoanálisis. *Boletín de la Asociación Psicoanalítica Argentina, 72*: 12.

Bolognini, S. (2006). Tutte le volte che . . . la repetizione tra passato, presente, futuro temuto e futuro potenziale nella esperienza analitica. V Encounter APA-SPI, Bologna.

Botella, C., & Botella, S. (1997). *Más Allá de la Representación* [*Beyond Representation*]. Valencia: Promolibro.

Botella, C., & Botella, S. (2001). *La figurabilité psychique*. Paris: Delachaux and Nestlé.

Botella, S. (2006). Rêver n'est-il pas également un se souvenir? Paris, II Encounter APA-SPP.

de M'Uzan, M. (1976). Contratransferencia y sistema paradojal. *Del arte a la muerte*. Barcelona: Icaria, 1978.

de M'Uzan, M. (1994). *La buche de l'inconscient*. Paris: Gallimard.

Engel, G. (1975). The death of a twin: mourning and anniversary reactions. Fragments of the ten years of self-analysis. *International Journal of Psychoanalysis, 56*(1): 23–40.

Faimberg, H. (2005). *The Telescoping of Generations*. London: Routledge.

Freud, S. (1894). Draft E. *S.E., 1*: 189–195. London: Hogarth.

Freud, S. (1895a). Project for a Scientific Psychology. *S.E., 1*: 295–397. London: Hogarth.

Freud, S. (1895b). On the grounds for detaching a particular syndrome from neurasthenia under the description "anxiety neurosis". *S.E., 3*: 90–117. London: Hogarth.

Freud, S. (1895f). A reply to criticisms on my paper on anxiety neurosis. *S.E., 3*: 123–139. London: Hogarth.

Freud, S. (1912c). Recommendations to physicians practising psychoanalysis. *S.E., 12*: 109–120. London: Hogarth.

Freud, S. (1914g). Remembering, repeating and working-through. *S.E., 12*: 145–156. London: Hogarth.

Freud, S. (1915c). Instincts and their vicissitudes. *S.E., 14*: 117–140. London: Hogarth.

Freud, S. (1915d). Repression. *S.E., 14*: 146–158. London: Hogarth.

Freud, S. (1915e). The unconscious. *S.E., 14*: 166–215. London: Hogarth.

Freud, S. (1920g). *Beyond the Pleasure Principle*. *S.E., 18*: 7–64. London: Hogarth.

Freud, S. (1923b). *The Ego and the Id*. *S.E., 19*: 12–66. London: Hogarth.

Freud, S. (1924c). The economic problem of masochism. *S.E., 19*: 159–170. London: Hogarth.

Freud, S. (1933a). *New Introductory Lectures on Psychoanalysis* (Lecture 29). *S.E., 22*: 7–30. London: Hogarth.

Freud, S. (1933a). *New Introductory Lectures on Psychoanalysis* (Lecture 31). *S.E., 22*: 57–80. London: Hogarth.

Freud, S. (1937d). Constructions in analysis. *S.E., 23*: 255–269. London: Hogarth.

Freud, S. (1939a). *Moses and Monotheism*. *S.E., 23*: 6–137. London: Hogarth.

Freud, S. (1941d). Psycho-analysis and telepathy, *S.E.*, *18*: 177–193. London: Hogarth.

Garma, A. (1954). *Génesis psicosomática y tratamiento de las úlceras gástricas y duodenales* [*Psychosomatic Treatment Of Gastric Duodenal Ulcers*]. Buenos Aires: Nova.

Garma, A. (1958). *El dolor de cabeza* [*The Headache*]. Buenos Aires: Nova.

Green, A. (1972–1986). *De Locuras Privadas* [*On Private Madness*]. Buenos Aires: A.E., 1990.

Green, A. (1973). *La Concepción Psicoanalítica del Afecto* [*Psychoanalytical Conception of Affect*]. Méjico, Siglo XXI, 1975.

Green, A. (1995). *La Metapsicología Revisitada* [*Metapsychology Revisited*]. Buenos Aires: Eudeba, 1966.

Green, A. (1998). *El retorno de lo reprimido teórico de la psicosomática, en Interrogaciones Psicosomáticas* [*Interrogations Psychosomatiques*]. Buenos Aires: A. E., 2000.

Green, A. (2000a). *Le Temps Éclaté*. Paris: Minuit.

Green, A. (2000b). La muerte en la vida. Algunos puntos de referencia para la pulsión de muerte. *Revista de Psicoanálisis*, *58*, 2, 2001.

Green, A. (2003). *Ideas Directrices para un Psicoanálisis Contemporáneo*. Buenos Aires, A.E., 2005.

Grubrich-Simitis, I. (1979). Extreme traumatisation as cumulative trauma: study of survivors. *Psychoanalitical Study of the Child*, *36*, 1981.

Laplanche, J. (1987). *Nuevos fundamentos para el psicoanálisis*. Buenos Aires: A.E., 1989.

Liberman, D., Aisemberg, E. R., D'Alvia, R., Dunayevich, B. J., Fernández Mouján, O., Galli, V., Maladesky, A., & Picollo, A. (1982). Sobreadaptación, trastornos psicosomáticos y estadíos tempranos del desarrollo. *Revista de Psicoanálisis*, *39*(5): 845–853.

Marty, P. (1990). *La Psicosomática del adulto*. Buenos Aires: A.E., 1992.

Marucco, N. (2007). Entre el recuerdo y el destino: la repetición. In: *Revista de Psicoanálisis*, *63*, 4 [reprinted: Between memory and destiny: repetition. *International Journal of Psychoanalysis*, *88*(2): 309–328, London, 2007].

McDougall, J. (1978). *Plaidoyer pour une certaine anormalité*. Paris: Gallimard. English edition: *A Plea for a Measure of Abnormality*, New York: International Universities Press, 1980.

McDougall, J. (1982). *Theatres of the Mind*. New York: Basic Books, 1985.

McDougall, J. (1989). *Theatres of the Body*. New York: Norton.

McDougall, J. (1995). *The Many Faces of Eros*. New York: Norton.

Pollock, G. (1970). Anniversary reactions, trauma and mourning. *Psychoanalytic Quarterly, 39*: 347–371.

Rascovsky, A. (1943). Consideraciones psicosomáticas sobre la evolución sexual del niño [Psychosomatic view of the sexual evolution of the child]. *Revista de Psicoanálisis, I*(2): 182–229.

Rascovsky, A. (Ed.) (1948). *Patología Psicosomática* [Psychosomatic Pathology]. Buenos Aires: El Ateneo.

Riolo, F. (2006). Ricordare, ripetere, rielaborare: un lascito de Freud a la psicoanalisi futura. V Encounter APA-SPI, Bologna.

Rosemberg, B. (1991). Masochisme mortifére et masochisme gardien de la vie. *Monografies de la Revue Française de Psychanalyse, 62, 5.*

Rousillon, R. (1991). *Paradoxes et Situations Limites de la Psychanalyse.* Paris: Presses Universitaires de France.

Winnicott, D. W. (1967). *Playing and Reality*. New York: Basic Books, 1971.

CHAPTER SEVEN

Particular vicissitudes of the drive confronted with mourning: sublimation and somatization*

Evelyne Sechaud

T he title I am proposing has its place within a thoroughly Freudian orientation, which is followed by the majority of French psychoanalysts. This perspective combines the drive and its object, whose importance never seems greater than when it is missing.

For Freud, the drive is the foundation of psychical life and constitutes the dynamic source of the psyche. He defined it in 1915c as

a frontier concept between the mental and the somatic, as the psychical representative of the stimuli originating from within the organism and reaching the mind, as a measure of the demand made upon the mind in consequence of its connection with the body. [p. 122]

The drive is, thus, the product and the basis of the work of transforming bodily excitation. The psyche–body unity, therefore, forms from the outset the locus of a movement of forces to which representations will give a meaning. The aim of instinctual impulses is

---

*Translated by Andrew Weller.

discharge, either via the short paths of action and somatization or via long paths which result in the binding of thing- and word-presentations and affects, opening out on to the most sophisticated forms of sublimation.

In the text of 1915c, Freud considers several vicissitudes of the drive, the double reversal, repression, and sublimation, but he does not mention somatization. This only appeared later as a manifestation of the negative therapeutic reaction, the need for punishment, and, finally, as an effect of the death drive. If the term death drive raises difficulties as a drive in symmetry with the sexual drive, it is easier to accept the idea of a primal destructivity directed both outwards and inwards, which remains unconscious most of the time. This destructivity is in the service of unbinding, which attacks linking, links with the object, links between representations and affects, whereas the life drive, Eros, is in the service of linking.

What is the place of the object? The drive–object pair is indissociable. Drive activity leads to the search for an external object capable of relieving the tension. The object is part of the drive organization in that it reveals the drive itself. Awareness of this object emerges in the hate aroused by its absence and its deficiencies, its inevitable failures to satisfy instinctual demands, and poses questions concerning the third party, "the other of the object" (Green, 1995, p. 252).

In this chapter, I want to examine the effects of mourning on the drive organization, when processes of sublimation or somatization follow an experience of mourning. By sublimation I also mean processes of creation. Sublimation is one of the ordinary transformations of the drive, while creation is an exceptional vicissitude. Both phenomena, sublimation and somatization, associated with an experience of mourning, are quite a common feature of ordinary clinical practice.

The crisis engendered by mourning

Mourning provokes a *crisis* in the psychical apparatus. It causes an internal upheaval, a breakdown of the prior state of equilibrium, which modifies both one's relations with oneself and with those around. The phenomenon is all the more important in that the loss is never limited to the current experience: each death echoes previous deaths, enters into resonance with earlier losses of all kinds, deaths, to be sure, but also renunciations, ruptures, and separations which have left their traces—traces of suffering, of wounds that are always ready to open up again, but also traces in the creation itself of the psychical apparatus, in the formation and differentiation of the agencies. The superego is notably a neo-creation resulting from Oedipal renunciation. Likewise, the loss, or, rather, the lack, of the primary object is at the origin of thinking, of representation and fantasy, which are inchoate forms of sublimation. All these experiences, which echo each other, are not just the result of successive additions (producing "cumulative trauma", according to Masud Khan), but give rise above all to operations of *après-coup* (*Nachträglichkeit*) that involve internal reorganizations. The outcome of this movement is uncertain: it may involve new distributions of investments, movements of symbolization, and movements of structural changes. Sublimation can come into play and facilitate a certain degree of release from the traumatic situation, or, alternatively, the movement may cause a more or less massive disorganization opening up the way to more or less serious somatizations. Both movements, which are apparently antagonistic, can coexist, owing to splits in the ego. The quality of the sublimations and the gravity of the somatizations are equally variable.

Sublimation is the result of a process of transformation that aims to bring about a change both in the aim and the object of the drive. The directly sexual aim is abandoned, although this does not imply, in my view, a real desexualization, because the sexual drive remains fully engaged: sublimation operates with part-drives and their physical anchoring in erotogenic zones. A new object is invested, such as work, artistic activity, politics, religion, etc., a cultural object which is valued socially. For a long time, sublimation appeared to be an elevated form of psychical development, an object of idealization. In reality, sublimation guarantees nothing, protects the subject from nothing, as Green (1993) has noted in his text on sublimation. In fact, some subjects can sublimate successfully by means of splitting, which allows the rest of the personality to function in non-neurotic modes.

On the contrary, somatization is a return to the body, or rather the soma, that is to say, a non-erotic body whose symptoms are not symbolized, unlike hysterical symptoms. The crisis of mourning can lead to somatic reactions of two different kinds. On the one hand, more or less benign and transitory reactions along the lines of a "somatic regression", which can occur in any sort of psychical organization; and, on the other, disorganizations of the type described by Marty as counter-evolutive disorganizations, which give rise to evolutive, serious illnesses that may lead to death. These somatizations correspond to a general movement of unbinding, which first affects psychical formations, and then somatic formations. They are part of the overall theoretical model of Marty, along with essential depressions, operational thinking, and operational forms of behaviour. However, Smadja (2001, p. 37) emphasizes the processual continuity that can exist between them.

The case of Jeanne

She has let herself drop into the armchair; she does not speak, not yet; she seems so tired and weary from the exhausting effort of the will to keep upright. She is a beautiful young woman; the short curls of her dishevelled hair, like the down of a young bird, accentuate the largeness of her eyes and her distressed gaze directed towards me in silent entreaty. The words are long in coming, but spoken rapidly; she has just undergone chemotherapy after a mastectomy for breast cancer, which had developed very suddenly. Her precise and distant words, resembling medical language, stand in contrast with the pain diffused by her gaze and the state of abandon of her body. She has also done an analysis, which ended well before the beginning of her illness. When I asked her why she had not returned to see her former analyst, a man, whom she said she had nice memories of, she replied, "I don't want him to see me like this!" But on that day, when I saw her for the first time, all that mattered was her current traumatic situation which had made her ask to meet me: "I need a place that can receive and contain my suffering . . . I need to cry somewhere . . ." In fact, she did not cry; she was shaken by short bouts of sobbing, which she suppressed; hoarse sobs which were a stifled cry, rather than a complaint. The affect she communicated to me was not anxiety, but pain, both physical and psychical, which reached me in my body like a surprise blow that stuns the mind. What we are confronted with here is a quantity of excitation which breaks in upon the mind, disrupting the limits of the outside and the inside. Her pain spoke to my body and pure affect threw into turmoil the thoughts and images it aroused in me.

Jeanne, who was then completely absorbed by acute piercing pain, had, in reality, been living for a long time in a state of unrecognized, long-term suffering, which organized her mode of being and thinking. Pain and suffering could be the colours of Jeanne's life, in the picture of it that she paints for me during her sessions, the significant objects of which are dead objects. But, hitherto, the dominant tonality had been more a neutral white, until the moment when the pain of the cancer suddenly gave violent colours to a life punctuated by successive bereavements which echoed each other. Eight months earlier, she had lost a baby, a little daughter, from a sudden death in infancy. In her quest for meaning, she was searching for the link between this event and her own history, a history of women, or, rather, mothers, over four generations, who, in turn, had abandoned or neglected a daughter because she was not a boy. She emphasized the identificatory repetition that marks the destiny of the daughters, and the death of her baby as the fulfilment of her unconscious infanticidal wishes: "I didn't cry; a criminal does not cry. I shut away my guilt in my breast"; but she brought the following association: "I was never welcomed by the maternal bosom." She described a depressive mother, who was constantly complaining, who appropriated her pain, dispossessed her of it, leaving her nothing but the void, the negative, in a state of anaesthesia that she feels today is deadly.

In the violence of her words, I could hear her murderous desire to kill the mother within in her, in the confusion of a primary identification where to kill the mother is to kill the child, from one generation to another.

Her father died when she was five years old: "I didn't see him dead . . . I didn't go to his burial . . . I was told I had to be strong and courageous . . ." She did not cry then, any more than she cries now as an adult; she was constantly tense due to her efforts not to show anything to those around her, and had managed to neutralize her affects until her current state of pain overwhelmed her, cracking open her customary defences.

Jeanne is a painter, as was her father. She only has a vague memory of her father, but he has always been present for her through the paintings that he left behind, like an untouchable idealized figure. She did not speak to me, at this stage, about her own work, except to express her fatigue and to say how her inspiration had dried up. On re-reading the description that I have just made of her spontaneously, I notice the references I have made to painting: is this an effect of primary identification or a defence against this fusion by using the father's pictorial material? She did not speak about her husband either, whom she had married during her first analysis, though she told me later on that he was kind but a bit weak, which I heard as meaning he was powerless to protect her against her mother. I surmised that her first analyst had been a paternal figure for her, and that a well-tempered seduction had allowed her to live her femininity but not to separate herself from her mother. The analysis seemed to have touched on Oedipal aspects while leaving the pregenital and omnipotent maternal figure in the shadows.

Pain

For the time being, in these sessions, I was wondering what kind of affect she was communicating to me: was it suffering; was it pain? Both words came to mind: pain, to designate the acute state; and suffering to denote the duration, but also a more unconscious dimension. Suffering means both undergoing experiences of pain and bearing one's pain, enduring it. The word pain comes from another root and designates more the blow, the wound. This nuance generally disappears in everyday usage where both words are frequently employed as synonyms.

In the Addendum C to *Inhibitions, Symptoms and Anxiety*, Freud writes, "Yet it cannot be for nothing that the *common usage of speech* should have created the notion of internal, mental pain and have treated the feeling of loss of object as equivalent to physical pain" (1926d, p. 171, my italics). Language has just one word for physical pain and/or psychical pain. The same word, pain, brings together the physical and psychical dimensions. Language serves to identify, in the sense in which it gives an identity to the experience, but for pain, more than any other affect, the designation of language is inadequate. One can add qualifications: the pain is acute, sharp, exquisite, or dull; it racks and pierces, invades and submerges . . . but the word does violence to the experience. Aulagnier (1975, p. 157) has identified the importance of "the necessary violence" involved for the child in having to link up a given experience or a particular affective experience with a universal nomination. Moreover, the search for adjectives or metaphors which are designed to circumscribe or evoke the painful experience cannot succeed in capturing it. The attempt to distribute the excessive quantity of affect into multiple word-presentations fails. One word, a single word, pain, condenses everything by itself, as the articulated beginnings of a cry in language. This single word introduces thought-identity, where perceptions grasp barely more than the quantitative. It is the same economic conditions, Freud says, which explain "the point of analogy which has made it possible to carry sensations of pain over to the mental sphere" (1926d, p. 171). Language blurs the distinction between the body and the psyche and, thus, takes over the effects provoked by pain.

Psychical pain is linked to the loss of the object and to its lack. As early as in the "Project" (1895a), Freud believes the absence of the breast constitutes the paradigmatic situation for the emergence of the reality of the object known through the experience of pain and hate. In "Mourning and melancholia" (1917e), Freud associates pain and the work of mourning. Pain is the sign that this work is under way. The subject separates himself from the object, memory after memory, bit by bit, marked by a painful feeling of "never again", indicating the reality of its disappearance. What is lost is not only the object, but also a part of the ego which disappears with the object. The loss is both narcissistic and object-related. The loss of a child, and even more so of a baby, comes within these two registers. In the Addendum C (1926d), Freud takes up the analogy between physical and mental pain within a perspective that remains economic:

> the intense cathexis of longing which is concentrated on the missed or lost object (a cathexis which steadily mounts up because it cannot be appeased) creates the same economic conditions as are created by the cathexis of pain which is concentrated on the injured part of the body. [p. 171]

Jeanne was all pain; I do not know what was worse, her pain or the mental suffering that revives lost memories and images. Hurting, she was really hurting; the pain radiated out from her breast into her back and her arm. She spoke, in a monotone voice, about the irrepressible bouts of vomiting, the exhaustion of her body broken by the treatment. And then she talked about the "sadistic" doctor, which allowed her to discharge her hate. She wanted to lodge a complaint against him, but refrained from doing so to avoid being a complainer like her mother.

Jeanne was suffering from a breast that was now absent, which reminded me of the sudden absence of her dead baby's mouth. I was thinking of the painful sensation of tight breasts, filled with milk, which suddenly became useless. The pain of a ghost breast was the negative of the pain of a breast that was too present now that the baby was missing. Neither her tears nor her milk could flow; they were blocked, held back. In me, a movement was set in motion that sought to link up this physical experience with communicable representations. A bond was formed, between her and me, uniting body and psyche, past experience with present experience. In her, the memory of the body that retains the trace of sensoriality linked to most memories was awakened. She let her mother take care of the baby's burial: "I had to be courageous and not think about it any more." Now she said, "I have buried my baby in my breast", and she was probably right. Can one speak here of a metaphor, a hysterical fantasy, acting as a vehicle of a symbolization? Or, on the contrary, is there a demetaphorization, with words being taken literally, with the dead child remaining incorporated, "encrypted" within her, blocking any work of mourning?

In Jeanne's case, her suffering had remained unconscious for a long time, allowing a sort of anaesthesia, a blank of affect to occupy the scene. The unconscious psychical pain became conscious through physical pain. The ill part of the body, the breast, allowed physical and psychical pain to come together. For Jeanne, at the time when these sessions took place, the painful breast made the transition from the body to the psyche possible. This breast that was removed also affected Jeanne at the deepest levels of her maternal and feminine identity. The material that emerged in the sessions concerned the dead baby initially; the loss of the child was a narcissistic wound that immediately echoed with the bodily affliction constituted by the most recent narcissistic wound. The death of a child marks the death of a mother as mother, a typically female form of castration anxiety. But this event in her adult life took Jeanne back to another death, that of her father when she was just a little girl. This death, too, could not be talked about, or even thought about, whereas the father's paintings, which were constantly before her eyes, represented a permanent sensorial presence. Only her mother had the right to be unhappy. Avoiding suffering allowed her to keep Oedipal guilt unconscious. Finally, beyond, or, rather, prior to, this thought prohibition there was the revived pain of an insufficient or distorted primary experience of satisfaction: "I was never welcomed by the maternal breast." This negative sentence, which was uttered in the very first session and linked to her demand, brought to my mind the fear of breakdown described by Winnicott: the possibility of breakdown owing to the eventuality of having to confront for the first time an unthinkable experience. The drive upsurge is a source of uncontrollable excitation without the help of an adult who could relieve the tension and fill the lack. Being faced with her impulses provokes a state of dereliction and a loss of the ego. This loss constitutes an empty space, a hole that could be portrayed by an open mouth that nothing comes to satisfy.

The sessions were very exhausting for me. Jeanne needed a particular mode of understanding from me based on a possibility for primary identification. Jeanne's pain spoke to my body, activating the memory of my own experiences of suffering. I could perceive the dimensions of her pain and I tried to make it representable for her. All pain takes us back to the primary distress of the infant and requires of the analyst a similar work to that which is accomplished by the mother, provided she is just good enough: in other words, she must be there, be attentive, think about the sick body and the mental suffering, and sometimes (not always) translate it into words as close to the experience as possible. During these sessions, Jeanne began to cry, with real tears, which left her exhausted but appeased. She also went for the first time to visit the grave of her father and of her baby.

During this period, Jeanne started painting again. She mainly paints abstract forms. I have never seen her paintings, but she talks to me at length about her work. She describes how she prepares herself, the choice of her brushes, the preparation of her colours, which she mixes herself, evoking joyfully the smell of the oil, the materiality of the colours, and the pleasures of rediscovering a sensory world linked to her father. She paints large canvases and stresses the movement that she tries to give to her forms: concentric movements of strong colours around a centre that she paints in white, but also with oblique, lightening-like flashes.

Psychical work

In mechanics, the definition of work associates force and movement. Force and movement are specific and essential characteristics of the sexual drive, whose other components, aims, and objects are vicarious, as sublimation shows. Psychical work involves the transformation of instinctual drive stimuli coming from the body by integrating them into the psychical apparatus and by establishing associative links between them. This associative work is missing in operational thinking, as described by Marty, owing to the lack of depth of the preconscious. Marty speaks of the "layering" (feuilletage) of the unconscious, which he imagines as a superposition of layers in which psychic elaboration takes place.

The words elaboration and working-through illustrate psychic work. Elaboration seems to me to denote the work which starts with the drive and moves towards consciousness: it is the dream work which produces dream-images out of latent thoughts by using the procedures of displacement, condensation, and symbolization, without forgetting secondary elaboration, which will give a coherent presentation. This work is absent in operational thinking. The psychical apparatus is, as it were, disconnected, and mentalization is eroded. In contrast, sublimation is the result of complex psychical work whatever the means used; it is a work of transforming part-drives, bringing into play the fantasy activity of infantile sexuality. The work of sublimation takes over the different operations of elaboration and working-through.

Working-through is a process in which the agencies of the conscious mind traverse all the levels of the psyche towards the drive sources. The work of mourning is a process of working-through, as several authors have argued (Pollock, 1977; Widlöcher, 1994). Indeed, "in mourning", writes Widlöcher, "the evident consciousness of the loss, the judgement of reality, gradually transforms the unconscious formations" (p. 155) Time is needed to draw the invasion of the present by the lost object back into the past: "The time needed for the judgement of reality to act on all the scenes connected with the lost object is identical to that of working-through" (*ibid.*, p. 160).

The work of sublimation implies this work of transformation and requires time and repetition: the time needed to appropriate this reality, time to assimilate and produce a new reality. Digestive, oral, and anal metaphors serve to illustrate this process, as do those of pregnancy and childbirth. Time is needed for thought to develop, but also for finding the optimal distance with regard to the period of excitation.

This long process of working-through concerns fragments. In the work of mourning, "each single one of the memories and expectations in which the libido is bound to the object is brought up and hypercathected, and detachment of the libido is accomplished in respect of it" (Freud 1917e, p. 245). The work of mourning is a work of decomposition. Its means consist in transposing on the human level the biological fact, that is to say, in "killing the dead person", to use Lagache's expression. Each fragment, however partial it may be, contains something of the lost object and gives the illusion of the possibility of finding it again. The slow working-through of the mourning process opens up the possibility of new associative links based on conscious memories and recreates a part of what has been lived through while giving it a new meaning. Sublimation is one of the possibilities of drive fulfilment when the object is lost. The new object created can then symbolize absence.

Jeanne speaks about her work as a painter, but her words could equally apply to the work of analysis. "I draw the void to get to the form . . . like that, the objects are within a space. And drawing counter-forms makes it possible to draw the form. That's how I emerge from blindness; by seeing the contour, I get to the form." It is a work on the negative that retraces the trajectory from her body to the lost objects.

The play of drive forces

The experience of mourning provokes an unfurling of instinctual forces; the violence is the symptomatic indication of it. This violence is particularly acute in Jeanne's analysis, the violence of what she is going through and of what she makes me go through. But violence is also one of the characteristics of somatization and, to a lesser degree, of sublimation.

According to Smadja, operational functioning results from incredible violence that is exerted on psychic life, and, when a somatization develops, on the patient's organic functions. This violence is also at work in sublimation. McDougall (2008) says that creativity involves extreme violence that is accompanied by profound anxiety and a great deal of guilt. She considers that violence is an essential element of creation and sees artists as violent individuals, in so far as they seek to exert their power over the external world, that is, to impose their ideas, their images, their dreams, or their nightmares.

This violence clearly reveals the play of instinctual forces on the ego: both libidinal forces and the forces of the death drive that are released by the unbinding set in train by mourning.

The loss of the object is a source of excitation, due both to the liberation of libido that was hitherto attached to the object, and to the libidinal co-excitation aroused by the wound of the loss. "In the case of a great number of internal processes sexual excitation arises as a concomitant effect, as soon as the intensity of those processes passes beyond certain quantitative limits" (Freud, 1905d, pp. 204–205; 1924c, p. 163).

The disappearance of the object concerning which the investment was ambivalent also favours the unbinding of the drives. In "Thoughts for the times on war and death" (1915b), Freud emphasizes the ambivalence that is inherent to every love-relation, and he enumerates: a parent, or a partner in marriage, a brother or sister, a child or a close friend, all are the object of our ambivalence. "There adheres to the tenderest and most intimate of our love-relations a small portion of hostility which can excite an unconscious death-wish" (p. 298). Love and hate are inextricably mixed, a situation which obliges love to remain "ever vigilant and fresh, so as to guard it against the hate which lurks behind it" (p. 299). The death of the object undoes the blend. The unbinding of the drives constitutes a critical moment whose evolution is uncertain. Either the subject embarks on the process of mourning, which leads to a new fusion of the drives, or he becomes immobilized in melancholia, prey to a superego which has become a pure culture of the death drive, or, alternatively, the path of somatization opens up to him, which may be an escape from melancholia but at the price of a repression of affects, an erosion of psychic life. In mourning, under the pressure of reality, the subject gives up the object ("Mourning impels the ego to give up the object by declaring the object to be dead" [Freud, 1917e, p. 257]), a difficult and painful process which includes a double renunciation: of what has not taken place, on both sides; of what one has received and what one has given, but also of what one has not received and waited for in vain and what one has not given and now regrets. But giving up the object, however painful that may be, does not mean giving up the possibility of making the new investments that are demanded by an exacerbated libido. The path of sublimation proposes a solution both for the libidinal drive and for the death drive by rediscovering certain aspects of the lost object in a form that is acceptable and even valued. In other words, the very movement of mourning brings into play what Green (1993, p. 237) calls the objectalizing function which "allows an activity to acquire object status and to be considered as a possession of the ego". In processes of somatization, defusion is maintained to the advantage of the death drive, that is, in the service of a disobjectalizing function that attacks all the possibilities of investment and aims at a lethal disinvestment.

However, the new blend of the drives employed in the object of sublimation is an unstable and variable blend. This instability of the new fusion with regard to the object of sublimation also lies in the nature of this object, which is fragile and remains at the mercy of its author who can always destroy it. Jeanne often destroys her paintings even before they are completed in an impulsive movement of rage and despair.

Jeanne has recently undertaken a series of self-portraits, which she says are motivated by her desire to show that she exists. But she also talks to me about her difficulties in executing them, explaining how she uses a "mirror that is never in the right place . . . When I paint, I can never manage to get close to my face . . . I paint the lack of balance." The analysis is still going on, swinging back and forth between opposing instinctual vicissitudes; the somatization seems to have stopped, while sublimation manifests the uncertainties of the transferential investments between presence and absence, between the forces of life and the forces of death.

References

Aulagnier, P. (1975). *La violence de l'interprétation*. PUF: le Fil rouge [*The Violence of Interpretation*, A. Sheridan (Trans.). London: Routledge & The New Library of Psychoanalysis, 2001].

Freud, S. (1895a). Project for a scientific psychology. *S.E.*, *1*: 281–397. London: Hogarth.

Freud, S. (1905d). *Three Essays on the Theory of Sexuality. S.E.*, *7*: 125–245. London: Hogarth.

Freud, S. (1915ac). Instincts and their vicissitudes. *S.E.*, *14*: 109–140. London: Hogarth.

Freud, S. (1915b). Thoughts for the times on war and death. *S.E.*, *14*: 273–300. London: Hogarth.

Freud, S. (1917e). Mourning and melancholia. *S.E.*, *14*: 239–258. London: Hogarth.

Freud, S. (1924c). The economic problem of masochism. *S.E.*, *19*: 156–172. London: Hogarth.

Freud, S. (1926d). *Inhibitions, Symptoms and Anxiety. S.E.*, *20*: 77–174. London: Hogarth.

Green, A. (1993). La sublimation. In: *Le travail du négatif*. Paris: Ed. de Minuit [Sublimation. In: A. Weller (Trans.), *The Work of the Negative*. London: Free Association Books, 1999].

Green, A. (1995). *Propédeutique*. Paris: Champ Vallon.

McDougall, J. (2008). *L'artiste et le psychanalyste*. Paris: PUF.

Pollock, G. H. (1977). Mourning process and organizations. *Journal of the American Psychoanalytic Association*, 25(1): 331–348.

Smadja, C. (2001). *La vie opératoire. Études psychanalytiques*. Paris: PUF [*The Psychosomatic Paradox. Psychoanalytic Studies*, A. Brewer (Trans.). London: Free Association Books, 2005].

Widlöcher, D. (1994). Deuil fini et deuil sans fin. *Le deuil*. Paris: PUF, Monographies de la RFP.

CHAPTER EIGHT

The place of affect in the psychosomatic economy*

Claude Smadja

Introduction

Affect has always occupied a place of prime importance in psychosomatic thinking. Even before psychosomatics became a discipline, the relation between affective life and illness constituted a common finding in medical thinking, first in German psychiatry of the nineteenth century, then in the work of a certain number of psychoanalysts.

The entry of medicine into the scientific era during the nineteenth century tipped the whole psychic dimension of illnesses over into the nosographical field of what henceforth came to be known as the neuroses—that is, clinical entities covering neurotic disturbances and nervous disturbances. Thus, psychopathology gradually took its place alongside somatic medicine. Within nineteenth century German psychiatry, two doctrinal movements developed, one of which was somatist or organicist, postulating the existence of micro cerebral lesions at the origin of psychical disorders; while

---

*Translated by Andrew Weller

the other, psychist or psychogenetist, linked psychopathological disorders to psychic conflicts in the patient's history. It was within the context of this second movement that the psychiatrist Heinroth proposed the term psycho-somatic to qualify somatic symptoms determined by conflicts of a psychic order. The development of Freudian psychoanalysis took its place within this movement of thought.

Although Freud was not explicitly interested in psychosomatics, he built a theory of the mind that supplied the theoretical and doctrinal bases on which all the movements of contemporary psychosomatics are based today. At the end of his life, in 1940, in a text entitled, "Some elementary lessons in psycho-analysis", he states unambiguously that "the fact could not be long overlooked that psychical phenomena are to a high degree dependent upon somatic influences and on their side have the most powerful effects upon somatic processes" (1940b [1938], p. 283). For Freud, the psychical phenomena involved in the modification of somatic processes always concern the instinctual drive economy and its transformations.

The metapsychology of affect and its theoretical implications in psychosomatics

Psychosomatic structure of affect

In his twenty-fifth Introductory Lecture on Psycho-Analysis in 1916–1917, Freud, having finished the elaboration of his first topography, takes up the theme of affect again and attempts to give a psychoanalytic definition of it:

> What is an affect in the dynamic sense? It is in any case something highly composite. An affect includes in the first place particular motor innervations or discharges and secondly certain feelings; the latter are of two kinds—perceptions of the motor actions that have occurred and the direct feelings of pleasure and unpleasure which, as we say, give the affect its keynote. [p. 395]

This definition contains several indications. The first is the distinction made by Freud between the bodily and psychical phenomena of affect. The second is another distinction made by Freud within the psychical phenomena of affect themselves between perceptions without qualitative value and feelings with qualitative value. Indeed, "the perceptions of the motor actions that have occurred", which Freud is careful to distinguish from direct feelings of pleasure and unpleasure, seem to be related, according to Green (1999, p. 308), to the unconscious level of the phenomenon:

> it is to be reduced neither to its somatic expression nor to its conscious experience, but might be conceived as perception of the unconscious Ego traversed by internal movements devoid of quality.

The third indication given by Freud in his definition is the notion of a hierarchical organization between bodily phenomena and psychic phenomena: "in the first place particular motor innervations or discharges and secondly certain feelings" (1916–1917, p. 395). So it may be noted that in Freud's conception there exists a somato-psychic structure of the affect. The two poles of this structure, one somatic and the other psychic, may be thought of as two destinations of the affect, one resulting from its integration in psychic formations and the other from its dispersion in different somatic modes of functioning. The factor that will play a major role in the choice of the destination of the affect towards either one of the poles is the quality of the structure of the ego, or, more generally, that of mental functioning. In his revision of the theory of anxiety in 1926, Freud, in fact, distinguishes two qualities of anxiety intimately related to the quality of the structure of the ego: one is a direct effect of the traumatic factor, and the other a signal announcing the reappearance of such a factor. In reality, these two qualities of anxiety encapsulate two modes of mental functioning that had been differentiated as early as 1895, that is, "actual" neurosis and neuropsychosis of defence. It is with regard to this dynamic and economic differentiation of mental functioning that the somato-psychic structure of affect truly takes on its meaning. We know that in actual neurotic functioning, psychic events largely escape the reign of the pleasure principle and that affect is dispersed essentially into bodily and somatic manifestations, whereas in neurotic (psychoneurotic) functioning, psychic events are governed by the pleasure principle and affects acquire a value of psychic differentiation.

Theoretical implications in psychosomatics

The first Freudian topography sets out a conception of affect that makes it an element that can be opposed to representation. Already, in the first texts, in particular (1894a, 1895a), Freud separates, in his initial concept of the drive, the quota of affect from the ideational representation or object-representation. In the metapsychology of 1915, each of these elements follows its specific vicissitudes. Affect may be subject to three different vicissitudes: repression, transformation into anxiety, and transformation into another affect. The repression of affect and its transformation into anxiety, particularly into diffuse anxiety, characterizes for Freud the mode of functioning in actual neurosis. This metapsychological conception of affect would be taken up by Ferenczi in his description of organ neurosis, and then, later, by Alexander, who made it the theoretical and doctrinal linchpin of his psychodynamic description of psychosomatic illnesses.

In the second topography, a new metapsychological conception of affect forced itself upon Freud. He no longer saw it as a first element opposable to representation, but as a second element arising from an initial drive state that Freud calls the psychical representative of the drive. Green (1999) has clearly shown in a text entitled, "Discriminating and not discriminating between affect and representation", that, in the context of the second topography, affect and representation may be said to be undifferentiated at the beginning of psychic life. This new conception of affect, corresponding to the second drive theory, allows for a theoretical approach to the most severe forms of psychosomatic illness. The notion of progressive disorganization, created by Marty in 1967, is a vast movement involving the effacement of psychical formations, which concerns both the affective dimension and the representative dimension. Thus, affects and representations undergo the same vicissitude: a process of radical negativation.

Psychosomatic clinical practice is very largely determined by the vicissitudes of affect. In the most benign forms, represented by symptoms of a functional order and an evolution that is as a rule critical and reversible, the repression of affect usually coexists with the preservation of an activity of representation at the heart of mental functioning. In the most severe forms, represented by somatic illnesses that are often grave and evolutive, the negativation of affects brings with it more or less profound distortions of representations and thought activity.

Psychosomatic illnesses and the economy of emotion

The notion of psychosomatic illness was introduced by the psychoanalyst James Halliday within the new movement of psychosomatics directed in the USA by Franz Alexander. It was entirely based on a theoretical conception that links somatic illness with a dysfunctioning of the emotions.

Franz Alexander developed his doctrine of psychosomatic medicine from the notion of organ neurosis. This was defined in 1926 by Ferenczi, who wrote,

> Many frequently occurring illnesses are mentally determined, though they consist of real disturbances of the normal functioning of one or more physical organs. They are called organ neuroses. The fact that they involve objective as well as subjective disturbances differentiates them from hysteria, though it is not possible to draw a sharp dividing line between them and hysteria on the one hand and a number of organic diseases on the other. [p. 22]

As can be seen, this definition is first and foremost clinical and nosographical. It relates the entity of organ neurosis to hysteria on the one hand, and to organic disease on the other. But it also gives an indication of an aetiological order, since it links this new entity with conflicts of a psychical order. We have here the essential elements of the constitution of the Freudian "actual" neurosis. It is worth recalling that actual neurosis is a psychical organization that is accompanied clinically by disturbances of a depressive and anxious nature and by diverse somatic disturbances affecting different organs, which are akin to what doctors refer to as functional disorders. Freud distinguished very early on the organization of actual neurosis from that of psychoneurosis of defence and in particular from hysteria, but at the same time he showed the importance of mixed forms between actual neurosis and defence neurosis, in particular in the combination of anxiety neurosis and hysteria. Generally speaking, Freud indicated early on that at the heart of every psychoneurosis of defence there existed a kernel of actual neurosis. Thus, there is good reason for identifying the organ neurosis with Freud's actual neurosis. In view of what I wish to say later on in this paper, let me emphasize now that what specifies the organization of an actual neurosis from a metapsychological stand-point is the interruption of the trajectory of somatic sexual excitations towards the psyche and the constitution of the drive. This interruption—and this is the important point—can be the result of a mechanism of repression. One of the major consequences of this metapsychological configuration is the development of a diffuse state of anxiety. The reflux of the sexual current towards different organs or different somatic functions leads them to be hyper-cathected by sexual excitation. Thus, the functional symptom can be defined, from the psychoanalytic point of view, as evidence of the erotic hypercathexis of a somatic function.

Under Franz Alexander's influence, Freud's view of actual neurosis underwent a theoretical deviation in the direction of a medicalization. This medicalization was based on three conceptual operations. The first was a change of theoretical referent. For the referent of the drive, Alexander substituted the referent of emotion. The second was a change in the dynamic conception of psychosomatic functioning. For the drive trajectory, Alexander substituted the trajectory linking emotion to the autonomous nervous system. The third was a change in the way the principles of mental functioning are envisaged. For the Freudian principle of constancy, Alexander substituted the principle of physiological homeostasis. He refers, in this connection, to the work and ideas of the biologist W. Cannon, and to his conclusions concerning the reactions of adaptation of the organism and of the different somatic systems to situations of danger.

On these new bases of a physiopathological and medical order, Alexander was to establish a new classification of psychosomatic illnesses. Generally speaking, they were conceived as deriving from a dysfunctioning of the psychosomatic path of an emotion or of a group of emotions. When an emotion finds itself repressed repeatedly at the psychical level, owing to certain conflicts, it follows the trajectory of one of the paths of the autonomous nervous system, either the sympathetic pathway or the parasympathetic pathway, and reaches an organ or a specific system of organs. It was this physiopathological schema that led Alexander to define two groups of psychosomatic diseases, those of a "sympathetic" and "parasympathetic" type. The first group includes diseases such as migraine, high blood pressure, hyperthyroidism, functional cardiac disorders, osteoarticular disorders, and diabetes. The psychical conflicts leading to the onset of these diseases involve the repression of hostile and aggressive emotions. Instead of finding an outlet towards motricity, the latter are diverted via the sympathetic pathway towards certain systems of organs, which, under normal conditions, prepare the organism for reactions of struggle and flight. The second group includes illnesses such as gastric ulcers, digestive disorders, states of colitis, but also asthma attacks. The psychic conflicts that lead to the onset of these diseases involve the repression of specific emotions linked to needs of dependency and protection by the object. Rather than finding a psychical and relational expression, by way of a regression to passivity, these emotions are diverted towards the parasympathetic pathway until they reach the systems of organs that, under normal conditions, are responsible for the restoration of the resources of the organism.

As we can see, Franz Alexander's psychosomatic approach attributes the somatic disorders of disturbed emotional states to certain specific psychical conflicts. This doctrine has, as a whole, been rejected by French psychoanalysts who have taken interest in somatic patients. The psyche–soma dualism which underlies it and its psychopathological conception constitute the main reasons for this rejection.

Psychosomatic illnesses and the economy of mental functioning

Pierre Marty and the Paris School of Psychosomatics have elaborated an original and rigorous conception of the processes of somatization, which rests on two theoretical foundations: the psychoanalytic evaluation of the patient's mental functioning and the economic dimension of the relations between the mind and the somatic systems. In order to show how affects are recognized and interpreted in psychosomatic praxis, I will elaborate Marty's economic conceptions on the affect of anxiety. Generally speaking, the clinical qualities of this affect cannot be dissociated from the quality of the mental functioning within which it develops.

For Marty, psychosomatic praxis is divided into two processes of somatization, which, in turn, are linked to two different levels of mental functioning. In the last work that he published, in 1991, *Mentalisation and Psychosomatique,* he defines them as follows:

We can consider, generally speaking, that:

— When the drive excitations prove to be of average importance and do not accumulate too much in a subject whose mentalization is otherwise good, one is fortunate in only witnessing the onset of somatic affections which in most cases are spontaneously reversible.

— When the instinctual and drive-based excitations prove to be important and accumulate in a subject, whose mentalization is otherwise poor, there is a risk of witnessing the onset of evolutive and severe somatic affections. [p. 41]

Thus, the process of somatization through regression is usually contrasted with the process of somatization through progressive disorganization.

Anxiety during the process of somatization along the regressive path

Regressive movements can affect both mental functioning as well as the somatic systems. In this case, they culminate in the development of somatic affections involving crises that the subject is accustomed to, and that are easily reversible and repetitive. These movements cannot be dissociated from the fixations to which they are linked. The major interest of these fixations, on the psychical as well as the somatic level, is to impede the course of the disorganizing movement and to give the subject possibilities of evolutive reorganization. Thus, they represent, from the psychosomatic point of view, the major defensive armature of the subject. During the process of somatization along the regressive path, the affect of anxiety may appear, but it is likely to be associated with mental representations. We then speak of object-related anxieties. This anxiety is marked by the qualities of the psychical regression concerned and the conflicts that are associated with it. The identification of the quality of anxiety in the patient presenting a regressive somatic affection, as well as the evaluation of his character during spontaneous reorganization, or under psychotherapeutic treatment, are of cardinal importance in psychosomatic practice.

Anxiety during the process of somatization following the path of progressive disorganization

The particularity of this process of somatization is that it develops in subjects whose regressive capacities are momentarily or chronically deficient. As the capacities of mentalization and symbolization generally go hand in hand with regressive qualities, the subjects present more or less severe deficits in psychical elaboration. The major clinical forms that are encountered in this context are behaviour neuroses and character neuroses that are insufficiently or poorly mentalized.

Referring to these organizations, Marty developed the notion of irregularity of mental functioning. It pertains to sudden transitions in these patients from forms of expression arising from psychical elaboration to other types of expression, such as characteropathic, behavioural, or somatic. These moments are often preceded or accompanied by violent and diffuse anxieties without mental representation. These anxieties may also be translated by a vague malaise or a diffuse feeling of discomfort.

When, as a result of traumatic circumstances, the disorganizing movement develops, rapid transformations of the quality of the psychic work marked by the immobilization and erasure of mental expression lead to the development of an essential depression. Marty writes,

> Diffuse anxieties often precede it. Automatic, and invasive, they could also be qualified as essential in that they express the individual's profound distress, a distress provoked by the afflux of instinctual movements that are not mastered because they cannot be elaborated nor expressed. The submerged Ego thus shows its defensive weakness, the insufficiency of its means of recourse, its disorganisation. Anxiety does not represent or no longer represents the alarm signal which usually ceases when mechanisms of defence appear. It is a permanent alarm. [1980, p. 61]

With essential depression, a state of operational life (*vie opéra-toire*) develops, which ensures a relative and fragile economic stabilization of the overall psychosomatic functioning. The anxieties then lose their intensity, or even disappear momentarily. In the absence of effective help, usually of a psychotherapeutic nature, there is a risk that the disorganization will continue and affect the somatic systems, giving rise to evolutive and severe affections.

Interruptive crises of mental functioning and the continuity of psychic investment

Having described the different qualities of anxieties that we encounter with patients and having emphasized the links with the different nosographical categories, it seems necessary to reformulate the question of anxiety from another perspective. This new way of posing the problem of anxiety in no way detracts from the clinical facts reported above. It simply enables us to apprehend them differently. We have seen that anxiety appears each time there is a break or interruption in the psychoanalytic work. It is when the latter is interrupted that anxiety emerges. Its quality then depends on the psychic tissue out of which it develops, and always in relation to the factor of time. These interruptive crises are often associated with changes in the economic register of mental functioning .

In contrast, the resumption of the continuity of psychic investment regularly goes together with the attenuation of anxieties, the transformation of their diffuse qualities into their object qualities, and even their integration within a neurotic symptom. This trend concerns, in particular, the psychical reorganizations that can be observed during psychotherapeutic treatment.

The coexistence of the two varieties of anxiety in the same patient is not exceptional. Thus, the identification of interruptive crises in mental functioning and resumptions of the continuity of psychic investment with qualitative transformations of the anxiety are among the best guarantees for appreciating the state of the patient's functioning during psychotherapies.

Marty recommends that such treatment should be conducted by a properly trained psychoanalyst. This requirement is linked to the observation that the onset and evolution of a somatic illness regularly indicates temporary or chronic psychic deficits. This is why

Marty insists on the importance of identifying and observing semi-ologically the psychic factors that generate or maintain the somatic disorganization. Thus, the aim of psychosomatic treatments is to help the patient establish or re-establish the optimal level of psychic functioning that it is possible for him/her to attain. In an unpublished text of 1988, he defines the handling of the therapeutic relationship by the formula: "from the maternal function to psychoanalysis". "The therapist's maternal function" consists in accompanying as closely as possible the patient's psychic movements, both verbally and non-verbally, and is based on the qualities of the analyst's identification with his patient. Braunschweig (1993) has proposed a metapsychological analysis of this maternal function of the therapist which clearly sets out what is at stake. For her, this function aims initially, and particularly with severely dementalized patients, to establish the counter-investments necessary for constituting primary repression, as well as to orientate differently and less dangerously for the patient the economy of these excitations. This function contributes towards the setting up of secondary repressions, in so far as the analyst sees it as his or her task to transmit to the patient the threat of castration by the father, a transmission that is conveyed as much by his analytic conduct and his interventions as by his sometimes anxious interest for the patient's health. This work, thus, has the aim of increasing the field of the dynamic unconscious.

Silence in psychosomatic praxis

The psychoanalytic treatment of somatic patients has led me to new considerations and new conceptions on the subject of the place of affects in the psychosomatic economy. Before introducing what I call "silence in psychosomatic praxis" (*une clinique du silence*), it would be useful to point out the extent to which in contemporary psychosomatic praxis questions relating to the affects are closely bound up with those concerning modes of thought. Thus, in my view, the operational state is a singular disturbance of thought in which the latter, for reasons that I am going to discuss, has become devoid of affect.

What is meant by "silence in psychosomatic praxis"?

By silence in psychosomatic praxis, I am referring to a set of phenomena which structure the patient's discourse and which are characterized by the failure to represent oneself psychically. These phenomena belong to the order of affect, fantasies, and representations, but also bodily perceptions. Furthermore, they have the peculiarity of arousing in the analyst, during the intersubjective dialogue with his patient, an unusual activity of representation and thought, as if he were obliged to produce representations and thoughts in his patient's stead. Silence in psychosomatic clinical experience is, to the highest degree, clinical experience of the negative.

I want now to clarify an important point from which the entire metapsychological understanding of silent phenomena results. Silence is not something flat and linear. It is not the equivalent of a flat electroencephalogram. On the contrary, it is the product of a rapport of psychical strength. It is sustained by an internal constraint, an imperious compulsion that maintains it constantly. It situates the phenomena it generates beyond the pleasure principle. It is worth recalling the warning of the authors of *L'Investigation psychosomatique* (Marty, de M'Uzan, & David, 1963) who wrote, in respect of "operational" patients, "that it was impossible for a human being really to be as flat and as defenceless as his way of being gave one to believe". A second point is called for here. I think that silence proceeds from a nodal, primary situation. This nodal situation is linked to the economy of affect. It concerns not only the most alive part of the person, but also the part that has the closest relations with the influences coming from the body.

Drawing on my analytic work with a certain number of somatic patients, whose degree of operational functioning is more or less extensive, I am propose a theoretical schema of the psychical phenomena which underlie silence in psychosomatic praxis. My thinking on this issue has its origin in some remarks of Freud, which opened up new perspectives in psychoanalytic research. These remarks can be found in his uncompleted text of 1938, "Splitting of the ego in the process of defence":

> I have at last been struck by the fact that the ego of a person whom
> we know as a patient in analysis must, dozens of years earlier,

when it was young, have behaved in a remarkable manner in certain particular situations of pressure. We can assign in general and somewhat vague terms the conditions under which this comes about, by saying that it occurs under the influence of a psychical trauma ... This success is achieved at the price of a rift in the ego which never heals but which increases as time goes on. The two contrary reactions to the conflict persist as the centre-point of a splitting of the ego. [Freud, 1940e (1938), pp. 275–276]

I want to focus on the relations Freud establishes in this text between, on the one hand, the constitution of a kernel of splitting in the ego and, on the other, the identification of an early traumatic situation during childhood. It is clear that for these links to be established, the postulated traumatic situation must have a sufficient determining value to create a rift in the ego at an early stage. Moreover, it goes without saying that this first defensive mechanism in the ego, owing to its early nature, precedes the establishment of repression.

The initial traumatic situation

The *initial traumatic situation* is the situation experienced at a very early stage and for a long period by the child, which will initialize all the psychic events that will lead to the construction of his state of subject. This situation, in fact, presents all the characteristics that are likely to constitute in the ego a first rift, or a centre-point of splitting. This situation may be defined as a state of phagocytosis of the child's id by the mother's ego. The adult patient describes throughout his (or her) sessions how his mind is invaded by his mother. When the mother is alive, it is on contact with the real mother that the ego is subjected to effects of immediate disorganization. A female patient told me that when she heard her mother on the telephone, the tone of her mother's voice immediately triggered a state of painful anxiety in her body. The permanent state of being invaded by the mother creates a state of internal confusion. Another female patient told me that her head was in a state of disorder and that she never knew if what she thought really belonged to her. What is at stake in this traumatic situation is the creation of a subjective psychic space of which the subject is deprived. Owing to an absence of withdrawal on the part of the mother, the entire process of disillusionment, in Winnicott's sense, is missing for the child. We know from André Green that it is in this space left vacant by the mother's withdrawal that the negative hallucination of her and the creation of a framing structure takes place. The depressed mothers of our patients oblige their children to be in a state of constant perceptual vigilance towards them in order to make sure that they are really alive.

Phenomena involving the negative hallucination of affect

This is the most important point concerning this silence in psychosomatic practice. I have always been surprised, if not fascinated, by the affective silence of these patients. The permanent complaints about their mothers or other persons in the current environment rarely give rise to real affective manifestations. When I happen to name an affect during a session, I sometimes hear my patient reply, "I understand, but I don't get it; I don't feel anything of that." To tell the truth, the problem is more complicated. It seems that, in the complex of the affect, a cut occurs between its ideational representation, or its word, and its quota or instinctual charge. A female patient told me, with regard to the anger that could well up in her concerning a conflict in her present life, that she had the idea of anger but that she was lacking the energy of anger. So, it is indeed the quota of affects, its instinctual force, which is barred from the ego's consciousness. The words "I don't feel anything" can, thus, be interpreted as a phenomenon involving the negative hallucination of the affect. There is silence concerning the affect. During analytic work, it often happens that faced with this silence, the analyst experiences a rich activity of representation concerning the affect that is missing in his patient.

Let us return now to the initial traumatic situation. One of the particular features of this situation of maternal phagocytosis, or maternal "colonization", is that the child is prohibited from experiencing his/her affects, which could represent a threat to the mother's psychic life. Is it not the case that these children often become "good", well-behaved children? They treat their mother gently and cause her no worries. I think that there is justification for supposing that in this situation that is traumatic for both the protagonists, the child operates a denial at the somatic frontier of his mind concerning primary affective and instinctual reality. This negative hallucination of affect, or this denial of internal perceptions of somatic and bodily origin, initializes the process of creating a rift in the ego and, thus, underlies the centre-point of splitting whose existence Freud postulated in 1938.

Phenomena involving the negative hallucination of internal perceptions

Many patients say that the perceptions coming from their body are not admitted by their conscious ego. They give the impression of being at war with what comes from their body, of trying to neutralize it. Some of them say that they have long become accustomed to not complaining, or to treating what comes from their body with disdain. Such manifestations are reminiscent in other fields of psychopathology of anorexic or melancholic patients. Here again, the silence concerning the body appears to be the result of a power struggle, of a conflict, the outcome of which is the barring from consciousness of what comes from the body. By contrast, we see patients who use psychical activity for self-calming purposes. Here, body care represents a search for calm and not for pleasure. All these phenomena that impose silence on the body at the level of both representation and thought might also be interpreted as phenomena of negative hallucination. However, with some of my patients, I have observed breaks in this silence of the body in the form of more or less serious crises of depersonalization. While a patient was talking to me about her mother and how she felt invaded by her, at the same time she felt invaded by what she called bodily fluids, which flowed from her head and her feet and converged towards the centre of her belly; these fluids would then disperse to the four cardinal corners of space. Another patient said how, during a conflictual situation in analysis, her ego withdrew to a position behind her body, which remained immobile. These phenomena of depersonalization are signs of a loss of ego boundaries and of a confusion between the inside and the outside. At the same time, it seems to me that they indicate a momentary weakening of the mechanisms of denial and splitting at the somatic frontier of the ego.

Thought-compulsion

This is an inner thought-activity, "operational" and permanent in character, which obeys an internal compulsion that the patient cannot interrupt.

Conclusion

Throughout the ages, the relations in medical thinking between the mind and the diseased body have taken affects into account. Emotion represented the first conceptual paradigm for establishing a bridge between psychic conflicts and organic diseases. The psychoanalysis of somatic illnesses, expanding on Freudian conceptions, has established relations between certain modalities of mental functioning and processes of somatization. In this context, the affect representative of the drive becomes the privileged target of the work of the negative, and its distortions regularly influence thought activity.

References

Braunschweig, D. (1993). Les implications techniques de la théorie en psychosomatique. *Revue Française de Psychosomatique*, 3: 144–160.

Ferenczi, S. (1926). *Final Contributions to the Problems and Methods of Psycho-Analysis*. London: Karnac, 1994.

Freud, S. (1894a). The neuro-psychoses of defence. *S.E.*, 3: 43–61. London: Hogarth.

Freud, S. (1895a). Project for a scientific psychology. *S.E.*, 1: 281–397. London: Hogarth.

Freud, S. (1916–1917). *Introductory Lectures on Psycho-Analysis. S.E., 16*. London: Hogarth.

Freud, S. (1940e [1938]). Splitting of the ego in the process of defence. *S.E.*, 23: 271–276. London: Hogarth.

Green, A. (1999). In discriminating and not discriminating between affect and representation. In: *The Fabric of Affect in the Psychoanalytic Discourse* (pp. 292–315), A. Sheridan (Trans.). London: Routledge.

Marty, P. (1980). *L'ordre psychosomatique*. Paris: Editions Payot.

Marty, P. (1991). *Mentalisation et Psychosomatique*. Paris: Synthélabo. Coll. Empêcheurs de tourner en rond.

Marty, P., de M'Uzan, M., & David, C. (1963). *L'Investigation psychosomatique*. Paris: Presses Universitaires de France.

CHAPTER NINE

The capacity to say no and psychosomatic disorders in childhood*

Gérard Szwec

T he conquest of negation significantly enriches object relations. Initially, the instinctual drives can be discharged only
through direct muscular activity. Once children develop the
capacity to make judgements, with the possibility of saying "yes"
or "no", they can discuss and negotiate. Their options are no longer
limited to fight and flight, and the reality principle prevails over the
pleasure principle. Saying "no" in order to signify one's opposition
to the object, to counter the other person, is a landmark stage in the
organization of the mind and the development of social relationships.

It is generally accepted that children who cannot communicate
their refusal of something to someone else have to find some other
way of doing so—one that involves the body.

However, since there is a whole range of physical phenomena
that could be seen as the body's response as a substitute for "no", I
must make it clear that my intention here is not to discuss what
generally goes under the heading of "body language" such as one

---

*Translated by David Alcorn.

sees in hysterical conversion with a symbolic meaning. I am talking here about the body that is somatically ill, not the erotic body.

In my consultation, I saw a nineteen-month-old boy who was disobedient; his parents were in a panic over the highly distressing somatic disorders that appeared as soon as anybody said "no" to him. There would be breath-holding spells with sudden loss of consciousness, and this had made people worry about the onset of sudden infant death syndrome. (In fact, the diagnosis of apparent life-threatening event [ALTE], with the possibility that it might lead to sudden infant death syndrome, had initially been envisaged but was later ruled out.) He would fall into this kind of state not only when he was stopped from doing something, but also when he fell or hurt himself. In addition, he suffered from severe asthma attacks, he refused to eat (in a way that evoked anorexia), had sleeping disorders, and was extremely hyperactive. During the consultation, he explored every inch of my office in a somewhat reckless way, moving all the furniture around; he would not tolerate any attempt to limit or prohibit what he wanted to do; he simply ignored such attempts and thus forced his parents to say "no" very often. Their saying "no" was a recurrent feature of the consultation, until one of their prohibitions was met by an incredible temper tantrum, with screaming and tears. On this occasion, the boy's tantrum did not end up in breath-holding and loss of consciousness, which is what his parents were expecting.

I shall come back in more detail to these refusals expressed with great violence by children through and by means of their own body—children who do not have the psychological wherewithal to make use of negation.

Negation and mentalization

For the psychoanalytic psychosomaticists of the Paris School, the mind and its workings—and negation plays a fundamental role here—have a protective function with regard to the *soma*. Their experience of treating adults and children has taught them that, if the mind cannot manage to find some way of discharging excessive mental excitation, this can lead to an increased risk of somatic breakdown. For this reason, they are very careful, in treating somatic patients, not to deprive them of a mental defence system that is perhaps the ultimate barrier.

Negation is essential to intellectual knowledge and to the capacity for abstraction. When children are able to use negation, they have access to repression as a mode of defence.

For Freud (1925h, p. 236),

> A negative judgement is the intellectual substitute for repression; its "no" is the hallmark of repression, a certificate of origin—like, let us say, "Made in Germany". With the help of the symbol of negation, thinking frees itself from the restrictions of repression and enriches itself with material that is indispensable for its proper functioning.

When, after the age of fifteen months, children shake their head to say "no", this implies that they have reached a judgement and are able to express it. That judgement has as much to do with their relationship to the outside world as with their own self, and this "leads to a progressive objectivation of mental processes", as Spitz puts it (1957, p. 399). They now possess the ability to carry out the mental operation that is negation, one that is based on an underlying capacity for abstraction. In other words, they are capable of symbolization.

With regard to the structure of the mind, the use of negation implies that passivity has been turned into activity, and also that repression has occurred; as Spitz points out, a new avenue for discharge of aggressiveness has been created.

When children can make use of negation, their capacity for object relations increases, and, above all, they no longer physically have to resist unpleasurable situations. They can express their refusal without having to have recourse to action or to the body.

Psychoanalytic psychosomaticists who work with children deal with a great variety of physical disorders that have to do with a refusal involving the body. Part of the psychosomatic pathology of infants can be understood in these terms.

Breath-holding spells

The breath-holding spells in the little boy described above are syncopal episodes following an apnoea. This usually occurs for the first time between six and eighteen months of age. In this little boy, it occurred in the first weeks of life.

In its ordinary form, a breath-holding episode can be described as a loss of consciousness that occurs in response to a frustration or a refusal that gives rise to anger or pain in the infant. The child begins to sob, and the loss of consciousness puts an end to that sobbing. When the child is revived, the reason for the frustration that brought about the loss of consciousness seems to have been forgotten. These attacks may occur whenever other similar frustrations arise.

As Kreisler (1996) says, "The attacks become more and more frequent, so that the child's family becomes increasingly worried; it can happen that nobody thereafter dares to frustrate the child, so that all authority is abandoned".

Breath-holding spells seem to occur as a somatic reaction when no psychic response is possible. This is true even after the age of fifteen months, which is when this capacity usually appears. With regard to the generally-observed reduction or disappearance of breath-holding spells at age eighteen months to two years, I would think that this is due to the fact that more appropriate ways of expressing disagreement have by then become available.

It is almost certainly repression—the necessary precondition for negation—that is defective. In children who have breath-holding spells, the perception that triggers the feeling of frustration cannot be made to disappear from consciousness by means of repressing it into the unconscious. Unable to respond via repression and, possibly, negation, the child makes the distressing frustration disappear by precipitating him- or herself into unconsciousness.

Falling into unconsciousness is an action, a somatic enactment. For the child, it is one way of interrupting the traumatic tension situation experienced with the parent; that situation is completely eliminated from the field of perception, as is the painful affect of displeasure that accompanied it.

The allergic object relation

The little boy of whom I have spoken also suffered from frequent attacks of asthma. During the consultation, no link was established between these attacks, his inability to tolerate a "no", and his own incapacity to say "no"; in other cases, however, the clinical picture has enabled such a link to be made.

As is well known, some children who suffer from asthma or eczema develop a way of functioning such that they do not have to deal with any of the frustrations or distress that intrapsychic conflicts generate (Szwec, 1993). In the allergic object relation as described by Marty (1958), the means employed is that of merging with the other, being that other person, without any differentiation between them—such that the relationship with that person is completely non-conflictual.

With respect to saying "no", the typical allergic person, in Marty's sense, is in an all-or-nothing situation. Such persons do not enter into conflict, so that they do not have to say "no". They develop such a degree of harmony in the relationship and become so indistinguishable from the other that the idea of any divergence does not even arise. They set up a relationship with a "host" object, who begins to resemble the mother figure in the undifferentiated dyad of the earliest period of life. They are completely faithful to the object, and if that relationship comes to an end, exactly the same kind of relationship is immediately set up with someone else.

However, if the object proves to be too different from the dyadic mother and the illusion of being merged with that object can no longer be sustained, there is still no possibility of saying "no" and putting up with conflict. Such people may then have an attack of their allergy-based somatization; sometimes, they will fall into a fit of rage. This kind of functioning in terms of "attacks" or "fits" has more to do with a physical expulsion of something from the body, an ex-corporation, than with a negation expressed within an object relation.

There is here a clinical convergence with Spitz's findings. He observed that babies with eczema often showed no anxiety when they saw a stranger's face—what Spitz (1965) called "eighth month anxiety" (his "second organizer of the psyche").

Such children maintain an equally familiar relationship with everybody, as though they were still functioning mentally in terms of the modalities of an earlier stage, that is, the smiling response to every face that appears during the third month of life (the first organizer).

When, in the second half of their first year of life, infants express their anxiety by refusing the stranger's approach, could that be described as an early form of negation? Spitz did not think so; for him, this is merely an expression of displeasure accompanied by withdrawal.

I would say that the refusal that is not yet a negation can be found also in behaviour and/or character traits that serve to dismiss any excessive psychological excitation when the mental avenue is obstructed. The behavioural form of refusal seems to repeat the responses that we see in frustrated babies, who make great use of their body through physical restlessness, emotional discharge, crying, or even somatic disorders.

The anxiety response in the presence of a strange face is not only an expression of distress. It is also the first sign of an (object-related) phobic fear indicating that primal repression has taken place. It serves as a counter-cathexis that enables the intolerable idea of the absence/loss/disappearance of the mother to be kept repressed in the unconscious. This, in itself, has a negating quality to it.

In the "typical allergic person", primal repression fails. ("Typical allergic person" is Marty's term. I am using it here to designate individuals, adults or infants, whose mental functioning has the same kind of typical features as we find in the allergic object relation described by Marty, or in the case of the baby with eczema who does not manifest stranger anxiety, as described by Spitz. This relation-based and identificatory functioning is not to be confused with an "allergy" in the strictly medical sense of the term.) This type of person will be inclined to deny otherness rather than confront the other person and say "no". Refusal, withdrawal, and avoidance are the main processes involved, but there is no identification with a prohibiting adult figure, which would imply turning activity into passivity.

This tendency to deny otherness, conflict, and separateness with respect to the object can be seen as a "tendency to deny having to say 'no'". When it becomes chronic, this tendency indicates severe deficiencies in the mental defence system, which seems able to assimilate only small quantities of libido and of aggressiveness. After a certain threshold is reached, the only outcome left is the somatic allergic attack. (The work of the negative as described by

Green highlights the common ground between a refusal or rejection involving the body and explicit negation.)

Anorexia nervosa in infants

The same little nineteen-month-old boy also refused his food. His eating behaviour was less worrying than his breath-holding spells, but it was another way of expressing his opposition. When infants are quite clearly anorectic, the rejection involving their body includes refusing food to the extent that the child's actual survival becomes an issue.

Early anorexia is a behaviour that appears most often to be a response to some event having to do with feeding: weaning, too much food being offered, offered at an inappropriate time, etc.

> Whatever the original pretext, the refusal has been met head-on; it is as though a reciprocal response system has been set up between the mother, with her inflexible attitude of constraint, and the infant, with a similarly inflexible attitude of opposition. [Kreisler, Fain, & Soulé, 1974]

This kind of refusal behaviour usually begins in the first six months, a period when object relations are being established. In severe cases that are resistant to treatment and remain persistent, the infant behaves as though hunger did not exist. Disobedience and a tendency to have tantrums are often part of the clinical picture.

In some cases, children seem to prefer the pleasure that they derive from refusing to the pleasure of food. In my clinical experience, refusing to be passive is a significant component of this disorder. Cases of anorexia without additional complications can improve and be cured once children manage to eat by themselves. It quite often happens that, much earlier than normally, anorectic babies develop a capacity for co-ordinating sophisticated motor functions such that they are able to feed themselves, in an attempt to manage without their mother or mother-substitute (Szwec 2002).

At an age when they are still unable to make use of negation, anorectic babies displace on to their feeding behaviour that first mental conflict indicated by the anxiety that they manifest when they see a strange face. Kreisler, Fain and Soulé (1974) has emphasized that this kind of displacement is an obstacle to mentalization. Anorectic babies do not succeed in taking their aggressive affects away from the mother by projecting them on to the stranger's face. The projection does not go all the way: it stops at the food, which is part of their image of their mother. The representations involving the relationship with the mother are ex-corporated, as if there were a need to fight against the threat of internalizing a bad object, the equivalent of food poisoning. The aim of this rejection is to enable some distancing from a mother who is experienced as a source of disruptive excitation.

Since no de-fusion of the mother's and stranger's faces has taken place, anorectic infants try to defend themselves against introjecting the image of a stranger by refusing to incorporate. Their refusal, less evolved than negation, is a deviant form of behaviour, set up under the threat of unbearable excitation that blocks any kind of representation of a mother–infant relationship in which a mother feeds her passive infant. It is this which, unlike the mental processes relating to phobic anxiety when a strange face is seen, turns the refusal to incorporate into a behaviour that runs counter to mentalization (Szwec, 2002).

Un-cuddly babies

Throughout the consultation, the little boy who could not stand being told "no" displayed his need for unremitting physical activity. This behaviour provoked many prohibitions, but he kept on investigating and examining everything until there came a time when he had a tantrum. I do not think that he particularly wanted to set up a power struggle or a sadomasochistic relationship. His hyperactive behaviour seemed more to be aimed at eradicating a relationship in which he would be the passive party. In spite of the fact that he moved around everything in my office that he could carry, not once did he climb on to his mother's lap for a rest. Unlike most children of his age when they feel tired, he never regressed on his mother's lap, sucking his thumb and day-dreaming.

Not only could he not tolerate "no", his whole behaviour manifested a permanent refusal of a certain type of relationship with the object. As a baby, he was distinctly "un-cuddly". (I have elsewhere [Szwec, 1998] described the clinical manifestations of, and theory underlying, the "un-cuddly baby" model, which involves both infantile psychosomatic elements and a withdrawal of object-cathexis.) If his mother took him in her arms, he would wriggle free. There was one consistent feature in his overall attitude: he refused to be passive in his relationship with her, whatever form that might take: giving him his bath, changing him, feeding him. He seemed to experience the "active mother" object as the source of all the excitation that he felt. He made use of his motor abilities to keep his mother at arm's length; this was not so much a feature of his relationship with his father.

By depriving himself of passivity as a drive-related possibility, his psychic development would always be shaky. Binding the drives and setting up a life-preserving masochism are jeopardized and, as is well-known, when destructive tendencies are not neutralized at the start through primary masochism, they tend to seek an outlet through motor discharge.

This child tried to calm the psychical excitation that was overwhelming him by having recourse to another form of excitation that had its source in physical restlessness. (I have described self-soothing procedures in my book, *Les galériens volontaires* [Szwec, 1998]. These consist in repetitive behaviour involving motor functions and/or sensoriality. Their aim is to control excitation that cannot be bound by more psychical means.)

His attempts to soothe himself through agitation were doomed to fail. They were no more than a diversion from representational thinking — in particular, the representation of the link to the object that had to be kept undone.

In attempting to suppress the idea of a relationship with the object, his behaviour made any kind of negation irrelevant. As Spitz has shown, the infant of fifteen months or more who shakes his or her head to mean "no" is making use of a signal targeted at the object. That gesture, in itself, signifies a refusal *to* someone. It is an intentional signal, with the aim of communicating that refusal to someone else. It is one of the infant's most important contributions to the setting up of a relationship with the object.

Self-soothing restlessness, on the other hand, does not have as its aim communicating something to someone. Indeed, it has no erotic value whatsoever, not even masochistic; self-soothing procedures replace the classical auto-erotic activities: these are either absent or insufficiently developed (Szwec, 1998).

When regressive behaviour replaces psychical regression, this implies a return to the kind of functioning that was prevalent in an earlier phase, that of non-differentiation; therefore, it falls well short of objectalization and, at the same time, lies beyond the pleasure principle. Unlike negation, which has the value of an act governed by the mind, regressive behaviour is not regulated by the mind; it acts against the mind, against thinking. In my view, this is an illustration of how the work of the negative in its destructive dimension can serve as a substitute for negation with its structuring quality (Green, 1993).

Refusing passivity

Once infants have learned to walk and are more independent, they hear adults saying "no" to them much more often than before. They are on the receiving end of more orders and prohibitions, and experience situations the repetition of which sets up a lasting memory trace of the word "no" and the gestures that accompany it. They combine this with a representation that is meaningful for their immediate circle by defensively setting up identification with the prohibiting adult. This identification is an early stage in the development of the superego.

None the less, every prohibition—by gesture, words, or both—gives rise to frustration, interrupting the child's activity. Spitz sees in this also a regression to the narcissistic organization of the ego, which runs counter to the progressive movement from the narcissistic phase to the establishment of object relations that are customary at that age. Children do not readily tolerate being forced back into passivity. In order to integrate passivity, it must not represent too much of a threat. This will depend on the messages internalized through the infant's contacts with the mother in the early stages of their relationship; these, of course, bear the hallmark of her own psychical conflicts between motherhood and other cathexes, in particular that of her sexual partner. In this triangulated situation, internalizing prohibitions has a structuring dimension in so far as it facilitates in the child some degree of mental integration around the maternal message about the threat of castration by the father. "If you do that again, I'll tell your dad" (Szwec, 2008).

This message enables bisexual identifications to unfold, but not if the passive position (and the feminine dimension that goes with it) is refused. The threat of castration will then be pushed aside by a character neurosis focusing on phallic narcissism, which, in adolescence, may give rise to an attempt at oneupmanship with regard to virile aspects, in both girls and boys.

Suppression

The various somatic manifestations that I have described in the nineteen-month-old boy who could not tolerate "no" evoke the kind of refusal that makes use of the body's physical resistance to unpleasant situations. These manifestations go hand-in-hand with limitations in object relations.

Generally speaking, if repression does not suffice, the child has recourse to other mechanisms in the struggle against the unpleasure and distress brought about by conflict and other vexations. One of these mechanisms, suppression (*Unterdrückung*), is of particular interest.

For Freud, repression is typical of neurotic structures, whereas suppression has to do with anxiety neurosis and the actual neuroses.

When the capacity to bind excitation is overpowered, suppression enters the picture, with the aim of cutting off sequences of representation and preventing excitation from being bound. Parat (1995) has pointed out that suppression focuses particularly on undoing any links between representation and affect, because it is the affect that is linked to certain representations which is feared.

When suppression is employed, the unwelcome representation is not repressed into the unconscious; it is neutralized. The corresponding affect is inhibited and maintained in stasis; this heightens the excitation, which can be discharged only through an anxiety attack, distress, or somatic means.

Like breath-holding spells, suppression of thoughts has as its aim the freezing or erasing of all affect. That said, breath-holding spells go further than the conscious or preconscious neutralization of thinking, because they involve the loss of consciousness that results from cerebral anoxia.

Suppression, as Marty (1951) has shown in the case of adults, may participate in the process that leads to cephalalgia. Psychotherapy with children and adolescents who suffer from headaches has highlighted just how much these young patients try to chase away or stifle any sexual and/or aggressive and angry thoughts.

In Freud's early writings, the suppression of sexual wishes for conscious reasons gives rise to orgasmic frustration leading to anxiety neurosis. Suppression appears to entail the extinction of the drive or of the need. Somatic sexual excitation is employed to an abnormal degree and the processing by the mind of that excitation is halted, thus leading to somatization.

Given Freud's final theory of the drives, we could consider the suppression of the aggressive drives that are liberated through the unbinding of the sexual drives in a similar light.

The "well-behaved child" neurosis

Children who suppress their sexual and aggressive drives are perfectly well-behaved. The stronger the suppression, the more well-behaved such children are; they succeed in strengthening repression to such an extent that there are no longer any derivatives.

In the "well-behaved child" neurosis, the classical neurotic symptoms are replaced by personality structures, given the powerful suppression of desire and aggressiveness. This point of view is based on Freud's idea that the suppression demanded by civilization, in particular through the way in which children are brought up, raises moral imperatives to such a high level that individuals are obliged to distance themselves more and more from their drive-related urges.

The personal moral code of these children, which usually mirrors that of their family, forms one of the motive forces behind suppression. It enables, for example, an aggressive or angry thought aimed at the Oedipal rival to be pushed aside, so that the relationship with that rival can remain affectionate.

For Freud (1924c, p. 170), "the cultural suppression of the instincts holds back a large part of the subject's destructive instinctual components from being exercised in life". The part played by the superego explains the turning back of sadism on to the subject in the form of secondary masochism and/or of superego sadism.

That said, this way of looking at the situation has to do with the binding of the instincts typical of the pleasure–unpleasure principle. In my view, we should look at it again in a way that goes "beyond the pleasure principle", taking into account the inadequacy of binding whenever drive-related excitation, of internal or external origin, goes beyond a certain threshold, with the risk that it may bring about a traumatic situation if it overwhelms the internal protective shield against stimuli. The solidity of that protective shield depends on what aspects of the maternal function have been internalized. In the infant's early development, the mother takes on the role of the agent of repression; this enables the child to have recourse to repression in order to avoid being overwhelmed in a traumatic fashion. From a very early stage, the mother incites her infant to repress, with the similar aim of avoiding trauma. When she says "no", she thereby encourages repression and/or suppression, depending on her own particular character traits. The same situation occurs in the infant's early relationships with other significant people.

Giving pride of place to suppression rather than to repression in the messages conveyed to the infant contributes to the "well-behaved child" neurosis; I tend to see in this an early form of character neurosis. When suppression becomes a habitual means of defence, it is accompanied by a high degree of idealization and prohibits any kind of regression. The too-well-behaved child, like those who are hyperactive or un-cuddly, refuses to have anything to do with regression. These children do not repress what gives them pain; they push it to one side in a very determined manner without letting any emotion get in their way.

To free themselves of their needs and drive-related urges, too-well-behaved children use suppression in an almost conscious way in order to remove affect from representations and thoughts. They will say that they are "emptying their mind". Emptying themselves of memories and projects, they live from day to day, in a concrete reality; at times, they seem to be on a kind of mental automatic piloting in which repetition is the dominant factor.

Too-well-behaved children are always measuring themselves against a terribly demanding ideal, and, as a result, their own narcissistic foundations are weakened.

Suppression impoverishes mental activity because it attempts to do away with any unconscious activity. Consequently, children who are subdued because of their continuous recourse to suppression often suffer from more or less severe somatic disorders. I agree on this point with Parat (1995), who argues that repression of representation results in the strengthening of character traits, while inhibition of affect leads to somatic disorders.

From the very beginning of life, children are subjected to the suppression that their parents impose on their drives. As Freud (1908d, p. 186) puts it: ". . . our civilization is built up on the suppression of instincts".

These prohibiting messages are made through various channels: facial expressions, words, etc. The child reacts with anger, refusals that at times may be quite strong, and, if the possibility does exist, by more mentalized means such as negation, which indicates that there is some identification with the prohibiting adult.

The messages that are transmitted in the course of bringing up children contain some degree of conditioning and training; this is most visible during toilet training. But, even in the mother's earliest relationship with her infant, her baby's rhythm does not necessarily correspond to her own or match the way in which she adapts to his or her needs. The manner in which she herself responds to frustration and the experience of needs being satisfied create the conditions for the hallucinatory satisfaction of wishes and contribute decisively to the construction of the infant's mind. It is the parents' mental functioning—and especially, perhaps, the mother's—that builds up the wherewithal which facilitates the child's earliest attempts not only at repression, but also at suppression. In bringing up her baby, the mother follows the principles laid down by her own superego and ego ideal.

When the suppression that upbringing entails becomes excessive because the parental superego is too harsh, the restrictions and constraints imposed on the infant will be excessive. These prohibitions can target motor functions, aggressiveness, language, sexuality, and, more specifically, the development of auto-erotic activity. The child simply has to bow down to the demands placed on him or her.

The risks involved when a well-behaved child becomes an over-conforming adult are not taken properly into account in our society. Yet, this kind of functioning may well become purely operational, reflecting a deadening of mental life that goes hand in hand with an increased likelihood of somatic disorders. Adults who were once too-well-behaved children go on inhibiting their mental functioning by attempting to repeat old recipes and ways of working in a purely operational way. Such people conform, and that is all. The over-conforming and over-rational people who have this kind of structure have a split-off emotional life. Their mental activity involving representations rooted in infantile sexuality is reduced to a minimum. The blind obedience to a purely administrative logic that we see in these individuals can, at times, reach the point of inhumanity (Arendt, 1963).

Conclusion

In this chapter, I have been discussing those young children who find it impossible to express their opposition to something through a mental process as negation and, therefore, signify it through physical means and by somatic disorders. I have also discussed those who make use of suppressing all mental activity and who, by that very fact, are increasingly likely to suffer some somatic breakdown or other.

While hyperactive children in the first category are often classified from a nosographic point of view as presenting behaviour disorders, those in the second group, well-behaved and over-conforming, are usually not considered to be pathological. Yet, all of these children may be prone to inadequate mental functioning, with the risk of somatization that this entails.

It bears repeating that the nosographic entity "disruptive behaviour disorders" is no more than a mishmash. Defined by purely symptomatic criteria (I am referring here to the suppression of the concept of neurosis in the *DSM* classification of the American Psychiatric Association, which is now the standard reference text for the world as a whole. *DSM* diagnoses are made on the basis of a combination [more or less] of symptoms that are no longer looked upon as the expression of invisible mental processes.), no distinction is drawn between situations in which the behaviour has to do with underlying thoughts and those in which it runs counter to, and even attempts to destroy, any possibility of thinking. No distinction is drawn between acts that are symptoms of a neurotic or psychotic structure and behavioural enactments that imply that any existing neurotic or psychotic means of defence is inadequate.

Those classified under this clinical heading, "disruptive behaviour disorders", and other similar disorders that are supposed to share the same "co-morbidity" (ADHD and oppositional defiant disorder), run the risk, it is said, of becoming antisocial personalities in adulthood. In order to offset that risk, behaviour modification programmes have been set up in several English-speaking countries, including the USA, with a momentum that is rapidly becoming worldwide.

Often, the idea is to identify as early as possible any deviant behaviour considered to be based on "bad impulses". This, in my view, amounts to a denial—the denial that antisocial and destructive tendencies exist in each and every one of us.

Whether these are suppressed by behavioural modification programmes, or through prescribing psychotropic medication with a tranquillizing effect, we can be sure that any child who is thereby muzzled will try to suppress all mental activity. This will be to the detriment of repression or other mental defence mechanisms, which, in turn, will leave the individual open to the kinds of danger that I evoked earlier, which are still largely underestimated.

References

Arendt, H. (1963). *Eichmann in Jerusalem: A Report on the Banality of Evil.* New York: Viking Press.

Freud, S. (1908d). "Civilized" sexual morality and modern nervous illness. *S.E., 9*: 179–204. London: Hogarth.

Freud, S. (1924c). The economic problem of masochism. *S.E., 19*: 157–170. London: Hogarth.

Freud, S. (1925h). Negation. *S.E., 19*: 235–240. London: Hogarth.

Green, A. (1993). *Le travail du négatif.* Paris: Editions de Minuit [*The Work of the Negative*, A. Weller (Trans.). London: Free Association Books, 1999].

Kreisler, L. (1996). Pathologies fonctionnelles néonatales alarmantes [Some alarming neo-natal functional conditions]. *Revue française de psychosomatique, 9*: 15–33. Paris: Presses Universitaires de France.

Kreisler, L., Fain, M., & Soulé, M. (1974). *L'enfant et son corps* [The Child and His/Her Body]. Paris: Presses Universitaires de France.

Marty, P. (1951). Aspect psychodynamique de l'étude clinique de quelques cas de céphalalgies [A psycho-dynamic aspect of the clinical study of some cases of cephalalgia]. *Revue française de psychanalyse, XV*(2): 216–252 [also in *Revue française de psychosomatique, 34*, 2008].

Marty, P. (1958). La relation objectale allergique. *Revue française de psychanalyse, XXII*(1): 5–35 [also in *Revue française de psychosomatique, 29*, 2006; The allergic object relationship. *International Journal of Psycho-Analysis, 39*(2–4): 98–103, 1958].

Parat, C. (1995). *L'affect partagé* [Sharing Affects]. Paris: Presses Universitaires de France.

Spitz, R. A. (1957). *No and Yes: On the Genesis of Human Communication.* New York: International Universities Press.

Spitz, R. A. (1965). *The First Year of Life: a Psychoanalytic Study of Normal and Deviant Development of Object Relations.* New York: International Universities Press.

Szwec, G. (1993). *La psychosomatique de l'enfant asthmatique* [The Psychosomatic Dimension in Children with Asthma]. Paris: Presses Universitaires de France.

Szwec, G. (1998). *Les galériens volontaires. Essais sur les procédés autocalmants* [Voluntary Galley-slaves. Some Thoughts on Self-soothing Procedures]. Paris: Presses Universitaires de France.

Szwec, G. (2002). L'enfant—organe hypocondriaque de sa mère [The child as the mother's hypochondriacal organ]. *Revue française de psychosomatique, 22*: 65–83.

Szwec, G. (2008). Je vais en parler à ton père ... [I'll tell your Dad ...]. In: D. Cupa (Ed.), *Image du père dans la culture contemporaine* [The Image of the Father in Modern Society] (pp. 141–144). Paris: Presses Universitaires de France.

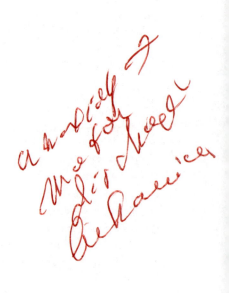

CHAPTER TEN

Symbolism, symbolization, and trauma in psychosomatic theory

Graeme J. Taylor

A fundamental premise in the field of psychosomatic medicine is that emotions and personality can influence bodily functions and contribute to the aetiology and pathogenesis of disease. This idea was emphasized in the eighteenth century by the eminent British physician William Falconer (1796), and a century later by Freud (1890a), who firmly believed that the health of the body can be affected by "violent affects" and by "persistent affective states of a distressing or 'depressive' nature" (p. 287). Cautious about extending psychoanalysis beyond the domain of mental disorders, Freud did not pursue an interest in somatic diseases; however, some of his followers began to apply the psychoanalytic method to the investigation and treatment of physically ill patients. Their work led to the development of several different psychosomatic theories, which initially had wide appeal, but subsequently were found to be of limited usefulness in their clinical application and as explanatory models of disease (Taylor, 1987).

Identifying the limitations of a theory provides an impetus for making revisions or developing a new theory. This certainly occurred in the broad field of psychoanalysis, when new findings began to question certain basic assumptions of traditional Freudian theory and led to important changes in theory and technique (Eagle, 1984). Psychosomatic theory has also changed, and continues to evolve as it integrates new ideas from developments in psychoanalysis as well as findings from research in the biomedical sciences. In this chapter, I show how some limitations of earlier psychosomatic theories have been surmounted by a contemporary theory, which places a greater emphasis on the adverse impact of traumatic events on the symbolizing function of the mind, a capacity that is essential for the cognitive processing and regulation of emotions and thereby helps protect the integrity of the body.

Psychosomatic theories of disease

During the middle decades of the twentieth century, the psychoanalytic approach to patients with somatic diseases was influenced, for the most part, by two psychosomatic theories. Both theories were based on Freud's concepts of repression and intrapsychic conflict; they differed, however, over the meanings (or lack of meanings) attributed to disease. One theory, which originated with Georg Groddeck, Smith Ely Jelliffe, and Wilhelm Stekel, and was further elaborated by Felix Deutsch, Melitta Sperling, and Angel Garma, assumed that somatic diseases have primary symbolic meaning. This theory was essentially an extension of Freud's view of conversion hysteria, in which somatic symptoms are considered an expression of an unconscious fantasy in "body language"; as such the symptoms carry "hidden" meaning which is considered directly accessible to psychoanalytic interpretation in the same way as a dream. Garma, for example, regarded peptic ulcer as a symbolic expression of an internalized aggressive mother.

The contrasting theory, which was formulated by Franz Alexander and his colleagues at the Chicago School, proposed that somatic diseases, like Freud's concept of the actual neuroses, are asymbolic (i.e., without meaning), and are a consequence of interactions between constitutional dispositions and physiological changes that accompany chronic states of emotional arousal. Alexander restricted his theory to a small group of seven diseases (the *vegetative neuroses*) and attributed chronic states of emotional arousal to specific intrapsychic conflicts that could be activated by certain life situations. Treatment was aimed at interpreting and resolving the unconscious conflicts thought to be maintaining emotional arousal.

A complicating factor for Alexander's theory is that bodily symptoms can become secondarily linked with fantasies and affects and, thereby, appear to give a somatic disease symbolic meaning. This was acknowledged much earlier by Glover (1939), who declared that "[psychosomatic disorders] have no psychic *content* . . . should they develop psychic meaning, it may be assumed that a psychoneurotic process has been superimposed on a psychosomatic foundation" (p. 173). As McDougall (1974) later observed, "any somatic event will tend to attach to itself ideas dealing with different aspects of the castration complex as well as fantasies concerning the early mother–child relationship" (p. 442). In her view, "theoretical confusion will result if we overlook the fact that *somatic processes and psychic processes are governed by different laws of functioning*" (p. 443). This does not imply that somatic disorders lack meaning and are beyond the reach of psychoanalysis, but, as McDougall argues, the bodily symptoms should be regarded as *signs* rather than symbols, since they do not take the place of something repressed.

During the 1970s, a third major psychosomatic theory emerged, which extended Alexander's theory by proposing that pathogenic states of emotional arousal are a consequence of impairments in the symbolic function itself. This theory, as Greco (1998) points out, shifts the focus from whether or not somatic diseases have psychological meanings to a higher level of abstraction in which explanations are sought for the subjective conditions that allow for the development of pathologies that lack symbolic meaning. In contrast to the two earlier theories, this theory gives important roles to trauma and dissociation, and has implications for therapeutic technique that go beyond interpretation of repressed conflict.

Before exploring the relationship between psychic trauma and physical health, let me clarify the distinction between symbolism and symbolization, which has been outlined in recent years by Aragno (1997), Freedman (1998), and Newirth (2003), although Deri (1984) wrote extensively about these two concepts in the 1980s.

Symbolism and symbolization

The traditional psychoanalytic view of symbol formation is derived from Freud's early work on the interpretation of dreams, and from his discovery with Breuer that the symptoms of hysteria carry hidden meanings (Freud, 1896c). This view is outlined in a classic paper by Jones (1916), who asserted that "only what is repressed is symbolized (in the true sense): only what is repressed needs to be symbolized" (p. 116). Thus, the emphasis is on unconscious representations of repressed libidinal and aggressive wishes that lie behind the manifest symbol (Deri, 1984). Dominated by primary process thought, this narrow view of symbol formation is referred to as *symbolism* (Freedman, 1998; Jones, 1916). It underlies the theory that somatic diseases express symbolic meanings.

Symbolization is a broader concept than symbolism, and emphasizes function rather than content; it includes secondary process as well as primary process thought, and is considered a process of linking and meaning-making (Aragno, 1997; Freedman, 1998). This understanding of symbol formation emerged primarily from the work of British analysts, including Rycroft, Segal, and Winnicott, who view the unconscious as an organization that creates meaning and generates new experiences, rather than simply "a container of disguised, immature, and hidden meanings" (Newirth, 2003, p. 8). The philosopher Susanne Langer (1942) described symbolization as "the fundamental process of [the] mind" that goes on all the time: "Sometimes we are aware of it, sometimes we merely find its results, and realize that certain experiences have passed through our brains and have been digested there" (p. 41). This process corresponds closely with Bion's (1962) concept of "alpha function", which he considered a kind of mental digestion that transforms emotional sense impressions (beta-elements) into alpha-elements that can be used in images, dreams, thoughts, and memories.

The distinction between symbolism and symbolization has important implications for treatment. Whereas, with symbolism, the analyst's task is to provide the *real* meaning for the symbol and thereby discard the symbol itself, with the broader concept, the aim of psychoanalytic treatment is to enhance the patient's capacity for symbolization, as both Green (1975) and Deri (1984) have emphasized. Clearly, the two concepts overlap; for example,

interpretations that lead to insight and an integration of the unconscious meaning of symbols into the conscious mind are an aspect of
symbolization as primary process thought is replaced by secondary
process thought.

By conceptualizing symbolization as a developmental achievement, psychoanalysts could begin to observe varying degrees of
impairment in this capacity, particularly in patients with histories
of deprivation or psychic trauma (Krystal, 1978). This occurred in
the field of psychosomatic medicine during the 1960s and 1970s and
paved the way for the development of the third psychosomatic
theory. While investigating the communicative style of patients
with the same type of diseases as Alexander studied, Nemiah and
Sifneos (1970; Nemiah, Freyberger, & Sifneos, 1976) observed that
many of the patients manifested a restricted imagination and a
deficit in the ability to symbolically represent and verbally express
emotions; they labelled this deficit *alexithymia*. They noted that the
paucity of fantasy, along with an externally orientated cognitive
style, correspond to the phenomenon of *pensée opératoire* described
by Marty and de M'Uzan (1963). Although subsequent research has
shown that alexithymia is not specific to, or an invariable feature of,
any group of diseases (Taylor, 2004), this construct made the symbolic dimension relevant to Alexander's theory by proposing that
the pathogenic impact of emotion on the body is a consequence of
a failure to adequately symbolize, and thereby contain, distressing
emotional states.

Symbolization and desymbolization of emotions

Our understanding of how emotional experience is represented
in the mind has increased over the past decade as a result of the
theoretical contributions and empirical investigations of Bucci
(1997a). In her multiple code theory of emotional information
processing, the fundamental organizing structures of human emotional life are referred to as *emotion schemas*. Bucci (2008, p. 57)
describes these as "particular types of memory schemas that
develop on the basis of repeated interactions with others from the
beginning of life and that form the basis of personality organization". They determine how we perceive and respond to others "and

are themselves continuously affected and changed by new interpersonal experience".

According to the multiple code theory (Bucci, 1997a), emotion
schemas begin to develop during infancy in a *non-verbal* form. This
includes *subsymbolic* processes, which are the patterns of sensory,
visceral, and kinaesthetic sensations and motor activity experienced
during states of emotional arousal, and also *symbolic imagery*, such
as the object or person associated with the emotion. As the child
develops language, *verbal symbols* (words) are incorporated into the
emotion schemas. The different components are connected, to varying degrees, by the *referential process* such that dominant emotion
schemas from the non-verbal systems can be translated into logi-
cally organized speech. This is not a transformation of one modality to another, but a connecting of the separate components of the
emotion schema, thereby allowing for a transformation of the
meanings represented in them (Bucci, 1999).

Normal emotional development depends on the integration of
sensory, visceral, and motoric elements in the emotion schema,
together with images and words. There are different degrees of integration among the subsymbolic and symbolic verbal and non-
verbal components in normal everyday functioning, with each
component able to function effectively in its own modality (Bucci,
2007). However, the integration within emotion schemas is significantly impaired in individuals who experience developmental deficiencies, serious conflict, or psychic trauma, as the connections
among the components are disrupted or even fail to form. The
dissociation or desymbolization within the schemas creates a potential for high arousal of the somatic and motoric components, as
these are no longer organized and regulated through links with the
symbolic components. As Bucci (1999, 2008) explains, dissociations
between or within the components, and the defences employed by
the person in an attempt to repair the schema, are likely to result in
pathological symptoms, the nature of which depends on the level
of dissociation and the strategies used to manage the affective
arousal when subsymbolic components are activated.

Bucci's (1997b) theoretical contributions have been extremely
helpful in developing a contemporary psychoanalytic understanding of somatic symptom formation. She proposes that when simply
the primary object of the emotion schema has been dissociated, in

the service of defence, the mind may try to repair the dissociation by using a part of the body to organize the schema, thereby creating a hypochondriacal or conversion symptom with symbolic meaning. More severe dissociations within the non-verbal elements of emotion schemas, as occur in post traumatic states, can result in states of prolonged activation of subsymbolic processes with upsurges of emotional arousal that are beyond the person's capacity to self-regulate (*ibid.*). Such dissociations may be triggered by stressful events or by cues related to the original trauma. Without the modulating influence of symbolic representations, a transition from health to a functional somatic syndrome (e.g., irritable bowel syndrome) or to structural organic disease may occur if the dysregulated emotion system dysregulates other biological systems in the body (Taylor, 1992). This type of event is illustrated by the personal experience of the psychoanalyst Parens (2004), which he describes in his autobiographical book, *Renewal of Life: Healing from the Holocaust.*

A case of eczema

At age twelve, Parens escaped from the Rivesaltes detention camp in Vichy France, having fled from Brussels to France with his mother a year earlier. He had been encouraged to escape from the camp by his mother, who was later murdered in Auschwitz. For the greater part of his life, Parens had resisted writing about his traumatic experience, but, at age seventy-three, and beginning on 14 August, 2002, which was exactly sixty years after his mother was sent to Auschwitz, he began to write down the memories from his childhood. Parens (2004) tells the reader that reliving and writing his Holocaust story was an excruciating process in which he reacted somatically as well as emotionally. For the first time in his life, and shortly before he began to write, he developed intense itching of his skin from an eczematous rash that suddenly appeared on his arms and chest and migrated to his thighs.

Parens was well aware of a link between the outbreak of eczema and the activation of intense emotions, including feelings of rage and hatred towards his French and Nazi persecutors and a profound aching sadness. Engaged in self-analysis, he reports an insight he gained four months after the onset of the ailment. He began to recall the misery and harsh conditions at Rivesaltes, in particular how at night he and the other detainees slept on coarse sackcloth mattresses and covered themselves with army-type coarse wool blankets. He wrote:

> For me, these torturous sleeping accommodations—so torturous in fact that I totally repressed this part of my Rivesaltes experience until this writing—plain and simple reflected the misery that was Rivesaltes. And, at this moment, I feel this specifically in my skin. [*ibid.*, p. 44]

Although Parens does not use the term symbolization, this mental process is implied in the following statement:

> This specific insight . . . will not immediately clear my skin. It will not clear it today because skin reactions of this nasty kind don't just wash away; they have to be, we might say, detoxified and metabolized by the psyche and by the body. (*ibid.*)

As we learned from Janet (1889), it is the "vehement emotions" that accompany extreme experiences that make them traumatic. Such emotions cause memories of the experience to be dissociated from consciousness, a defensive manoeuvre that involves disruption of the referential connections between the symbolic and subsymbolic components within the emotion schemas. The retrieval of the memories, however, especially images, activates subsymbolic components associated with the original experience, thereby generating states of arousal and feelings that are once again experienced as intolerable. This is evident in Paren's description of how he experienced the loss of his mother. Looking back to when he was a seventeen-to-eighteen-year old adolescent and first heard the news that his mother had been murdered in one of the death camps, Parens acknowledges that the need to protect himself against excessive pain led him to suppress and set aside mourning the loss of his mother. He employed the defence of dissociation: "My mother was sent to Auschwitz on August 14, 1942. I have repeated that sentence in an effort to inscribe it in my brain. My brain resists its inscription. But it's there, even though I often can't find it" (*ibid.*, p. 116). And, a few paragraphs later,

To this past year, this past August 2002 to be exact, I have not been able to remember on which day my mother was sent with other internees—like cattle—from Drancy to Auschwitz. Live stock is sent in wagons to be butchered, so that we can eat. Just to be gotten rid of! I just realized that I am scratching my arms and my head as I write this. [*ibid.*, pp. 117–118]

At age twenty-four, Parens had the opportunity to visit a woman who had been with him and his mother in Rivesaltes. She told him that his mother had been sent away on one of the selections of internees destined for an extermination camp in Poland.

I heard the jarring news. I knew the fact; but to hear her say it, she who was there, I collapsed inwardly; soon I was numb. Time slows as I write about it; nearly immobilized now, pensive, dulled feelings, heavy, sad—words don't tell well enough; I don't tell well enough. A heavy amorphous pain, lying on top of rage that is sequestered right now. [*ibid.*, p. 127]

We can surmise that the retrieval of traumatic memories, as Parens was writing his personal memoir, activated intense and overwhelming emotional states that were initially not well managed cognitively and resulted in dysregulation of biological systems that maintain the integrity of the skin. As he was able gradually to tolerate and contain the dreaded affects, and link them with verbal representations as he continued thinking and writing, Parens presumably reduced the painful activation, which then allowed healing of his skin.

Relationship between trauma and disease

Several retrospective studies with very large samples have yielded strong support for an association between childhood trauma and the development of somatic disease in adult life. The Adverse Childhood Experiences Study in San Diego, California (Dube et al., 2009; Felitti et al., 1998), for example, and the National Comorbidity Survey in the United States (Goodwin & Stein, 2004), found that self-reported childhood trauma was associated with an increased risk for a broad range of physical illnesses, including cardiovascular, digestive, respiratory, and autoimmune diseases, which could arise many years after the exposure. The types of trauma included sexual, physical, and emotional abuse, as well exposure to household dysfunction such as parental separation or divorce, domestic violence, and parental substance abuse or mental illness. There is evidence also that traumatic experiences in adulthood can have consequences for physical health in later years. Several follow-up studies of Vietnam War veterans with chronic post traumatic stress disorder have reported a higher lifetime prevalence of various somatic diseases as many as twenty years after military service (Boscarino, 1997, 2004; Friedman & Schnurr, 1995).

Notwithstanding the importance of these correlational studies, they do not explain how emotions associated with unsymbolized psychic trauma may contribute to changes in physical health. The causal mechanisms are likely to be complex and involve various co-existing pathways, including a direct effect of emotions on other biological systems, as well as adult health behaviours such as smoking, alcohol or drug use, and overeating, which traumatized individuals often employ to regulate distressing affects without awareness of their origin (Bucci, 2008; Felitti et al., 1998; Friedman, 2008). There is now substantial evidence that emotional stress directly affects the nervous, endocrine, and immune systems; moreover, these systems communicate with one another via bidirectional pathways, thereby forming an arrangement of reciprocally regulating subsytems within the body that interface via the brain with mental processes and with the larger social system (Eskandari & Sternberg, 2002; Glaser & Kiecolt-Glaser, 2005; Kiecolt-Glaser, McGuire, Robles, & Glaser, 2002; Sternberg, 2000; Taylor, 1992). In earlier contributions (Taylor, 1987, 1992), I proposed a psychobiological dysregulation model of disease in which perturbations in one or more components of the feedback loops between the various bodily systems (including the emotion system) may lead to changes over time in the rhythmic functioning of one or more of the systems, thereby creating conditions conducive to disease activity. In the case of eczema, for example, emotional stress activates the hypothalamic–pituitary–adrenal (HPA) axis and the sympathetic nervous system, which release neurohormones that reach the skin via the bloodstream and produce an overproduction or changes in the regulation of cytokines and other neuropeptides that normally regulate inflammatory and immunologic processes in the skin (O'Sullivan, Lipper, & Lerner, 1998; Seiffert & Granstein, 2006).

Because of dissociation, people often fail to remember the details, or even the occurrence, of childhood traumas. Traumatic memories, however, are encoded in the procedural or implicit memory system, which is mediated, at least in part, by the amygdala, which does not forget (Yovell, 2000). Even though early trauma has a distorting effect on the developing personality, memories of traumatic childhood experiences may lie dormant for decades, but eventually be awakened by an appropriate stimulus, such as a stressful emotional state, perhaps associated with separation, loss, or personal threat (Siegel, 1995). The emotional memory may be experienced somatically only, and not attributed to past childhood events, especially when it is dissociated from verbal and non-verbal symbolic components in the emotion schema which are necessary for an explicit memory of the original trauma (Bucci, 2007, 2008; Siegel, 1995).

Treatment implications

Consistent with contemporary recommendations for the psychoanalytic treatment of traumatized individuals (Cohen, 1980; Bromberg, 1998), Bucci (2007, 2008) emphasizes that to bring about changes in the organization of the emotion schemas it is necessary that the patient experience some aspects of the affective core of the dissociated schema in the therapeutic sessions. Since the mode of mental organization following psychic trauma is repetition-compulsion, some aspect of the original trauma will inevitably re-emerge in the transference, with a potential for enactments and for retraumatization if the analyst is perceived as the original predator and is provoked to act. In the context of the new interpersonal relationship with the analyst, however, and aided by his or her containing function, there is the opportunity to gradually symbolize the dissociated painful emotion by connecting somatic experiences with imagery and language. As imagery initially heightens activation of subsymbolic elements in the schema, patients are likely to experience the affective arousal as overwhelming and disorganizing, and sometimes fear that they are going mad. There is also a risk that activation of the sympathetic nervous system and HPA axis will aggravate a patient's somatic disorder, and even be a threat to life. It is, therefore, important for the analyst to regulate the intensity of the emotional arousal while enhancing the referential process, and, together with the patient, reflect on the retrieved memories and the meanings the patient has given to them.

To illustrate the process of symbolization in psychoanalytic therapy with somatically ill patients, I describe some aspects of my work with two men who suffered from cervical dystonia (spasmodic torticollis), which is a form of *focal dystonia*. Although the aetiology of this disorder is not fully known, genetic factors or peripheral injury have been implicated in some cases, as well as an abnormality in the basal ganglia of the brain involving a dysregulation of dopaminergic and/or cholinergic pathways (Besson et al., 1988; Dauer, Burke, Greene, & Fahn, 1998). Scaer (2005) links the disorder directly with trauma by relating the head turning to the *orientating reflex* that mammals developed as part of an "early-warning system" for detecting threat from predators prior to initiating a flight response. He suggests that "torticollis may actually be an aborted orienting reflex, where the instinctual head turning that occurs with the evaluation of a potential threat becomes fixed due to the subsequent traumatization that occurred in that victim" (p. 238). From this perspective, cervical dystonia may signify an instinctual bodily response to threat that is now organized by the repetition-compulsion.

Case 1

Jorge, a forty-five-year-old married man, developed cervical dystonia following a minor head injury. He sought analysis after obtaining only mild and temporary relief from various medications aimed at relaxing the muscles of his neck. I learnt that he was from a Latin American country and had been raised, along with two older sisters, by his mother, his father having abandoned the family when Jorge was aged four. In the second month of the analysis, and with considerable embarrassment, he was able to tell me that he had been seduced sexually on two occasions by his football coach when he was aged fifteen. Having grown up yearning for the love and guidance of a father, he had attempted to befriend the coach, who persuaded him that fellatio was like shaking hands. Jorge said that he had buried the memory of the events to keep them out of his mind; I was the only person he ever told. He recounted that following the seductions he became deeply depressed, failed his courses, and was expelled from school. After immigrating to North America in his early twenties, he began to experience panic attacks and often dissociated with out-of-body experiences and an unpleasant taste in his mouth. Following the session, Jorge cried and felt intense shame, humiliation, and disgust with himself.

During the months following this disclosure, Jorge became distressed in the sessions whenever he tried to recall details of the sexual abuse. As subsymbolic components of emotion schema were activated, he experienced the sensation of a steel rod from the top of his head down his upper spine and tremendous tension in the muscles of his neck; these symptoms were often accompanied by a headache and an urge to vomit, and he usually cried. He reported awakening in the mornings with a feeling that he contained "a deep black hole" which felt "like a pot of undigested emotion".

Since adolescence, Jorge had experienced a sense of masculine inadequacy and feared that he might be a latent homosexual. We came to understand that this fear reflected a personal meaning he had created to explain why he had been caught unawares and allowed himself to be abused by the football coach. Although the involuntary torsion of his neck became secondarily linked with castration anxiety and neurotic conflicts over phallic aggression, Jorge's dystonia lacked primary symbolic meaning. Instead, it was associated with "unmodified primal repressions" (Cohen, 1985) that underlay his sense that he contained a black hole of undigested emotion. Grotstein (1990) suggests that the experience of a black hole in the psyche "represents the ultimate traumatic state of disorganization, terror, chaos, randomness, and entropy" (p. 377). For Jorge, this included the anguish and bewilderment of himself as a helpless four-year-old boy who had suddenly lost his father, a trauma that also had to be relived in the transference.

Case 2

Tom, a thirty-one-year-old single man, developed a gradual onset of cervical dystonia one month after the death of his closest male friend in a motor vehicle accident. He was referred to me to help him cope with his illness, as he had become depressed and suicidal after being given a poor prognosis by his neurologist. (I have reported a comprehensive account of my treatment of Tom elsewhere [Taylor, 1993]; in this brief summary I focus specifically on the issue of symbolizing dissociated childhood trauma.) Early in the treatment, I discovered that Tom responded somatically to criticism, especially from his supervisors at work. Whereas before developing the illness he had responded mainly by passive–aggressive and acting out behaviours (such as frequent lateness for work), he now responded almost entirely at the somatic level, with an intensification of spasm of his neck muscles and no awareness of any underlying fantasies. This somatic response was repeated in the transference, with Tom seeming to experience me as attacking when I made some exploratory interpretations of possible phallic or other symbolic meanings for his dystonia. Tom also had difficulty identifying subjective feelings associated with the narcissistic injuries induced by criticism.

Gradually, I was able to trace the origin of Tom's somatic response to the cumulative trauma of intense and frequent ridiculing and teasing by his parents throughout childhood and adolescence, and also in his adult life. Even when Tom developed cervical dystonia, his mother showed no empathy for his embarrassing disability. Completely unattuned to her son's emotional distress, she mocked and teased him whenever she found him looking in a mirror, just as she had done during his adolescence when she accused him of admiring himself before the mirror. Tom had also been deprived of warmth and affection from his mother, who was only sixteen years old when he was born (his father was eighteen).

Towards the end of the second year of treatment, Tom began to experience disturbing dream and fantasy images, which played a pivotal role in symbolizing the dissociated childhood traumatic experiences. He described the images as "brutal and nasty" and "not the kind of images one would want to see . . . they are pornographic and involve killings and death." He feared he was going mad. I remained receptive to hearing Tom describe the frightening images and simply reflected the subjective feeling component of the various emotional states suggested by the images and also by Tom's facial expressions and bodily postures, especially states of anger, anxiety, sadness, or profound shame. At the same time, I helped him identify and accurately label these feelings for himself. By transforming the frightening images and emotions into meaningful feelings and desires, we were able gradually to reconstruct traumatic episodes in Tom's childhood, including numerous instances when he had painfully experienced the absence of love and warmth from his parents and their humiliation and shaming of him rather than positive mirroring.

As Tom slowly acquired a capacity to contain and modulate intense affects, and to use the symbolic system of language to think and talk about emotionally painful childhood experiences, there was a parallel steady improvement and eventual disappearance of his dystonia.

Conclusion

As McDougall (1974) has stated, it is the capacity for symbolic functioning that enables human beings to bind or cope with the physical and mental pains that we all inevitably encounter throughout life. This capacity breaks down when adults experience massive psychic trauma, but more commonly in individuals who experience serious traumatic events in childhood and there is no parent who is able to contain the overwhelming affects and render them bearable for the child. Unable to mentally represent the unbearable emotional states so that they can be "digested" through dreaming and thinking, the traumatic emotions are dissociated, but are prone to return by way of somatic illness. Psychoanalytic therapy of somatically ill patients requires identification and activation of dissociated emotional states so that unsymbolized trauma, with the aid of the analyst's containing and symbolizing ("alpha") functions, can be transformed into psychic structure.

References

Aragno, A. (1997). *Symbolization: Proposing a Developmental Paradigm for a New Psychoanalytic Theory of Mind*. Madison, CT: International Universities Press.

Besson, J. A., Ebmeier, K. P., Gemmell, H. G., Sharp, P. F., McFadyen, M., & Smith, F. W. (1988). Brain imaging and treatment response in spasmodic torticollis. *British Journal of Psychiatry, 153*: 399–402.

Bion, W. R. (1962). *Learning from Experience*. London: Heinemann.

Boscarino, J. A. (1997). Diseases among men 20 years after exposure to severe stress: implications for clinical research and medical care. *Psychosomatic Medicine, 59*: 605–614.

Boscarino, J. A. (2004). Posttraumatic stress disorder and physical illness: results from clinical and epidemiologic studies. *Annals of the New York Academy of Science, 1032*: 141–153.

Bromberg, P. M. (1998). *Standing in the Spaces. Essays on Clinical Process, Trauma, and Dissociation*. Hillsdale, NJ: Analytic Press.

Bucci, W. (1997a). *Psychoanalysis and Cognitive Science*. New York: Guilford Press.

Bucci, W. (1997b). Symptoms and symbols: a multiple code theory of somatization. *Psychoanalytic Inquiry, 17*: 151–172.

Bucci, W. (1999). Response to the comments of Bouchard and Lecours. *Canadian Journal of Psychoanalysis, 7*: 23–29.

Bucci, W. (2007). Dissociation from the perspective of multiple code theory: Part II. The spectrum of dissociative processes in the psychoanalytic relationship. *Contemporary Psychoanalysis, 43*: 305–326.

Bucci, W. (2008). The role of bodily experience in emotional organization. New perspectives on the multiple code theory. In: F. S. Anderson (Ed.), *Bodies in Treatment* (pp. 51–76). New York: Analytic Press.

Cohen, J. (1980). Structural consequences of psychic trauma: a new look at "Beyond the pleasure principle". *International Journal of Psychoanalysis, 61*: 421–432.

Cohen, J. (1985). Trauma and repression. *Psychoanalytic Inquiry, 5*: 163–189.

Dauer, W. T., Burke, R. E., Greene, P., & Fahn, S. (1998). Current concepts on the clinical features, aetiology and management of idiopathic cervical dystonia. *Brain, 121*: 547–560.

Deri, S. K. (1984). *Symbolization and Creativity*. New York: International Universities Press.

Dube, A. R., Fairweather, D., Pearson, W. S., Felitti, V. J., Anda, R. F., & Croft, J. B. (2009). Cumulative childhood stress and autoimmune diseases in adults. *Psychosomatic Medicine, 71*: 243–250.

Eagle, M. N. (1984). *Recent Developments in Psychoanalysis*. New York: McGraw-Hill.

Eskandari, F., & Sternberg, E. M. (2002). Neural-immune interactions in health and disease. *Annals of the New York Academy of Science, 966*: 20–27.

Falconer, W. (1796). *The Influence of the Passions on Disorders of the Body.* London: Dilly & J. Phillips.

Felitti, V. J., Anda, R. F., Nordenberg, D., Williamson, D. F., Spitz, A. M., Edwards, V., Koss, M. P., & Marks, J. S. (1998). Relationship of childhood abuse and household dysfunction to many of the leading causes of death in adults. *American Journal of Preventive Medicine, 14*: 245–258.

Freud, S. (1890a). Psychical (or mental) treatment. *S.E., 7*: 283–304. London: Hogarth.

Freud, S. (1896c). The aetiology of hysteria. *S.E., 3*: 189–221. London: Hogarth.

Freedman, N. (1998). Psychoanalysis and symbolization: legacy or heresy? In: C. S. Ellman, S. Grand, M. Silvan, & S. J. Ellman (Eds.), *The Modern Freudians* (pp. 79–97). Northvale, NJ: Aronson.

Friedman, H. S. (2008). The multiple linkages of personality and disease. *Brain, Behavior, and Immunity, 22*: 668–675.

Friedman, M. J., & Schnurr, P. P. (1995). The relationship between trauma, post-traumatic stress disorder, and physical health. In: M. J. Friedman, D. S. Charney, & A. Y. Deutch (Eds.), *Neurobiological and Clinical Consequences of Stress: From Normal Adaptation to Post-traumatic Stress Disorder* (pp. 507–524). Philadelphia, PA: Lippincott-Raven.

Glaser, R., & Kiecolt-Glaser, J. K. (2005). Stress-induced immune dysfunction: implications for health. *Nature Reviews Immunology, 5*: 243–251.

Grotstein, J. S. (1990). Nothingness, meaninglessness, chaos, and the "black hole" II: the "black hole". *Contemporary Psychoanalysis, 26*: 377–407.

Glover, E. (1939). *Psychoanalysis.* London: Staples.

Goodwin, R. D., & Stein, M. B. (2004). Association between childhood trauma and physical disorders among adults in the United States. *Psychological Medicine, 34*: 509–520.

Greco, M. (1998). *Illness as a Work of Thought. A Foucauldian Perspective on Psychosomatics.* London: Routledge.

Green, A. (1975). The analyst, symbolization and absence in the analytic setting (on changes in analytic practice and analytic experience). *International Journal of Psychoanalysis, 56*: 1–22.

Janet, P. (1889). *L'automatisme psychologique*. Paris: Alcan.

Jones, E. (1916). The theory of symbolism. In: *Papers on Psychoanalysis* (5th edn). Baltimore, MD: Williams & Wilkins.

Kiecolt-Glaser, J. K., McGuire, L., Robles, T. F., & Glaser, R. (2002). Psychoneuroimmunology: psychological influences on immune function and health. *Journal of Consulting and Clinical Psychology, 70*: 537–547.

Krystal, H. (1978). Trauma and affects. *The Psychoanalytic Study of the Child, 33*: 81–116.

Langer, S. K. (1942). *Philosophy in a New Key* (3rd edn). Cambridge, MA: Harvard University Press, 1957.

Marty. P, & de M'Uzan. M. (1963). La "pénsee opératoire". *Revue Francaise de Psychanalyse, 27*(Suppl): 1345–1356.

McDougall, J. (1974). The psychosoma and the psychoanalytic process. *International Review of Psycho-Analysis, 1*: 437–459.

Nemiah, J. C., & Sifneos, P. E. (1970). Affect and fantasy in patients with psychosomatic disorders. In: O. W. Hill (Ed.), *Modern Trends in Psychosomatic Medicine, Volume 2* (pp. 26–34). London: Butterworths.

Nemiah, J. C., Freyberger, H., & Sifneos, P. E. (1976). Alexithymia: a view of the psychosomatic process. In: O. W. Hill (Ed.), *Modern Trends in Psychosomatic Medicine, Volume 3* (pp. 430–439). London: Butterworths.

Newirth, J. (2003). *Between Emotion and Cognition: The Generative Unconscious*. New York: Other Press.

O'Sullivan, R. L., Lipper, G., & Lerner, E. A. (1998). The neuro-immuno-cutaneous-endocrine network: relationship of mind and skin. *Archives of Dermatology, 134*: 1431–1435.

Parens, H. (2004). *Renewal of Life: Healing from the Holocaust*. Rockville, MD: Schreiber.

Scaer, R. (2005). *The Trauma Spectrum: Hidden Wounds and Human Resiliency*. New York: Norton.

Seiffert, K., & Granstein, R. D. (2006). Neuroendocrine regulation of skin dendritic cells. *Annals of the New York Academy of Science, 1088*: 195–206.

Siegel, D. J. (1995). Memory, trauma, and psychotherapy. *Journal of Psychotherapy, Practice, and Research, 4*: 93–122.

Sternberg, E. M. (2000). Does stress make you sick and belief make you well? The science connecting body and mind. *Annals of the New York Academy of Science, 917*: 1–3.

Taylor, G. J. (1987). *Psychosomatic Medicine and Contemporary Psychoanalysis*. Madison, CT: International Universities Press.

Taylor, G. J. (1992). Psychosomatics and self-regulation. In: J. W. Barron, M. N. Eagle, & D. L. Wolitzky (Eds.), *Interface of Psychoanalysis and Psychology* (pp. 464–488). Washington, DC: American Psychological Association.

Taylor, G. J. (1993). Clinical application of a dysregulation model of illness and disease: a case of spasmodic torticollis. *International Journal of Psychoanalysis, 74*: 581–595.

Taylor, G. J. (2004). Alexithymia: 25 years of theory and research. In: I. Nyklíček, L. Temoshok, & A. Vingerhoets (Eds.), *Emotion Expression and Health: Advances in Theory, Assessment and Clinical Applications* (pp. 137–153). New York: Brunner-Routledge.

Yovell, Y. (2000). From hysteria to posttraumatic stress disorder: Psychoanalysis and the neurobiology of traumatic memories. *Neuro-Psychoanalysis, 2*: 171–181.

Afterword

Madeleine Baranger

In praise of pluralism

We are very grateful to Marilia Aisenstein and Elsa Rappoport de Aisemberg from the moment their intellectual exchanges and longstanding friendship caused them to engage and commit to compile this book: an introduction, perhaps a confrontation, of the psychoanalytic thoughts of ten authors—themselves included—coming from most parts of the world, be it Europe, USA, Canada, or Latin America, in this way bringing in diverse psychoanalytic orientations.

I recall perfectly well that the first book published by APA (Argentine Psychoanalytic Association) gathered all the first studies on psychosomatics in a time when this subject was not widely taken into account. Even several years later, many European analysts, for example, in France or the UK, were not at all inclined to hear or even discuss it, probably because of a suspicion that there existed an anti-analytic basis in this approach.

It would be needless to summarize or value each work that appears in this book. All these writings deserve a careful reading: they develop and detail different clinical and/or theoretical aspects of the subject matter, interweaving subtle touches that reflect varied psychoanalytical orientations complementing each other as a means to understand (represent) a natural or therapeutic evolution. The title of my Afterword attempts to express the merits of this book.

Several authors revisit the history of the birth of psychosomatics, starting with its discovery in Chicago by Franz Alexander. Many others take the time to remark on the correlation of the interest in psychosomatics with ideas already posed by Freud, essentially the consideration of all manifestation of the patient (those of somatic nature included) as an expression of an unconscious conflictive stance that the subject cannot resolve because of his/her incapacity or denial to assume or recognize.

Because the authors belong to different psychoanalytical schools, and have a certain divergence of ideas with regard to the development and evolution of the psyche, we are exposed to varied interpretations of certain phenomena that could pave the way, as often happens, to fundamental discussions on the theory of what psychoanalysis considers as properly human and on the practice and theory it requires.

What is even more fascinating about this book is the abundance of precise clinical material, sometimes very dramatic indeed, that allows the reader to see represented the method of thinking, interpreting, and theoretical stance of the analyst, exposing the case by a temporal and partial identification with his/her intellectual processes.

This material is a real gift to the reader, psychoanalyst and researcher alike, and entices us over and over again to rethink our own account of phenomena and theories.

The wide variety of clinical material is analysed and worked through mostly by reviewing and studying it in detail in the light of the basic psychoanalytical concepts (Freudian), thus encouraging the reader to exercise his/her analytic thinking, and often proposing new resources for his/her practice, and even guiding him/her to revise or, moreover, correct his/her own analytical stance. In reality, it is the only way in which any science or knowledge flourishes, starting from doubts and contradictions in a person who has been exposed to other thinkers' ideas on the same subject.

In passing, I have mentioned the sheer amount of clinical material presented by our ten authors. It is invaluable because of the richness of the variety of the cases presented in this book. Some patients featured are children, and, in one case, a baby; others are adults of varying ages, including adolescents. There is, too, a variety in age and sex, in origins and social position, that could lead to a comparative study on the influence of these specific circumstances and the importance that each analyst can place or suppose on each. This is an inexhaustible book.

In their Preface, the two compilers present their conception of psychosomatics as an extension of psychoanalysis that constitutes the real core of contemporary psychoanalysis. Each of the editors makes clear their conviction in their respective chapters in the book. Their conceptions do not overlap. I believe we can profit by contrasting one with the other.

Elsa Rappoport de Aisemberg points out that the somatic and the neurotic functioning very often coexist in psychosomatic patients. Her hypothesis is that psychosomatic manifestations come from a proper unconscious (that was never conscious) while the psychoneurotic one belongs to the repressed unconscious. Somatosis would come from primitive traces, sensory, potentially traumatic, pertaining to events that took place before the appearance of language. These events were not transformed and remain, so to speak, between soma and psyche (in the id of Freud, deeply embedded in the soma); not being able to be transformed into drive, it expresses itself in the soma in something like a short circuit.

Marilia Aisenstein addresses those texts of Freud that signal the many ways in which the libido can be distributed between organic maladies and psychic symptoms.

Both authors refer to basic concepts of Freud, expressed in the metapsychology papers, in order to understand somatosis. Although they arrive at a somewhat different ideological understanding as to how they see somatosis, this does not prevent or hinder the dialogue between them or their essential collaboration.

The virtual dialogue among all the authors of the book is something else that I consider to be of especial merit.

INDEX

Adverse Childhood Experiences Study, 189
affect, xxii, 14, 17, 23, 28, 31, 33, 38–39, 41–42, 49–50, 54, 56–58, 60–61, 65, 113, 116–119, 126, 132, 134–138, 143, 145–149, 151–152, 154–156, 158–160, 166, 170, 173, 175–176, 181, 183, 189–191, 195 *see also*: development
aggression, 96–100, 113, 115, 151, 165, 168, 170, 174, 176, 182, 184, 193–194
Aisemberg, E. R., xxi–xxii, 90, 112–115, 117–118, 124, 126–127, 129, 201, 203
Aisenstein, M., xxi–xxii, 56, 58, 61–62, 64, 72, 74, 89–90, 94, 96–97, 102–103, 107, 201, 203
Alexander, F., xvii, xxi, 112, 127, 148–151, 182–183, 185, 202
American Psychiatric Association, 177
Anda, R. F., 189–190, 196–197

Angelergues, R., 70, 74
anger, 25, 57, 61, 81–82, 85–86, 158, 166, 174, 176, 194
anxiety, xvi, 21–23, 36, 40, 56–58, 60–61, 66–69, 71, 73–74, 93–94, 99, 102–103, 114–115, 118–120, 134, 142, 147–155, 157, 167–169, 173, 195 *see also*: death
annihilation, 94–95
castration, 139, 193
claustrophobic, 66, 73, 101–102
dissolution, 98
hypochondriac, xvi
multiple, 98
neurosis, 36, 57, 115, 119, 149, 173–174
paranoiac, 73
phobic, 170
primitive, 93, 103, 105
separation, 66, 99
stranger, 167–168
Anzieu, D., 70, 72–75, 87, 90
Aragno, A., 183–184, 195
Arendt, H., 177–178

Argentine Psychoanalytic
    Association (APA), 201
arousal
    affective, 186, 191
    emotional, 182–183, 186–187,
        192
Augustine, 78, 90
Aulagnier, P., 10, 137, 144
Auschwitz, 187–189 see also:
    Holocaust
automatism, 8, 11–12
autonomous nervous system, 150

Baranger, M., xxiii, 106–107, 113,
    119–120, 123, 127
Baranger, W., 106–107, 119–120,
    123, 127
behaviour see also: well-behaved
    child
    destructive, 105–106
    disruptive, 177–178
    hyperactive, 170
    refusal, 169
    regressive, 172
Bell Atlantic, 82
Besson, J. A., 192, 196
Bick, E., 70–71, 75
Bion, W. R., 3, 14, 31, 43, 65, 71–72,
    75, 93–94, 99, 102–103, 105–108,
    123, 127, 184, 196
Bion's
    H, 94, 106
    K, 94
    L, 94
Bleger, J., 121, 127
Blos, P., 97, 108
Bohleber, W., 120, 127
Bollas, C., 54, 62
Bolognini, S., 114, 127
Boscarino, J. A., 190, 196
Botella, C., 96, 108, 123, 127–128
Botella, S., 96, 108, 122–123, 127–128
Bouvet, M., 4, 59, 62
Bowen, M., 79
Braunschweig, D., 155, 160
breath-holding, 164–166, 169, 173

Breck, J., 79, 90
Breck, L., 79, 90
Breuer, J., 49–50, 62, 184
Bromberg, P. M., 191, 196
Bronstein, C., xxii, 64–65, 73–75, 99,
    108
Bucci, W., 185–187, 190–191, 196
Burke, R. E., 192, 196
Burns, J. P., 78, 90
Buske-Kirschbaum, A., 87, 90
Bustamante, A., 114, 127

Cahn, R., 95, 97, 108
Carpinacci, J., 74–75
case studies
    Jeanette, 85–88, 90
    Jeanne, 134–136, 138–143
    Jorge, 192–193
    Joseph, 80–85, 87–90
    Juana, 124–126
    Katia, 16–21
    Livio, 100–106
    Martha, 66–69, 72–74
    Mrs B, 80, 89
    Patient A, 21–27
    Patient B, 26–27
    Patient C, 27–28
    Patient D, 28–29
    Tom, 193–195
Cassirer, E., 93–94, 108
Castoriadis-Aulagnier, P., 95, 108
cathexis, xvi, 58, 137, 171–172
    counter-, 54, 168
    hyper, xvi, 5, 18, 150
Chicago School of Psychosomatic
    Medicine, xvii, 182
Cohen, J., 191, 193, 196
conscious(ness), 2, 18, 20, 33, 38–42,
    53–54, 66, 102, 116, 121, 138,
    140–141, 147, 158–159, 164, 166,
    173–175, 185, 188, 203 see also:
    ego, unconscious(ness)
causality, 37
Corfield, D., 88–91
countertransference, 17, 24–25, 54,
    57–59, 66, 89, 104–105, 119,

121–122, 125 *see also*:
    transference
Croft, J. B., 189, 196

D'Alvia, R., 112, 129
D'Aniello de Calderon, H., 114, 127
Dauer, W. T., 192, 196
David, C., xviii, 6–7, 10, 45, 156, 161
de M'Uzan, M., 6–7, 10, 23, 45, 64, 88, 91, 123, 128, 156, 161, 185, 198
death *see also*: Thanatos
    anguish, 98
    anxiety, 99
    drive, 65, 71, 89, 117, 132, 142–143
    instinct, 64
    threat(s), 74
    wish, 142
depression
    essential, xviii, xxii, 4, 6, 43, 64, 134, 153–154
    melancholic, 4
    position, 10, 12
    primary, 4
Deri, S. K., 183–184, 196
Descartes, R., 77–79, 89
development(al)
    emotional, 186
    of affect, 54
    psychic, 171
Dube, A. R., 189, 196
Dunayevich, J. B., 112, 129

Ebmeier, K. P., 192, 196
Eckell de Muscio, I., 114, 127
Edelstein, C., 74–75
Edwards, V., 189–190, 197
ego, 8, 12, 15, 20, 33, 41, 55, 57, 70–72, 87, 116, 133, 137, 139, 142–143, 147, 153, 156–159, 172, 176
    conscious, 38
    super, 18, 38, 133, 142, 172, 175–176

element(s)
    alpha, 65, 94, 184
    beta, 65, 71, 94, 99, 184
Engel, G., 112, 128
envy, 22–23, 86
    penis, 24
Eros, 90, 117, 132
Eskandari, F., 190, 197

Fahn, S., 192, 196
Faimberg, H., 124, 128
Fain, M., xviii, 6, 9, 45, 64, 169–170, 179
Fairweather, D., 189, 196
Falconer, W., 181, 197
fantasy, 18, 20, 25, 60, 70–71, 99, 101–104, 120, 133, 138, 140, 156, 183, 185, 194 *see also*: life, unconscious
Farber, E. M., 83, 90
Felitti, V. J., 189–190, 196–197
Ferenczi, S., xvi–xvii, 148–149, 160
Fernandez Moujan, O., 112, 129
Ferro, A., 101, 106, 108
Fine, A., 64, 75
Freedman, N., 183–184, 197
Freud, S., xv–xvi, xxi–xxii, 2–4, 6, 10, 12–13, 15, 29, 31–34, 36, 40–41, 43–44, 47–56, 59–62, 64, 78, 89–90, 94–95, 97, 108, 111, 113–119, 122, 128–129, 131–132, 136–137, 141–144, 146–150, 156–157, 159–160, 165, 173–174, 176, 178, 181–182, 184, 197, 202–203
Freyberger, H., 88, 91, 185, 198
Friedman, H. S., 190, 197
Friedman, M. J., 190, 197

Galli, V., 112, 129
Garma, A., xix, xxi, 112, 129, 182
Garma, E., 64, 75
Geiben, A., 87, 90
Gemmell, H. G., 192, 196
General Telephone and Electronics
    Corporation (GTE), 82

Geneva Association of
    Psychosomatics (AGEPSO), 1,
    29, 44
Glaser, R., 190, 197–198
Glover, E., 12, 183, 197
Goodwin, R. D., 189, 197
Granstein, R. D., 191, 198
Greco, M., 183, 197
Green, A., xxi–xxi, 4, 12, 40, 44,
    52–53, 55, 57, 59, 62, 73, 90,
    95–96, 105, 108, 111–114,
    117–119, 121, 129, 132–133,
    143–144, 147–148, 158, 160,
    168–169, 172, 178, 184, 197
Greene, P., 192, 196
Grotstein, J. S., 193, 197
Grubrich-Simitis, I., 120, 129
guilt, 28–29, 74, 135, 139, 142

Hellhammer, D., 87, 90
Holocaust, 120, 187 see also:
    Auschwitz
hysteria, xv, 21–22, 50, 57, 60, 88,
    115, 134, 138, 149, 164, 182, 184

id, xvi, 7, 35, 38, 49, 55, 60–61, 114,
    116–117, 157, 203
instinct(ual), 11, 18, 31, 33, 43,
    47–49, 51–52, 55, 59–60, 64,
    131–132, 140–143, 146, 152–153,
    158–159, 163, 174–176, 192
    see also: death, sexual
International Psychoanalytical
    Association (IPA), xxiii
introjection, 71, 94, 99, 105, 170
Isaacs, S., 64–65, 75

Janet, P., 188, 198
Jeammet, P., 96–97, 99, 103, 108
Jeanson-Tzanck, C., 16–21, 44
Jones, E., 184, 198

Kalinish, L., xxii
Kernberg, O., 89, 91
Kiecolt-Glaser, J. K., 190, 197–198
Klein, M., xxii, 10, 12, 64, 71, 75
Koss, M. P., 189–190, 197

Kreisler, L., 166, 169–170, 178–179
Kristeva, J., 65, 75
Krystal, H., 120, 185, 198

Langer, S. K., 184, 198
Laplanche, J., 111, 118, 129
Leader, D., 88–91
Lerner, E. A., 191, 198
Levy, R., xxii
Liberman, D., xix, xxi, 112, 129
libido, xvi, 27, 37, 40, 50, 57, 59–60,
    64, 66, 97, 99, 119, 141–143, 168,
    184, 203
  aggressive, 37
  erotic, 37
  narcissistic, xvi, 37
life see also: Eros
  emotional, 177, 185
  fantasy, 8, 27–28
  mental, 4, 7–8, 15, 31, 48, 52, 177
  operational, 6, 16, 154
  threatening event (ALTE), 164
Lipper, G., 191, 198
Lombardi, R., 65, 75
Louppe, A., 98–99, 108
Lutenberg, J. M., 106, 108

Maladesky, A., 112, 129
Marks, J. S., 189–190, 197
Marty, P., xxi–xxii, 1–18, 29–30,
    35–38, 42–45, 56, 64, 75, 88, 91,
    94, 96, 99, 102, 108, 111–112,
    129, 134, 140, 148, 151–156,
    160–161, 167–168, 174, 179, 185,
    198
Marucco, N., 114, 129
masochism, 26, 28, 48–49, 52, 60,
    96–97, 99, 104–105, 113, 116,
    171–172, 175 see also:
    sadomasochism
Mason, A., 73, 76
Mayell, H., 85, 91
McDougall, J., xviii, xxi, 16, 88, 91,
    101, 108, 111–112, 115, 118,
    120–121, 124, 129, 142, 144, 183,
    195, 198

McFadyen, M., 192, 196
McGuire, L., 190, 198
Meltzer, D., 65, 76, 94, 99, 108–109
mentalization, xxii–xxiii, 12, 14–15,
        20–21, 26–27, 29, 52, 56, 93–94,
        96–97, 99, 102–103, 105–106,
        140, 152–153, 155, 164, 170, 176
metapsychology, 9, 32, 47, 61,
        93–94, 126, 146, 148, 150,
        155–156, 203
Mom, J., 119–120, 127
mother
    figure, 167
    –infant relationship, 70, 118, 123,
        170, 183
    –substitute, 169
mourning, xxii, 74, 111, 124–126,
        132, 134, 137–138, 140–143, 188

Nall, L., 83, 90
narcissism, 23, 27–28, 37, 60, 72, 88,
        97–99, 103–104, 111, 121, 137
narcissistic wound, 21, 24, 28, 138
National Comorbidity Survey, 189
Nemiah, J. C., 88, 91, 185, 198
neurosis, xv–xvii, 149, 153, 173–175,
        177, 182 see also: anxiety
    psycho-, xix, 149–150
Newirth, J., 183–184, 198
Nordenberg, D., 189–190, 197
NYNEX, 82

object, 12, 28, 32–34, 36, 39–40,
        42–43, 49–50, 55, 58, 60–61, 65,
        71–74, 94–99, 102–107, 113–121,
        124, 131–133, 135–137, 140–143,
        148, 151, 154, 163, 167–168,
        170–171, 186
    external, 42, 64, 71, 73, 132
    internal, 72, 96, 99, 105
    lost, 137, 141, 143
    presentation, 16, 31–34, 39
    relations, 9, 41–42, 99, 137, 152,
        163, 165–169, 172–173
    skin, 72
objective/objectivity, 97, 117, 149, 165

O'Donnell, P., 114, 127
Oedipal ideas/theory, xv, 22, 105,
        115, 120–121, 124, 126, 133, 136,
        139, 174
Ogden, T. H., 71, 76
Ornish, D., 80, 84, 91
O'Sullivan, R. L., 191, 198

pain
    mental, 136–137, 195
    physical, 23, 27, 134, 136–138,
        195
    psychic, 119, 124–125, 134,
        136–138
Palleja, O., 74–75
Parat, C., 173, 176, 179
Parens, H., 187–189, 198
Paris Institute of Psychosomatics
        (IPSO), 29, 59
Paris Psychoanalytic(al) Society,
        xviii, 16, 44
Paris Psychosomatic School/Paris
        School of Psychosomatics,
        xviii, xxi, 47–48, 51, 64, 151
Pearson, W. S., 189, 196
phantasy, 55, 64, 70–73, 87
    unconscious, 63–65, 71
Pichon Rivière, E., xix, xxi
Picollo, A., 112, 129
Pirke, K.-M., 87, 90
pleasure
    principle, 59, 114, 118, 147, 156,
        163, 172, 175
    –unpleasure principle, 52–53, 59,
        175
Pollock, G. H., 112, 130, 140, 144
preconscious, 2–3, 15, 17, 33, 38, 41,
        53–54, 57, 116, 140, 173 see also:
        conscious(ness),
        unconscious(ness)
projection, xvi, 18, 30, 64, 71–73,
        106, 170, 175
projective
    identification, 64–65, 69, 71–73,
        99, 106, 123
    reduplication, xviii, 7

psyche, xviii–xix, xxi, xxiii, 2, 4,
    29–30, 41, 43, 47, 51–53, 55, 59,
    79, 87, 89–90, 112, 115, 117–123,
    131, 137–138, 140, 150–151, 167,
    188, 193, 202–203
  pre-, xxii, 2, 10–11
Psychosomatic Institute of Paris
    see: Paris Institute of
    Psychosomatics (IPSO)

rage, 23, 57, 81, 86, 88, 100, 143, 167,
    187, 189
Rascovsky, A., xix, xxi, 112, 130
regression, xvi, xviii, 13–14, 42, 60,
    98, 105, 134, 151–153, 170, 172,
    175
representative
  carnal, 30
  ideational, 31–33, 35, 39, 41, 116,
    148, 158
  psychical, 1, 16, 29, 31–35, 39–41,
    47, 52, 131, 148
repression, xv, xvii, 1, 5, 14–15, 33,
    35, 50, 53–56, 115–118, 121–122,
    126, 132, 143, 148, 150–151, 155,
    157, 165–166, 168, 173–176, 178,
    182–184, 188, 193, 203
Riolo, F., 117, 130
Robles, T. F., 190, 198
Rosemberg, B., 97, 99, 109, 113,
    130
Rosenfeld, H., 64, 72, 76
Rousillon, R., 114, 120, 130

sadomasochism, 99, 104–105, 117,
    170 see also: masochism
Scaer, R., 192, 198
Schnurr, P. P., 190, 197
Segal, H., 65, 76, 184
Seiffert, K., 191, 198
self
  analysis, 112, 122, 187
  preservation, 116
  -regulation, 187
  soothing, 171–172
sexual
  abuse, 120, 193

discomfort, 85
drive, xvi, 116, 118, 132–133, 140,
    174
excitation(s), 70, 115, 142, 150,
    174
inhibition, 88
instinct, 48
transmitted disease, 87
trauma, 120
sexuality, xv, 23, 48, 50, 67, 88,
    103–104, 116, 119, 124, 176
  homo-, 22, 26, 193
  infantile, 50, 113, 115, 124, 140,
    177
Sharp, P. F., 192, 196
Siegel, D. J., 191, 198
Sifneos, P. E., 88, 91, 185, 198
Smadja, C., xxii, 39, 49, 62, 134, 142,
    144
Smith, F. W., 192, 196
soma, xviii, xxi, xxiii, 2, 4–5, 12,
    15–16, 34–35, 37, 40–43, 47, 57,
    64, 77, 79, 89–90, 96, 99,
    102–103, 105, 112–115, 117–121,
    124, 133, 151, 164, 203
somatic, xv–xix, 2, 7–8, 10–11,
    13–14, 26–27, 31, 33–34, 36–40,
    42, 49–50, 52–53, 56–57, 59–61,
    64, 79, 90, 95–96, 102, 105,
    112–113, 115–116, 118–119, 124,
    131, 134, 145–147, 149–156,
    159–160, 164–166, 168,
    173–174, 176–177, 181–184,
    186–187, 189–192, 194–195,
    202–203
somatization, xviii, xxii, 14, 21, 28,
    35–36, 43, 132–134, 142–143,
    151–153, 160, 167, 174, 177
somatopsychic, 2, 38
somatosis, xix, 103, 106, 112, 114,
    117, 121–122, 124, 126, 203
Soule, M., 169–170, 179
Spillius, E. B., 65, 76
Spitz, A. M., 189–190, 197
Spitz, R. A., 72, 165, 167–168,
    171–172, 179